The Changing Politics of Education

The Changing Politics of Education

Privatization and the Dispossessed Lives Left Behind

Michael Fabricant
and
Michelle Fine

Paradigm Publishers
Boulder • London

Copyright © 2013 Paradigm Publishers

Published in the United States by Paradigm Publishers, 5589 Arapahoe Avenue, Boulder, CO 80303 USA.

Paradigm Publishers is the trade name of Birkenkamp & Company, LLC, Dean Birkenkamp, President and Publisher.

Library of Congress Cataloging-in-Publication Data

Fabricant, Michael, author.
  The changing politics of education : privatization and the dispossessed lives left behind / Michael Fabricant and Michelle Fine.
     pages cm
  Includes bibliographical references and index.
  ISBN 978-1-61205-271-7 (pbk. : alk. paper)
  1. Privatization in education—United States. 2. Public schools—United States. 3. Educational equalization—United States. I. Fine, Michelle, author. II. Title.
  LB2806.36.F33 2013
  379.10973—dc23

                                                          2012039110

Printed and bound in the United States of America on acid-free paper that meets the standards of the American National Standard for Permanence of Paper for Printed Library Materials.

Designed and Typeset by Straight Creek Bookmakers.

17 16 15 14 13   1 2 3 4 5

*To Harriet Kasindorf-Fabricant, a North Star
who guided me to places where passion birthed justice*

and

To Rosie and to a much better tomorrow

Contents

Acknowledgments

This book grows out of our friendship and shared political commitments, but would never have been possible without the strong encouragement of Dean Birkenkamp at Paradigm. Dean was able in conversation to affirm our enthusiasm for the project and help us sharpen parts of the narrative that were elusive. Laura Esterman at Paradigm has consistently offered sharp, clear answers to our questions about the stages of production. Her clarity helped to quell our anxiety in the final stage of the project.

Dawn Panokien was an extraordinary gift to the project. After multiple drafts of the manuscript she helped us both smooth out the rough edges and elevate critical theme. Sue Delgiorno provided a very sure hand in systematically addressing the mountain of detail associated with the referencing. Her capacity to track down even the most obscure citation was much appreciated. In the process of developing the manuscript Niki Werner Fabricant read early drafts and offered insightful feedback that contributed to the shaping of parts of the narrative.

We began the manuscript as our mothers, Harriet Fabricant and Rosie Fine, closed their eyes for the final time. They are both missed, always and deeply.

We ended the book carried by the fierce commitments of the Chicago Teachers Union and the parents who mobilized with educators, insisting on education as it must be.

So with Harriet and Rosie in our bellies and CTU in our hearts, we appreciate the opportunity to be in conversation with others who struggle to sustain public spaces of dignity, care, equity, and justice.

Introduction

We are concerned about the dismantling of public education occurring before our eyes. At the same time, we are encouraged by the ever-more frequent, if staccato, waves of organized push back from educators, youth, communities, labor, and immigration and civil rights advocates across the country.

Presently there is a struggle between the forces of privatization who have money and media capital and grassroots forces mobilizing citizen bodies to advance democratic and equitable public schooling. At the moment it is clear that privatization is rolling over public schools—and increasingly universities—in the form of testing, standardization, attacks on tenure and academic freedom, charter networks, vouchers, virtual charters, online education, school closings, stealth invasion of Boards of Education or Boards of Trustees, and heavy investment in policing and private security forces on site. Simultaneously a national wave of resistance moves across the nation as youth and educators walk out of Detroit public schools protesting school closures and create freedom schools; as parents and educators mobilize in New York City against high-stakes testing and school closings; as the Chicago Teachers Union call a strike vote in defense of strategic investment for democratic, equitable public education; as the American Federation of Teachers (AFT) builds labor and community collaborations to defend neighborhood schools; and civil rights organizations and immigrant rights groups caution the proliferation of charter schools, the defunding of public education, and demand a moratorium on the high stakes testing of children.

New alliances are being sutured together between parents and educators; education, juvenile justice, and civil rights organizations; public universities and our K–12 allies. We witness labor unions taking seriously the need to defend the fragile capillaries of democracy we call public education and collaborate with communities for racial and economic justice.

We offer this text to provide a lens for analyzing the current moment in educational history, with a dual focus on the structural design and strategic implementation of privatization as state policy, and the highly uneven impact on the lives of educators, parents, and youth on the ground. We believe that by interrogating both structure and lives we can understand the strategic dismantling of the public sector and be in conversation with movements for economic and racial justice in education.

And so we commit ourselves, in this book, to address the economic and political genesis of our current circumstances—while simultaneously chronicling the profoundly dangerous consequences of those circumstances for public institutions, poor communities, and communities of color—and tracking the eruptions of powerful sites of resistance launched by new coalitions of political allies. We write this book in three dialects: the structural narrative seeks to create an accessible analysis regarding the interplay between economic decline, the policy choice of austerity, and a systematic carving of the public out of public institutions; second, the dispossession narrative reviews the vastly differential consequences of public education policy by class, race/ ethnicity, and neighborhood on the ground, on schools, teachers, students, and our democracy; and third, the mobilization narrative seeks to chronicle an archive of alternative forms of resistance and policy. This last segment of the analysis is intended to trace not only the circuits of dispossession but also emergent spaces of protest, new solidarities, and alternate policies. How these distinct spaces are being welded together to restore and transform a public sphere of educational possibility is also explored.

While books have been written on American economic decline as well as on how neoliberal "reform" has constrained the public sphere—and, in turn, the intellectual, political, and social development of youth, particularly poor youth of color—rarely are these two themes explored together. Analyses of neoliberalism and austerity have largely been separated from analyses of lives and institutions on the ground. Thus, critical arguments about educational injustice have typically been crafted with little attention paid to lives on the ground—educators, parents, community members, youth, and advocates and even less attention to the mobilization of social movements for economic and racial justice. And so, that is exactly the task we have set for ourselves: to examine the genesis of, document the collateral damage from, and highlight sites of resistance to the privatization of US education that now result both from neoliberal policymaking and the intensifying dissolution of American empire.

THE CRISIS IN PUBLIC EDUCATION

For decades politicians, scholars, journalists, educators, activists, and others have been warning us about the growing crisis in public education. Test scores and other "objective" indicators of decay and decline validate their claims. The indicators highlight readily visible achievement gaps separating students of low-income communities from those of high-income communities, an inconsistency that is of particular concern to residents in communities of color. Even so, educational crisis is rarely discussed in terms of structural conditions of poverty and racism—a silence that is especially curious given that the magnitude of the achievement gap is so very stark. Anyone engaged in objective inquiry into the conditions of public schooling, past or present, will note that poor neighborhoods and especially poor neighborhoods of color are sites of severe underinvestment, fewer experienced educators, higher turnover, and often better equipped to police or recruit for the military than to educate. In the past, policymakers addressed growing crisis through experimentation and modest forms of strategic intervention never mobilized to resolve systemic issues, but rather to create, at best, small, highly localized improvements to student academic performance. In contrast, a language of crisis now emanates from the centers of power and wealth, stirring momentum for a radical restructuring of public education, often exploiting the "tragedy of the miseducated black child" as a figleaf, or foreplay, to privatization. Indeed, today's policymakers, emboldened by substantial philanthropy and in the driver's seat, refuse to address poverty, economic inequality, finance inequity, or racism and instead insist on investing in the privatization of testing, curriculum, teacher development, teacher evaluation, achievement networks, online curriculum development as well as virtual education. What is it about this moment that has produced such radical discourse, and then, in response, rapid, and far-reaching re-/de-formations of the public sector? For decades, calls for renewed investment and sweeping reform in education were largely ignored. And there is ample evidence that when investment has been strategic, achievement has risen; racial, ethnic, and class gaps have narrowed; and schools have improved. Yet, since 2003, political movements have emerged, legislation has been drafted, and new forms of practice created that are altering the structure of public education. This reform is predicated not on increased investment but rather on assumptions that education—like capitalist industry—can be made more economically efficient through market reforms and privatization. By demanding higher levels of productivity from professional staff, reformers assume they will, in turn, be able to lower education costs. Some, including Bill Gates, Eli Broad, David and Charles Koch, and other new reformers from the private sector, contend that the problem with public education today is not money but the dearth of innovation, assessment tools, virtual technology, and school choice. Reformers from afar, those who are geographically, economically, and experientially divorced from the day-to-day challenges of public education in very poor communities, argue that technology and the market will resolve our complex problems, even as the budgets of public schools are slashed in every part of the country, as teachers and students are placed under testing surveillance and humiliation, as public schools are closed and charters reopen with selective admissions in their place. The bleeding and twinning of conservative philanthropic interests with government has bred circumstances in which accountability, transparency, and quality schooling for all are deeply threatened.

At the same time, those who live in poor communities of color, who are affected by educational inequity in their daily lives, are most attentive to ramifications they see stemming directly from underinvestment in their local schools: "My child is struggling to learn but the size of her class has increased in the past year and so she can't get the kind of individual attention she needs," said Marion. She was a concerned mother with whom Mike spoke on the playground of a South Bronx elementary school, when conducting ethnographic research in January 2005. Her friend added, "In the past year, text books are just not available; in my son's class, his friends are sharing books." A third parent explained that she was concerned because

"I know how important writing is to his education, but he is getting very little of that in the schools. Everything seems to be about testing." After several minutes, a parent standing to the side of the group entered into our conversation, showing even greater frustration than the other women, "Look, my kid can't even go to the bathroom, the toilets have been broken for months, and faucets don't work. I am going to try to get her into a charter school next year."

The teachers who spoke that day on the playground, too, described the outcomes of economic divestment in their school. "Did you hear that Smith and Rollins have resigned? How many does that make in the last year?" A colleague indicates, "I think those two make it ten of our seventy teachers since last October." An older teacher added, "I've never seen the morale so low, between the teacher assessments, which hold us accountable for things we can't control, our reduced health care, having no freedom in the classroom to do anything but teach to the test, and the size of our classes growing, you don't feel like getting out of bed to come here. Bottom line is anyone with another option is leaving. We're losing our best and brightest teachers."

Those tasked with educating poor children describe the daily experience of public education in far different terms than the speakers we hear in the media. As of March 2012, a full 27 percent of surveyed educators indicated that they plan to leave the field within a few years, a record high. Their counter-narratives suggest, unsurprisingly, that disinvestment, overtesting, and the constant critique of schools and educators matters desperately to youth and to those educating them. Many new educational reforms have made the success of educators more difficult. The increasingly singular emphasis on testing and assessment leaves students underprepared and drives many creative, effective teachers out of the profession. Nevertheless, the media, legislators, and economic elites have, almost without exception, aligned with the new reformers, while ignoring the voices of parents and branding teachers and their unions as self-interested and inattentive to the needs of poor children. Our question becomes: Why have the new reformers and their agenda for change gained so much traction in the past decade, despite the ethnographic and empirical evidence suggesting that fixes such as less funding and more testing do not work? In what follows, we argue that current US education reform must be understood in its broader political-economic context, a context that is shaped, at present, by neoliberal ideology and accelerated economic decline.

NEOLIBERALISM DEFINED

Neoliberalism is a political, economic, and ideological system that privileges the market as the most efficient platform for distributing social goods, minimizes the role of government responsibility in assuring collective well-being and highlights instead personal responsibility for assuring individual well-being (Harvey 2004). By facilitating market-driven reform to determine how and for whom to redistribute opportunities and burdens, neoliberal policies tend to facilitate the upward flow and control of resources, opportunities, and power toward wealthy communities and corporate interests. Simultaneously, a downward drip of surveillance in the form of testing, policing, and restricted access to quality institutions for working-class and poor youth is stimulated.

Neoliberalism operates through various mechanisms of material and power consolidation. Geographer David Harvey distinguishes *capital accumulation,* the processes by which elites and corporations generate, sustain, and consolidate power from *accumulation by dispossession,* a set of practices by which elites or corporations repossess formerly public goods or services and convert them into individually held private goods. In both instances, as concentrations of capital grow for elites through accumulation so, too, does the immiseration of the poor. Once these processes are unleashed and inscribed in law or policy, Harvey argues, those who are dispossessed are typically left to fend for themselves, with policymakers assuming their misfortune is self-induced.

The present foci of educational reform, as well as the discourse of the new reformers, make sense when interpreted as products of this neoliberal moment. Neoliberal thought itself begins to make a new kind of sense when examined in light of our declining American empire.

AMERICAN EMPIRE IN DECLINE AND THE RECONFIGURATION OF THE STATE

According to Harvey, US hegemony in the production and distribution of goods began to erode during the 1960s and 1970s. Once this occurred, the US tried to maintain international dominance by positioning itself at the head of the global financial sector. Although the United States remains powerful in this sector today, Harvey notes "that financial power is flowing out of the US." Our expansive debt is increasingly held by foreigners, and disproportionately by Asian banks. One consequence, he asserts, is that the US is, one day soon, "actually going to have to pay out to the rest of the world, rather than extracting a kind of tribute." The recent debacles in Iraq and Afghanistan suggest that US military power—another primary pillar of US empire production—is in decline along with its financial power. This seems an apt moment, therefore, to ask: How is the erosion of US empire, and our shifting position in the international realm, affecting the position of the state as social provider and implementer of domestic policy? (Harvey 2004, 3–4).

The kinds of autonomy historically accorded to the state are disappearing, in domestic matters just as in international matters, replaced by an ever-more nakedly transparent corporate agenda. As the power of the state yields to the power of unconstrained capital, the policy landscape radically shifts—again, domestically, as well as internationally.

One of the most important outcomes of the decline of American empire is global capitals' deeper penetration of state functions and the "trading favors to secure the right to precious resources previously held in the public domain" (Klein 2007, 18).

Corporate America's search for new ways to profit at a time in which the state seeks to mitigate economic crisis has created a magnetic-like attraction between private sector entrepreneurs and state assets. Naomi Klein has described what is happening as a second colonial pillage: "In the first pillage the riches were seized from the land, and in the second they were stripped from the state" (Klein 2007, 308). Ultimately, Klein suggests that "the government is deconstructing itself—hacking off great chunks of public wealth and feeding them to corporate America, in the form of tax cuts on the one hand and lucrative contracts on the other" (372).

This has produced a number of outcomes that strike at the heart of any democratic project. Inequality of wealth and income are a hallmark of this historic epoch, now equaling that of the Great Depression and continuing to grow. Statistics indicate high rates of employment and homelessness, dismal access to health insurance for US citizens, and rampant degradation of public schools during an era of budget cutting, providing innumerable vivid examples of social dispossession, as the bodies and minds of already marginalized populations are deemed even less valuable.

Critically, politicians' and policymakers' continued commitment to austerity and budget cutting, the kinds of reform hailed by neoliberalism, is likely to produce social disruption and unrest, widening inequalities and severely truncating the life trajectories of our nation's most impoverished young people. It is within this context that control and surveillance assume an ever-larger role in the compressed repertoire of state functions. As the state is stripped of its capacity to develop services, social supports, or redistributive policies in response to intensifying need and economic crisis, it is left with the unbalanced and costly response of ever-more militaristic forms of social control.

The state, as it is remade, is positioned to accommodate corporate interests on two fronts. First, it must reconfigure social services to fit ever-more austere budgets. In education, lower teacher and administrator pay, larger classes, more uniform curricula, and degraded facilities, for example, are part of this restructuring. Second, the state can distribute public sector assets in such a way that they enable private sector profit and plunder, providing corporations a new means by which to achieve historic rates of return on their surplus capital.

Four primary themes emerge from an analysis of empire decline and the resultant restructuring of state domestic policy: (1) inequality grows; (2) greater percentages of the population are rendered "disposable"; (3) the state's role in control and surveillance over persons in poverty and the state-funded professionals who have jobs in education, social service, and health care assumes new importance; and (4) public wealth, space, and opportunities get privatized. Each of these is a powerful element in the remaking of public education policy at present.

Redefining the Crisis

The historian Eric Hobsbawm has remarked, "As the century ended it became evident that the media were a more important component of the political process than parties and the electoral process and likely to remain so" (Hobsbawm 1994,

581). Media power to sell particular narratives of crisis and ignore others has been a powerful explanatory factor in the masking of economic crisis, as driving both the starvation of public services and the consequent eroded services. Rather, the crisis has been relocated from the larger market economy to an "inefficient public sphere" and the unions protecting unproductive, incompetent workers. The structure and staffing of hospitals, schools, and social services are cast as the villainous characters in this melodrama. The commonsense solutions are to create new standards for professional practice, promote market choice by inventing alternatives to present public agencies such as charter schools, demand greater productivity of staff, and direct more public resources to the development of new technologies to improve efficiency and productivity.

Clearly, issues of obdurate bureaucratic resistance to needed innovation and improved classroom instruction are preventing the remaking of public education. That said, bureaucratic behavior and teacher performance have been significantly impaired through fiscal starvation. Strategic disinvestment in public education has been the most critical factor in degrading academic rigor and outcomes in the poorest communities of color. The first stage of any corrective to the present breakdowns in public education must involve substantial strategic investment. Instead, what is being proposed are diminished budgets with a significant reallocation of remaining resources out of the public system, to private or quasi-private institutions. In effect, the presumption is simple: if you reallocate to the private sector, while intensifying staff monitoring, the "product" of education will be invigorated. Consider the new Council on Foreign Relations Independent Task Force report on US Education Reform and National Security (Associated Press 2012): "Educational failure puts the United States' future economic prosperity, global position, and physical safety at risk," warns the Task Force, chaired by Joel I. Klein, former head of New York City public schools, and Condoleezza Rice, former US secretary of state. The country "will not be able to keep pace—much less lead—globally unless it moves to fix the problems it has allowed to fester for too long," argues the Task Force. The report notes that while the United States invests more in K–12 public education than many other developed countries, its students are ill prepared to compete with their global peers.

The lack of preparedness poses threats on five national security fronts: economic growth and competitiveness, physical safety, intellectual property, US global awareness, and US unity and cohesion, says the report. Too many young people are not employable in an increasingly high-skilled and global economy, and too many are not qualified to join the military because they are physically unfit, have criminal records, or have an inadequate level of education. "Human capital will determine power in the current century, and the failure to produce that capital will undermine America's security," the report states. "Large, undereducated swaths of the population damage the ability of the United States to physically defend itself, protect its secure information, conduct diplomacy, and grow its economy."

While the crisis has been articulated in a discourse of threat, risk, and dangerous insecurity, the recommendations are oddly familiar—standards, choice, and data-driven surveillance:

- Implement educational expectations and assessments in subjects vital to protecting national security. "With the support of the federal government and industry partners, states should expand the Common Core State Standards, ensuring that students are mastering the skills and knowledge necessary to safeguard the country's national security."
- Make structural changes to provide students with good choices. "Enhanced choice and competition, in an environment of equitable resource allocation, will fuel the innovation necessary to transform results."
- Launch a "national security readiness audit" to hold schools and policymakers accountable for results and to raise public awareness. "There should be a coordinated, national effort to assess whether students are learning the skills and knowledge necessary to safeguard America's future security and prosperity. The results should be publicized to engage the American people in addressing problems and building on successes."

The question we must ask at this moment is: What forces are driving this redefinition of crisis and these enactments of solution? Who is making money, and equally important, what will be the consequences for public education?

THE WITHDRAWAL OF CONCENTRATED WEALTH FROM COLLECTIVE LIFE

At present, a cross section of wealthy individuals and their foundations are intent on remaking the public sector and, more specifically, public education. Their goals and interests may vary. For example, the Koch brothers' agenda to dismantle the public sector is different than Bill Gates's desire to remake teacher performance through new forms of technical assistance, technology, and monitoring. What they do have in common, however, is an unwillingness to acknowledge, either on the basis of political ideology or technological belief, that the larger economic crisis, regressive tax policies, and budget cutting are factors driving the accelerating degradation of public education, and an unwillingness to imagine strategic public sector investment as a remedy to educational decline. Across the political spectrum of concentrated wealth, the naturalized landscape of austerity, diminished budgets, privatization of public agencies, and reification of market solutions to public problems has hardened. We have been told since the 1980s there is no alternative to a neoliberal free market world, and if we don't succeed in that world, it's our own fault (Harvey 2004).

A Compelling Question

What explains the behavior of those who control concentrated wealth? Why are the elite willing to eviscerate services such as quality public education essential to sustaining both economic opportunity and growth? Present policymaking represents a flight by the very wealthy from collective life. We have witnessed concrete expressions of such flight as the affluent withdraw to the safety of privately policed gated communities. A fiscal sign of such withdrawal is the devolution of the tax system from a progressive to regressive system placing less and less obligation on the wealthy, and, in turn, ever greater responsibility on the middle class. The intensifying call for the radical restructuring of public education represents a withdrawal from collective life through a dismantling and capitalizing of public assets. Resources are shifted from public systems to private networks, such as charter schools; new entrepreneurs penetrate the emergent market of public education through, for example, testing technology and curricula; and the experience of public education is cheapened and hollowed out through ever-more mechanized forms of classroom instruction. These trends represent a flight from a collective life, by effectively abandoning what Harvey describes as a common or collective responsibility:

> The corporatization and privatization of hitherto public assets … indicate a new wave of enclosing the commons. As in the past the power of the state is frequently used to force such processes through even against popular will…. The reversion of common property rights won through years of hard class struggle to the private domain has been one of the most egregious of all policies of dispossession…. [It is within this context that] capitalism internalizes cannibalistic as well as predatory and fraudulent practices. (Harvey 2004, 148)

Surplus capital that "lies idle with no profitable outlets," according to Harvey, represents a great danger to the economy (148). In effect, if capital is restrained so that it cannot beget additional capital, the entire system is at risk of collapsing in on itself. He concludes, "If capitalism has been experiencing a chronic difficulty of over accumulation since 1973, then, the privatization of everything makes a lot of sense as one way to solve the problem. Over accumulated capital can seize hold of public assets and immediately turn them into profitable uses" (149).

Naomi Klein, in her book *The Shock Doctrine* (2007), describes how disaster and fear have also infected the behavior and thinking of the wealthy.

> Already wealth provides an escape hatch from most disasters…. It buys bottled water, generators and rent a cops…. If we continue in this direction, the images of people stranded on New Orleans roof tops will not only be a glimpse of America's unresolved past of racial inequality but will also foreshadow a collective future of disaster apartheid where in which survival is determined by those who can afford to pay. (528)

There are other reasons for the affluent class's withdrawal from collective life. Robert Trivers (2011), author of *The Folly of Fools: The Logic of Deceit and Self-Deception in Human Life,* argues that in fact human capacity for denial may explain the continued commitment to certain types of policy promotion despite empirical evidence of their failure. The powerful influence of denial in setting and sustaining reform course in this political moment is described by John Horgan as follows: "And the more we believe our own lies, the more sincerely, and hence effectively, we can lie to others. 'We hide reality from our conscious minds the better to hide it from onlookers,' Trivers explains. But our illusions can have devastating consequences, from the dissolution of a marriage to stock market collapses and world wars" (Horgan 2011).

Eric Hobsbawm (1994), in *The Age of Extremes,* describes the convergence of a weakened state, the demands of capitalist accumulation, and the impact on essential welfare state functions, in the late twentieth century.

> Western governments and economic orthodoxy agreed that the cost of public social security and welfare was too high and must be reduced and mass reduction of employment in the hitherto most stable sectors of the tertiary occupations of public employment . . . became common. (572)

> The nation state was eroded in two ways from above and below. It was rapidly losing power to and function to various supra national entities . . . (such as global corporations). It was also losing its monopoly of effective power and its historic privileges within its borders. (576)

> Social distribution and non-growth would dominate the politics of the new millennium. Non-market allocation of resources or at least a ruthless limitation of market allocation was essential. (578)

Derrick Bell, critical race theorist and legal scholar, was more explicit about the racial motives behind the sustained commitment to inequality gaps when he wrote, in his book *Faces at the Bottom of the Well: The Permanence of Racism* (1992): "Black people will never gain full equality in this country. Even those herculean efforts we hail as successful will produce no more than temporary 'peaks of progress,' short-lived victories that slide into irrelevance as racial patterns adapt in ways that maintain white dominance. This is a hard-to-accept fact that all history verifies" (12).

The impact of these policy trends has been especially profound for public education. To begin with, both the size of the teaching workforce and its base salaries have been systematically slashed over the past five years. Simultaneously, the boundary between public and private forms of education is rapidly disappearing as charter schooling, and entrepreneurial profit-making centers, drive school reform. As a result, the autonomy of the state in setting public education policy has been largely supplanted by the intensifying corporate desire to capitalize public education resources, on the one hand, and their foundation allies' focus on legitimating through research and policy work the corporatization and privatization of schooling, on the other. Critically, the makeover of public education is not class and race neutral. Rather, the most rapid and dramatic changes in public education are occurring in the poorest communities of color. Cornel West was remarkably prescient twenty years ago in naming the decaying underpinnings of American empire as choking off democracy and needed social reform in every sector of the society, especially public education. If you listen closely you can hear the present echo of his words:

Republicans played the old racial card to remain in office and liberal Democrats lacked the courage to tell the truth about the new levels of decay and decline engulfing us. Instead, we as a people tolerated levels of suffering and misery among the disadvantaged (especially among poor children of all colors, caught in the vicious natural lottery! [see charter schools, testing etc.]), lost faith in our money-driven political system ... as the racial divide expanded and the gaps between rich, poor, and working people increased. We now find ourselves hungry for quick solutions and thirsty for overnight cures for deep economic, cultural, and political problems that were allowed to fester for decades. And, most sadly, we seem to lack the patience, courage, and hope necessary to reconstruct our public life—the very lifeblood of any democracy. (West 1993, 158)

THE STRUCTURE OF THE BOOK

The argument of this book will unfold in the following seven chapters. Chapter 1 explores the relationships among the decline of American empire, growing rates of inequality within the United States, ever-more draconian disinvestment in all things public, and the expansion of a disposable citizenry in need of surveillance and containment. In turn, the growing policing of the expansive number of estranged citizens less and less able to turn to the state for any form of service sustenance, reliance on the technologies that have the patina of science to legitimate policies of gradual service starvation to the poorest communities, and perhaps, most importantly, the capitalization of the public sphere into a site of profit making can be traced back to the nexus between wealth redistribution to the most affluent and the restructuring of the state. The chapter will argue that these themes have powerful implications for the welfare state and, more specifically, public education. Ultimately, the new radical reform agenda for education is to colonize public schooling through the capitalization of assets, corporatization of school culture, and production of cheaper forms of instruction as well as curricula. The particular impact of these themes on the instruction, organization, culture, and outcomes of public education will be explored in the following four chapters.

Chapter 2 considers how the trends outlined in Chapter 1 are influencing public school teachers and teaching. The recent right-wing attack on teachers collectively (in unions) and individually (as professional laborers) is particularly germane to this moment. The disposability of the teaching profession, disinvestment in its salary base, public humiliation through gross evaluation formula, and degradation of the skill and autonomy necessary to build an instructional craft are currents that run through the past decade. Of particular importance are high teacher turnover rates, especially in urban areas. The contradiction between present policy and the development of the stable and skilled teaching workforce necessary to improve academic performance in the poorest communities of color will be examined. Of central concern is explaining the tension between the articulated aspiration of improved learning and the intensifying derogation of the teaching profession.

Chapter 3 explores the new forms of schooling that increasingly dot much of the public education reform landscape. Charter schools, virtual learning, and the reemergence of vouchers will be discussed. The particularly important function of charters in evolving a decentralized, relatively autonomous alternate public education system is the primary focus of the chapter. The increasingly transparent intention of charters to capitalize public education assets and its practices, which, in turn, grows ever-greater strains of education inequality, will be explored. Finally, the nexus between the political momentum for charter reform, the economic support of concentrated wealth in proliferating a market-based public education, and the selling of these alternative systems to desperate, very poor communities is the analytic spine of the chapter.

Chapter 4 provides a brief glimpse into narratives of dispossession. The stories of individuals caught up in the web of dispossession are especially critical. Perhaps most salient are the institutional experiences of school closings and their impact on communities and students. It is with this in mind that the story of Brandeis High School's genesis over the past thirty years—as a site serving high concentrations of very poor students, to a contested terrain for relatively affluent parents, and finally its closure—will be told.

Chapter 5 focuses on testing as both the red dye that tracks teacher performance and the lever controlling their classroom pedagogy. It represents a trigger and source of scientific legitimacy for the present radical reform of public education. In turn, the "science of testing" provides the cover for closing urban neighborhood schools, forcing students to drop out, extolling charter programs, and directing the work of teachers in the classroom. It is testing that legitimates and reproduces a shell game of scientific reform without strategic investment. Equally important, it has the disquieting impact of justifying increased investment in control and surveillance while increasing class size and contracting instructional budgets in the same schools. Keeping your eyes on the pea of test scores and taking your eye off of the context of investment in poor communities of color is a reform shell game that offers simplistic answers to complex social problems. The question we must ask ourselves: Why is such an approach being emphasized in a moment that finds American empire in crisis domestically and internationally?

Chapter 6 explores the dispossessing consequences of present public education policy: How does the present reform direction create circuits of dispossession that lead students out of public education, often invisibly, to illicit and secondary labor markets, the military, and prison? How does the present direction of reform ensure the intensifying estrangement of the overwhelming majority of students of color from public schooling? What are the psychological and physical consequences of these outcomes for individuals and communities of color? How have these processes and outcomes intensified over the past decade as market and testing reforms are scaled up? The outcome of more systematically slotting estranged students to the lowest rungs of the job market, the military, prisons, and street life is part of a production system that is growing an ever-larger pool of disposable citizens in an era of economic and political crisis. As Hobsbawm and other historians have remarked, these disposable citizens represent an increased threat to social stability.

Chapter 7 reviews the intersecting layers of education reform and the aforementioned themes of capitalization of public assets, the testing "sciences," legitimation of growing inequality, accelerating disinvestment in public services, and ever-greater reliance on surveillance and control to monitor estranged students. The absence of the political will to enact progressive forms of taxation and consequent strategic investments in public education is also examined. The kinds of investments empirically proven to increase academic performance in the poorest communities of color will be described. Most critically, the myth that investment does not matter will be dissected and the attendant politics of despair and demobilization associated with such mythology discussed. Finally, the kinds of political struggle, contested terrain, and movement formations that have successfully waged campaigns for strategic investment in public education close the book.

FOR FURTHER READING

Barkan, Joanne. "Got Dough? How Billionaires Rule Our Schools." *Dissent* (Winter 2011). http://dissentmagazine.org/article/?article=3781. Accessed April 7, 2011.

Miner, Barbara. "The Ultimate Superpower: Supersized Dollars Drive *Waiting for Superman* Agenda." October 12, 2010. http://www.rethinkingschools.org/archive/25_02/25_02_miner.shtml.

Peterson, Bob. "Big City Superintendents: Dictatorship or Democracy?" http://www.rethinkingschools.org/archive/24_01/24_01_paulo.shtml.

Weiss, Dale. "Teaching Budget Cuts to Third Graders." http://www.rethinkingschools.org/archive/25_04/25_04_weiss.shtml.

Chapter 1

The Radical Restructuring of the State and the Dissolution of the American Economy

The language of empire is a powerful tool for explaining the reach of the American economy and culture. The economic, political, cultural, and military power of the United States has straddled the globe over the last century. We cannot wade into a discussion of empire without first defining its meaning. This is not intended to be a definitive explication of empire. Rather, it is a starting point, a place to offer a frame of understanding regarding the basic character of empire and its historic relationship to colonialism. This is especially critical because for some, the language of empire simply cannot be applied to the American democratic project. This scaffolding, in turn, will provide the basis for erecting a structure for our larger argument about the nexus between empire, economic crisis, and present education policy.

The distinguished historian William Appleman Williams noted the basic properties of empire in his book *Empire as a Way of Life*. To begin with it creates

> a union of initially separate but politically and socially related units under one central authority. The resort to force by one or more of those entities may or may not be a major element in that process, but in either case the result is an empire governed by an imperial system. The will, and power, of one element asserts its authority. In the United States this aspect of empire is illustrated by ... the government created by the constitution over the original and significantly independent states of America. (Appleman Williams 1980, 6)

Appleman Williams also describes a second dimension of empire as "the forcible subjugation of formerly independent peoples by a wholly external power, and their subsequent rule by the imperial metropolis. One thinks here of the First Americans and of the northern half of Mexico seized by conquest in the 1840's, by the US and integrated into its imperial system" (4). In the last century and a half, one might add other territories including, but not limited to, the Philippines, Puerto Rico, and Hawaii.

David Harvey has asserted that empire is a particular focus on global reach that may or may not include the acquisition of territory. In describing, for example, the US appetite for empire, he notes, "There has never been an interest in particular territories, it has always been interested in global power. We have to see . . . always an attempt to construct a global regime of power with the US at the centre and able to pull the strings" (Harvey 2005, 1). Neil Smith (2009) has supported the proposition that US imperial strategy has been global all along.

Conjoined with empire is an imperial drive and colonization. Appleman Williams notes that the term imperialism does have irreducible meaning: the loss of sovereignty-control over essential issues and decisions by a largely agricultural society to an industrial metropolis (Appleman Williams 1980, 15). Clearly, the American imperial drive has expressed itself from the eighteenth century to its present interests over oil, which has ultimately led to the subjugation of Iraq to American interests.

Critically, the relationship between America and empire can be traced back to the very origin of the nation. The American quest to expand and consolidate its global empire continues to this date. That said, the reach and influence of American empire has begun to wane over the past fifty years. Equally important, the decline of America has accelerated significantly over the past decade. It is to the question of American empire and decline that we will now turn our attention.

American economic dominance internationally was both ascendant and unparalleled in the decades following World War II. Then, in 1973, a unilateral decision by OPEC to increase the price of oil threatened American economic hegemony. This moment marked a more general turning point in which less developed parts of the world increased costs for the first world countries extracting, exporting, and consuming their natural resources. More recently, the decline of the US manufacturing sector along with skyrocketing debt financed largely by China have intensified global competition and further weakened the international reach and influence of American empire.

Tellingly, historian Alfred McCoy (2010) noted:

> Under current projections, the United States will find itself in second place behind China ... in economic output around 2026, and behind India by 2050.... By 2008, the US had already fallen to number three in global merchandise exports, with just 11% of them compared to 12% for China and 16% for the European Union.... Similarly, American leadership in technological innovation is on the wane. In 2008, the U.S. was still number two behind Japan in worldwide patent applications with 232,000 but China was closing fast at 195,000 thanks to a blistering 400% increase since 2000.... In 2009, the U.S. hit rock bottom in ranking among the 40 nations surveyed by the Information Technology and Innovation Foundation when it came to "change" in "global innovation-based competitiveness" during the previous decade.

The nexus between the dissolution of American empire internationally and domestic policymaking, specifically public education, is at the core of this chapter. The explanatory frame of empire more or less disappeared from American discourse in recent years. As historian William Appleman Williams noted, *empire* has been a largely forbidden term in explaining either American aspiration or circumstance for reasons relatively apparent. To be defined as an empire connoted a power, self-interest, and willingness to exploit that contradicted the popular imagination of America as a reticent economic power whose principal interest was in protecting and expanding democracy. On occasion, popular culture established connection between empire and America. This was the case, for example, in the 1960s, when John Lennon noted that New York City, like Rome in an earlier era, was the center of global culture and commerce. His reference was to empire. "Why would one want to live anywhere else?" he concluded. These moments that broke through the veil of ignorance about American empire, however, had little cultural or political traction. They burned bright for a moment and quickly disappeared in the larger firmament of cultural and political discourse. In the present moment, that veil is again being pulled back.

At a time of political and economic crisis (think of the debacles that unfolded in Iraq and Afghanistan, or of the ongoing intensification of the 2008 economic meltdown), as the discourse surrounding crisis grows more radical and facilitates reform that is, as we have said, rapid and far-reaching, the language of American empire has become more acceptable. Perhaps, this is a consequence of the increasing concern of ruling elites from other nations, most notably China, filling the void. The decline in US international power and economic strength has produced an ever-more radical discourse on the Right about how to restore the influence and competitiveness of America. A *Newsweek* article warned that "steep debt, slow growth and high spending kills empires and America could be next" (Ferguson 2009, 1). Meanwhile, in contradistinction to those who use empire either nostalgically or as a national status in need of preservation are many critics. A number of eminent scholars, including Michael Hardt and Antonio Negri, Neil Smith, Cindi Katz, Adolph Reed, and David Harvey, have applied the frame of empire imaginatively in their analyses of US power and its repercussions. Equally important, writers as varied as journalist Charles Blow of the *New York Times* and novelist Richard Ford have used the language of empire in their writings. Many of these critics have explored the domestic consequences of American power internationally, depicting in their works the redistribution of resources resulting in ever-greater concentrations of wealth, an increasing magnitude of inequality, the intensification of poverty in communities of color, and an ever-expanding cohort of citizens defined as expendable.

The imperiled political and economic situation of American empire is a particularly salient context for exploring a series of compelling policy issues that have been examined, to date, almost exclusively through a center-right lens. Critically, and perhaps contradictorily, the remainder of this chapter will not explore US policy or action internationally. Global trends are being analyzed by experts with greater competence. Rather, we wish to investigate the relatively untilled ground that begins with the following questions: How has the decline of American empire as an international economic engine affected the role of the state and the policies it has championed domestically? Specifically, how has the new global economy and US economic decline within that economy influenced public education policy decision-making? What new role is being assumed by the state in our global economy? What new roles are the super rich playing in shaping domestic policy? How is the state's long-term strategic planning function affected? What are the costs and benefits to the larger society as a result of the state's changing roles and programming?

The remainder of this chapter will raise these questions as a prelude to the discussion of public education policies and issues that runs throughout the book. We will survey the vital interconnections between the decline of American empire, globalization, and the ever-more compromised role of the state. This dynamic is essential if we are to locate both the intent and impact of present social policies within the larger context of the contradictory push-pull of capital and American empire. Our intention is not to explore all social policies. As indicated above, our focus will be on the nexus between these political and economic forces and recent education policy. It is our expectation that this discussion will provide the necessary scaffolding to erect a fuller understanding of recent, dramatic shifts in education policymaking. It is our contention that the lessons in education can be applied to other sectors of the state such as health care and social services.

THE ROLE OF THE STATE

In the past, imperial structure has depended on state subjugation of other places and peoples in a colonial relationship. Subjugation cheapened the costs of labor and resources to facilitate the expansion of profit and the power of empire. Today, however, the technology and communication advances that speed up processes of globalization are of key import to empire building, allowing it to take qualitatively different form than in the past. Technology advances have accelerated the hypermobility of capital, a property that now underpins the accelerating, expansive concentration of wealth in a relatively small number of financial institutions around the globe. The rapid movement of money has significant implications for the stability of economic institutions, jobs, and the tax base of the state. The accelerated movement of capital across a heterogeneous global landscape—one in which labor laws, labor protection, and costs of living are far from standardized—provides part of the legitimacy for reducing "vestigial" national regulations that impede rapid financial decisionmaking and threaten corporate profits. Organized labor is particularly imperiled in this environment; today, in the time it takes to click a mouse, company heads can move thousands, if not hundreds of thousands of jobs from the United States to South Asia. Finally, as dollars flow from one region to another, the tax base of the state is rapidly destabilized. The nexus between American empire and globalization has effectively reduced the power of organized labor and the state. On the other side of the ledger, corporate power has grown exponentially during this same period.

As state power is reduced, supplanted by global corporations, and economic crisis deepens, the practices of empire grow more nakedly aggressive. One new role of the state becomes the utilization of military power to control territories for the benefit of private interest. While US military power remains both unparalleled and omnipresent internationally, US corporations are now outperformed by companies in Western Europe, China, and India. Faced with diminishing economic, political, and social strength, the American state grows dangerously reliant on both mercenary and public military forces to stabilize its international standing. Even when free trade and other international policies legalize corporate land-grabs and the extraction of precious resources such as oil in foreign regions, the US military oversees the wealth transfers. We might think of US interactions with Iraq in recent decades. Clearly, the American military is playing an ever-more aggressive role to stabilize US corporate influence internationally.

THE POLITICS OF CONCENTRATED WEALTH, GROWING INEQUALITY, AND THE DECLINE OF GLOBAL EMPIRE

Billionaires such as the Koch brothers, the Broad family, and Bill Gates, both individually and through their foundations, are crossing boundaries that once insulated government policymakers and policymaking from the individual agendas of the nation's wealthiest and most powerful citizens. Not only this, but the wealthy are now more likely than ever to be the very elected officials who are making policy decisions.

As Jacob Hacker and Paul Pierson have noted in their recent book *Winner-Take-All Politics*:

> By the time Rahm Emmanuel reached Capitol Hill, his understanding of politics had crystallized. In a summary that would have warmed the heart of Mark Hanna, the great political fixer of the Gilded Age, Emmanuel reportedly told staffers:
> "The first third of your campaign is money, money, money. The second third is money, money and press. The last third is votes, press and money. That is money 6 votes to 3." (Hacker and Pierson 2011, 252)

In this moment when the costs of a political campaign have skyrocketed, there is an especially powerful and growing connection between financing and electoral outcomes. More specifically, waging a successful campaign—in particular, affording the multimedia promotion of a candidate—is far more expensive than in the past. Money today may be even more vital to political campaigns than it was over a century ago or during the Gilded Age.

Who can most easily and expeditiously finance national and state political campaigns in this era? The wealthiest sectors of American society are the only groups capable of raising such large sums in relatively short periods of time. Especially relevant is the fact that exponential increases in the cost of political campaigns are occurring simultaneous to the most rapid shift of wealth and income in the society since the late nineteenth century. According to Robert Lieberman, "The share of total income going to the top one percent [of US earners] has increased from roughly eight percent in the 1960's to more than 20 percent today" (Lieberman 2011, 154).

This concentration of wealth produces a disproportionate political influence on electoral politics.

It appears increasingly obvious in the United States that the role of the state or, more concretely, central government as protector of the people, especially of those at the bottom of the social order, is an artifact of an earlier era, perhaps historic fantasy. For example, in the US during the Great Depression, a number of expanded or new state functions were codified through redistributive tax codes, regulatory functions, and social entitlements as well as services, although human rights were still legally and formally divided along racial lines. Historically, government performed vital functions, helping, on the one hand, to legitimate the large social order through the provision of specific kinds of social programming such as supports for the aged or homeless while, on the other, strengthening the workforce presently and over time through education, housing, and other services. As well, the government played a key role in making both the strategic assessments and large resource investments necessary for the continual accumulation of wealth. The development of highways, mass transit systems, genetic research, and banking regulations are but a few examples of this state function. Finally, we would be remiss not to mention the state's role in regulating and controlling society, whether owning and operating prisons, sustaining domestic police forces, or deploying armed forces internationally. Today, however, in an era of declining empire and increasingly powerful forces of globalization, a number of these basic functions are being called into question by economic and political decisionmakers (Gough 1979; O'Connor 1973).

At present, the US government's many roles are being evaluated and often redefined. Increasingly, the government is depicted as a failed institution, interfering with the efficiency of free markets. All public services, from education to medical treatment to policing, it is argued, are better privatized and then purchased through the marketplace. Some members of the super-affluent, such as billionaires David H. and Charles G. Koch and Wisconsin governor Scott Walker, call for the liquidation of public services and the transfer of public sector responsibility as well as funding to private companies. Simultaneously, they and many others believe that public institutions must become more akin to corporations by adopting new measurements of success that emphasize efficiency, heightened productivity, and worker accountability. The reconstituted culture of public agencies and the transfer of public wealth to private corporations is joined to a call for austerity. Public agencies and their private sector counterparts, it is asserted, must do more with less, producing ever-greater efficiencies and productivity in a world where resources for public services are increasingly constrained. State policy, debt, and a declining economy all reduce tax revenue. Consequently, budgets for a range of government services are slashed, public workforces reduced, and practices cheapened by the adoption of ever-more rote and mechanized forms of work. Meanwhile, expectations for worker output only rise. Policies of disinvestment in state functions and the abandonment of the public sector, along with calls for ever-higher, more easily quantified standards of service is a political cornerstone of this era.

As functions long performed by the state, such as schooling, are corporatized, transferred to the private sector, or downsized through policies of austerity, the very meaning of the state and the services it provides are radically reworked. State capacity to hire teachers and retain them, create stimulating learning environments, prevent overcrowded classrooms, and develop school-based leadership that can innovate on the basis of experience is, at best, stunted and, at worst "disappeared." Such a trend is not restricted to public schools but also coursing through the arteries of hospitals and other service providers. These patterns are often presumed by the larger public to be unavoidable consequences of a fixed economic political landscape. And yet we know that the landscape changes. Tax policies over the past thirty years, which lightened the obligations of the wealthy and increased costs for the middle and working classes, have only gained momentum. The explosive growth in debt financing by the federal government increasingly crowds out other service provisioning, diminishing investment in the poor and working classes. These are not consequences of natural forces but rather of an explicit lobbying campaign waged by the interest groups most likely to benefit from such changes: the already wealthy and powerful. The corporatization, capitalization, and cheapening of services provided by the state have a singular outcome: they hurt the poor and middle class while advantaging the very wealthy in the short and long terms.

THE RISE OF THE FINANCIAL SECTOR

The redistribution of wealth and income to a thinner and thinner slice of the top tier of Americans is in part explained by the explosive growth of finance capital and high-tech industries. In the financial sector, hedge funds and security swaps became both a new media language and the glitter that lit up Wall Street. Forty-one percent of officially declared US corporate profits emanate from finance capital. But what does such reliance on finance capital and profit mean? Smith (2009) suggests that this uneven distribution of profit is likely symptomatic of a budding crisis:

> The financial sector becomes flooded with capital.... With less and less capital devoted to the production of social value, and more and more capital devoted to the legalized gambling of the financial system, the discrepancy between the paper value of capital and its social value in terms of actual work is increasingly wide. At some point, the claims that paper capital makes to produce social value in the form of stocks, hedge funds, derivatives, debit-credit swaps, currency and so forth have to be rationalized with the actual value of what is produced; paper claims value and real value have to be brought back to commensurability, generally requiring a massive devaluation of paper capital. A crisis in capital is quite predictable. (63)

Smith describes precisely what occurred in the 2008 stock market meltdown when the Dow Jones fell from over 14,000 to below 7,000. The meltdown was a result, in part, of subprime lending practices that began in the United States but were replicated around the globe as banks ignored the risks associated with new financial tools. In the case of the United States, when the house-price bubble burst in 2006, tens of millions of overextended homeowners lost all or most of their investments, and many were forced to default on loans. Banks on the other sides of those loans began to fail almost immediately, first in the United States and then in Europe. The overreliance on showing a profit, even if only on paper; the evisceration of regulations such as Glass-Stegall, which might have created a firewall between banks and financial houses, thus at least slowing the spread of this economic virus; the ideological veneration of "wealth managers"; and the ever-greater influence of captains of the finance industry on state decisionmaking boards combined to produce the crisis of 2008. What that crisis will mean for the US economy, and empire, in the long term, remains unanswered.

Increased dependence on the financial sector to undergird and propel the economy is troubling for multiple reasons. First, it betrays shrinking industrial or service sectors and thus exacerbates diminishing diversity of employment positions in the US job market. Compounding this, the financial industry lends itself to far greater income inequality than either industrial or service sectors. Finally, the movement of more and more capital to the financial sector to produce increased rates of profit represents a crisis of overaccumulated capital to find other outlets for profit making fundamental to market need (Harvey 2004). An overreliance on finance industries to generate profit in the United States is both untenable (the search for ever-greater rates of profit through finance industries produces bubbles such as the subprime debacle) and indicative of the decline of other sectors of the US economy. This is to say, the movement of more and more capital and economic activity to the financial sector tells of declining US competitiveness in agriculture, industry, and perhaps even service production in the global marketplace.

ECONOMIC DECLINE, THE CAPITALIZATION OF PUBLIC ASSETS, AND TRANSFORMATION OF THE STATE

Capitalism requires the continual generation of capital, in the form of profits, while preventing overaccumulation from undermining value. Some part of the ongoing choreography of capital requires stretching the boundaries of space and time. According to Harvey (2004), surpluses can be absorbed by (a) temporal displacement through investment in long-term capital projects or social expenditures (such as education or research) that defer the reentry of capital values into circulation into the future; (b) special displacement through opening new markets, new production capacities, and new resource, social, and labor possibilities elsewhere; or (c) some combination of (a) and (b). Surpluses generated in the present and absorbed, for example, by long-term capital projects, can be productive only if they contribute to the long-term productivity or profitability of capital. As Harvey notes, this can happen when a more educated labor force or communication system expedites a next round of accumulation. But this theory does not always work. Overinvestment in built environments of, for example, housing, or social expenditure on public education, can result in devaluations of those assets or difficulties in paying off those debts. In part, such investment is a bet on a society's future in both the short and long terms.

The preparedness of a society to make such a bet in moments of larger economic crisis, as in the United States today, has proven to be politically and socially difficult. Progressive taxation policies that either freeze or reduce debt and grow various forms of public investment have historically been a primary means for absorbing over-accumulated wealth. However, new taxation policies, in so far as they redistribute wealth from top income earners to the middle and bottom do not win electoral or financial support from the affluent class. Without such taxation, overaccumulated capital must find other outlets. As a result financial institutions have played a more and more prominent role: easing the movement of capital to markets in new geographic spaces such as China or to growth industries such as high tech. Further, the creation of financial instruments such as the subprime mortgage bundles that preceded the economic crisis in 2007 promised to reduce the risks of capitalism's cycles of boom or bust. We saw instead that greater reliance on short-term returns from financial institutions creates an ever-more imperiled economic cycle of profit bubbles, bursts, and deepening crises, especially when accompanied by reduced investment in state projects that are both long and short term.

THE DECLINE OF EMPIRE AND RESTRUCTURING OF THE STATE

The rapid globalization of the circuitries of both economic production and distribution has had a number of significant consequences. Perhaps no outcome has had greater reverberation than an unmooring of individual and corporate identity from place. What we are witnessing is an increasingly vagabond capitalism that with greater impunity can ignore its collective social responsibilities. The rapidity with which capital is rerouted globally is matched only by the speed with which it sheds its commitments to social reproduction. In describing this, Cindi Katz (2001) noted that social reproduction "is always less mobile than production. At worst, this disengagement [by capitalism from social responsibility], hurtles certain people into vagabondage; at best it leaves people struggling to secure the material goods and social practices associated with social reproduction" (255).

Various social reproduction functions of the state, such as public schooling, are abandoned, creating the basis for policies that capitalize and redistribute formerly public assets to the private sector, while proliferating, for example, testing cultures as a cheapened substitute for other forms of education. Present educational policies are decreasingly able either to produce meaningful academic growth or to avert students' dropping or being pushed out of school. Instead, local schools are underfinanced and pedagogically constrained, providing ever-more degraded learning environments that lead students to early decisions of exit and dead-end jobs. Residents in the poorest communities of color who depend on public education to build the academic capacity and market competitiveness of their children are rendered even more marginal than in the recent past. The continued extraction of capital from the "commons" (regressive tax codes, budget cutting, capitalization of public schooling) only further delegitimates public institutions in the eyes of individuals struggling to carve a better life out of ever-more hostile environments.

The full retreat from social responsibility is not simply a consequence of global-ization and economic crisis. Although the objective circumstance of the deepening international and domestic economic crisis of America is indisputable, the flight from social responsibility enacted through budget cutting policies is largely the result of lower taxes for the very wealthy. Progressive income taxes and revenue generation as an alternative to budget cutting to reverse state debt and make strategic social reproduction investments in, for example, education and health care, to strengthen the economy in the short and long term, has largely been ignored by policymakers.

Instead, along with the decline of American empire has come a radical restruc-turing of tax codes. If capital can move with ever-greater rapidity from one place to another, the state is held hostage to the ever-present threat of industries relocat-ing, which, in turn, potentially degrades the tax base. The alternative has been for the state to accede to lower taxes on the wealthy and industry in exchange for the increasingly hollow promise of greater commitment to place. As noted earlier, the lessened obligation on the wealthiest sectors of society has occurred contradictorily at precisely the moment when concentrations of wealth and income have exploded. Importantly, the threats and greater mobility of the wealthy have resulted in more of the tax burden being shouldered by the middle class, which, in turn, has produced increased political resentment of the state. Critically, this cycle of upward tax redis-tribution, the growing tax burden passed onto the middle class, and the consequent resentment of the state is but one frame for explaining the steady erosion of both state financing and legitimacy. Anxiety about decline and an uncertain economic future has promoted an ever-more vulture-like ideology among dominant economic groups that leaves little room for policies guided by anything other than self-interest. The intersection between globalization and anxiety about the evaporation of accumulated wealth at risk in an ever-more unstable American empire has created much of the political momentum for silencing any political discourse that advances as its agenda the increase of taxes on the wealthy. Equally important, the consequent imposi-tion of regimes of austerity on state programs have degraded the quality of what is offered and resulted in an ever-greater rationing of what remains. This, in turn, has perpetuated popular notions of state programming as both wasteful and ineffective.

The new tax wars are but one expression of an increasingly hobbled state. As was noted earlier, the state's autonomy to carry out a range of strategic and social reproduction functions is also being challenged by an ideology that sanctifies the market, vilifying all things public. This market ideology dictates that the state be remade in the image of the corporation, thus emphasizing measures of productivity, efficiency, and outcome. Equally important, business practices are imported wholesale from corporations to centralize practices, create new command and control systems, incorporate monitoring technology into the practices of public agencies, track the performance of practitioners with complex evaluation schemes (education), moni-tor productivity through the levels of reimbursable dollars accumulated (health and social services), and within this corporate culture evolve administrators trained more in business techniques than the content or quality of the services being delivered. The tradeoffs of this exchange are rarely noted. The autonomy and discretion of public decisionmakers to make best choices in complex circumstance are rendered invisible. The distinct skill sets of relationship-building and substantive expertise that, for instance, distinguish the best practitioners in fields as disparate as public school teaching and medicine are rarely noted. As well, the embedding of these services in local communities and the potential experience of the state as proximate, democratic, and collective is lost; moving rapidly toward becoming a forgotten alternative, a sense of the commons, exemplified by the public sector, is dimming from collective memory.

That loss of a commons, however, is not simply a consequence of a makeover of the culture of government. Privatization, hereafter in this chapter described as capitalization, is perhaps the most troubling consequence of recent efforts to marketize all things public. We have entered a new phase of outsourcing or privatizing public resources. In the last ten years, the rhythm and nature of this transfer of public wealth has accelerated. Entire sectors of the social reproduction side of the welfare state, most critically in health care and education, are being rapidly capitalized as entrepreneurs search for new profitable markets. In public education, we have witnessed the ascent of charter schools, virtual learning, market curricula development, and an expansive number of firms engaged in the measurement and assessment of teachers, with a host of entrepreneurs making large and small profits. More specifically, profit making extends from publishers capitalizing on the new standards-based testing curricula, to high-tech companies experimenting and testing their curricula interventions, to real estate operators leasing property at exorbitant fees, to alternative certification programs, and finally for-profit schools. Each of these fragments, pieces of profit making, are part of a new "gold rush" to capitalize the $500 billion of public assets being redistributed from neighborhood K–12 public schooling to the marketplace. The transformation of education would not be complete, however, without at least mentioning for-profit higher education. The for-profit sector of higher education has rapidly increased in the past decade. So much so, that at this moment, the University of Phoenix's student population of approximately 250,000 is second only to that of the New York State University system. For-profit colleges in the trades also have exploded in size, according to both enrollment and share of market. The for-profit sector's intrusion into education complicates understandings of public versus private, as it has been financed, in large part, through federal loan programs or public assets. Approximately 80 percent of the operating revenue of these for-profit schools can be tracked back to federal loan programs.

The ever-more rapid redistribution of public assets to for-profit entrepreneurs in education and health care cannot be explained outside a context of empire decline. In general, as US companies lose their capacity to compete in a range of markets they have historically dominated, other options have been systematically opened to recirculate overaccumulated capital. Most importantly, high-tech companies developed and expanded a range of service industries and the finance industry became an ever-more critical part of the circuits of capital and profit making. Critical to this discussion, the entrepreneurial gaze was cast upon public assets. The state controls a treasure trove of cash that heretofore had only been available to the market in the most circumscribed ways. The need to create new markets for overaccumulated capital desperate for new sites of profit making converged with the intensifying ideological assault regarding the state's historic inefficiencies and lack of productivity. The battering ram of ideology or market solutions to public problem, over time, opened up the gates of the larger treasury of the public sector. More to the point, ideological warfare has increasingly given way to a rapid material redistribution of public assets to private entrepreneurs.

One might argue that the project of capitalizing public assets, or the commons, is the most primitive form of capitalism. It feeds with ever-greater ferocity off of the accumulated pain and dispossession of the poor and middle classes by redistributing resources upward. It might also be argued that it represents an end point, regarding the presumption that the state has an independent sovereignty. As its boundaries are pierced by a private sector promoting profit, deregulation, and corporatized practices as well as the resetting of policy direction by the extraordinarily wealthy, the state has effectively surrendered its status as a public space, or commons. Instead, it has been transformed into a catch basin of wealth increasingly unregulated as a result of market ideology and its assets redistributed to powerful political and economic interest groups. It is within this context that schools and health care agencies, for example, are starved and, in turn, increasingly provide ever-more degraded services to the poorest communities, while contradictorily private interests swallow an ever-greater proportion of the state's public assets.

One clear consequence of this dynamic is that the state is increasingly unable to meet its most basic social reproduction functions in poor and working-class communities. The health, job readiness, and critical thinking abilities of the largest part of the citizenry are increasingly being sacrificed at the altar of capitalization. These trends erode the legitimacy of welfare state institutions, as they are increasingly unable to provide basic services adequately. This downward spiral is produced largely by neglect but spun by the private sector, the media, and political allies as a consequence of a fundamental coding flaw in the DNA of the state, which they argue is programmed to produce bureaucratic inefficiency and ineffectiveness.

Importantly, the public health care and education that achieves some measure of adequacy, if not excellence, is reserved for a smaller and smaller slice of the population. We will address this question of excellence and accountability regimes in the second half of the book. Quality services are available, for example, on the basis of class privilege to those who can supplement what the state subsidy provides, for example in the area of health care. In education, the wealthiest communities have always received a disproportionate share of public resources. Recently, this class structure has been braided to a social meritocracy of test scores. On the basis of recent social policy, poor and working-class students of color who are best able to produce strong test scores are most likely to access programming, receiving greater public and private investment. In general, they are more likely to be admitted to charter schools. Consistently, high scores ensures survival in charters. Those who do not sustain their performance on standardized tests are over time "transitioned" back to traditional public schools. In this way, the basic legitimacy of capitalization policy can be sustained, at least, in the short run, through exemplar narratives of extraordinary success. The dynamic of ever-more selective targeting of enriched reproduction investment and an intensified legitimating of such initiative is a hallmark of both present policymaking and public discourse.

This transfer of wealth upward may be a signal that ruling groups have effectively given up on the future of American empire and opened a fire sale on what remains of its assets. In that sense, we may be witnessing the cannibalization of our children's future as their public assets are being sold to private sector bidders. No matter what this phenomenon signifies, about either the economy or assumptions about the future of American empire, this we do know: the encircling of the commons by dominant economic groups is not a new phenomenon. The loss of a commons public sphere is not without historic precedent. As Christopher Hill in *The World Turned Upside Down* has noted, "These struggles unfolded in seventeenth century England, as the forces of private power and landownership clashed repeatedly with multiple and diverse popular movements pointing away from capitalism and privatization towards radically different forms of social and communal organization" (Harvey 2004, 162).

THE LOGIC OF DISASTER, SURVIVAL, AND DISPOSABILITY IN LEGITIMATING POLICIES THAT CAPITALIZE THE COMMONS

As American empire teeters, searching for new markets and expanding profits to stabilize itself, the public sector has become the latest source of capital for the profit engines of the private sector. As the redirection of public money accelerates, policy tradeoffs have become more transparent. For example, in education the redistribution of public assets to charter schools has had a range of consequences that will be described in the next chapter of the book. Of particular significance is a logic, or Gramscian "common sense" understanding, among many poor parents of color that the schools in their neighborhoods and the fate of their children are braided to a "disaster." Thus, they choose to decouple their child's fate from that of the raging fire of degraded public education in the larger community in an attempt to ensure individual survival. The movement from collective efforts to solve collective problems to individual exit to charter schools to solve the problem of degraded public schools has, in large measure, been a product of an ideological campaign waged by the Right to delegitimize public institutions and policymaking that offer ways out to a select few.

These policies of exit ultimately reinforce the phenomenon of survival of the fittest. Parents capable of gambling on the charter school lottery and children who, once admitted, are able to post the test scores to make it over the long haul are declared as most fit. Survival as we have come to understand it in the poorest communities of color has to do with both parental engagement and student testing performance. But what is the fate of those students who have neither actively engaged parents nor testing skills? They are not granted "survival" exit visas. Instead, they are relegated to the ever-more barren and starved sector of traditional public education. Shock and awe media reports celebrate charter schools and the test scores of the 1–5 percent of poor students of color who make up their census while overlooking the 90–95 percent of students of color who remain in underfunded and failing traditional public schools.

The powerful interplay between disaster, shredding of safety nets, market ideology, and disposability is vividly illustrated in New Orleans in the aftermath of Hurricane Katrina. Policies of privatization and capitalization following Katrina were especially evident in the area of public education. Entire neighborhoods were rapidly transformed into experiments in vouchering and charter education. The language of natural and public education disaster was conflated as right-wing advocates such as Clint Bolick of the Alliance for School Choice announced, "If there could be a silver lining in this tragedy, it would be that children who had few prospects for a high quality education, now would have expanded options" (Saltman 2007, 138). Brian Riedlinger, director of the Algier Charter School Association, stated, "I think the schools have been a real albatross. And so I think parents are given the hope of wiping the slate clean and starting over" (138). The fundamentalist language of cleansing and redemption does not translate very well to complex public institutions. The proposals fashioned by the "new public education reformers" of New Orleans were not intended to rebuild but rather to replace public systems of education with private, relatively unaccountable, and cheaper forms of education.

We continue our description of post-Katrina New Orleans for its ability to provide especially powerful reminders of how recent policies circulate within the poorest communities.

> Six months after Hurricane Katrina damaged all 124 New Orleans Public Schools (NOPS), only 20 had reopened. Approximately 10,000 of the 62,227 students enrolled in NOPS before the storm had re-registered for school in the district. While the state floundered, privatization experts were explicit in communicating their desire to undermine public control over education decision-making, with spokespersons from organizations such as Freedom Works arguing that imposing a voucher system at that moment would be hard to overturn later. (142)

As Bolick noted, a prime reason for introducing vouchers in New Orleans was to save money. New Orleans "received an already very low per pupil funding of roughly 5,000 dollars (per pupil funding in surrounding wealthier communities was double and triple this amount), while Bush's voucher scheme pays only 750 dollars per student" (143). Equally important, the charter school miracle in New Orleans has been made available to a vast majority of present residents, producing little if any impact on academic testing outcomes. Perhaps, most importantly, the 52,000 students who migrated elsewhere in the aftermath of the storm have been of little interest to policymakers exclusively focused on privatizing and capitalizing the New Orleans school system. Kenneth Saltman (2007) describes the reworking of NOPS as the largest experiment ever in school vouchers, allowing for enormous profits in education rebuilding and the replacement of a universal system of education with a charter school network.

The continued underfunding of traditional public schools, rationing of access to charter schools, and disinterest in those students who have been permanently dispossessed from New Orleans schools as politicians, developers, and investors seek a market solution to a social problem is troubling. As education writer Henry Giroux notes:

> Katrina revealed with startling and disturbing clarity, that if you are poor and black, society neither wants, cares about, or needs you. African Americans occupy the poorest sections of New Orleans . . . ghettoized frontier zones created by racism and coupled with economic inequality. Cut out any long-term goals and a decent vision of the future, these are the populations . . . who have been rendered redundant and disposable. (Giroux 2006, 188)

The rapacious behavior of capital and dominant political, as well as economic, interests during this epoch is unbridled. Importantly, the intention to plunder and loot the public purse and degrade the commons is producing profound contradictions, which we will enumerate in a moment. The intensifying dispossession and disposability of large sectors of the population, in large part due to a radical restructuring of the state, raises questions about the viability of both present policies and the society. Clearly, this form of primitive or barbaric capitalism is not without historic precedent, but we may be entering a period of especially harsh destruction stemming from new "vulture" forms of capitalism, free of state regulation, and further, positioned to pillage what remains of the independent and fiscally solvent state. According to Harvey, vulture capitalism "is as much about cannibalistic practices as it is about achieving harmonious global development" (Harvey 2004, 136).

Vulture capitalism signals a rapid disintegration of the fragile wall that separates long-term state functions from the short-term and circumscribed interests of corporations or the market. As this wall falls, the "civilizing function" of the state in providing public education, health care, and social entitlements is ever-more likely to give way to policies of austerity and profit making. The interplay between the disfiguring of the state and the disintegration of culture is briefly described by Zsusza Ferge (2000): "The functions of the state in the last centuries seem to describe a bell curve. The ascending side promised a virtuous circle, forcing the state to complete its self-serving and coercive functions with more responsibility for the common good. The descending side may lead to a vicious circle giving free rein to a process of decivilization" (201).

Indications of decivilization are evident as the state loses political legitimacy and the power to guide social reproduction. The crisis of capital within American empire has forced a choice between short-term private sector capitalization of public assets and longer-term state investment in social reproduction. In a political environment dominated by corporate interest, and where working-class social movements are at best weak and at worst nonexistent, it is the former policy option that has prevailed. That option, however, although addressing some of the short-term interests of concentrated wealth, is not likely to serve the short- or long-term interests of the overwhelming number of Americans or the larger economy. The incompatibility between short-term plunder or capitalization of public education and the short- and long-term needs of the society in relationship to social reproduction, political legitimation, and economic accumulation are key indicators of decivilization.

THE CONSEQUENCES OF RECKLESSLY CAPITALIZING PUBLIC EDUCATION: THE IMPERILED FUTURE OF THE AMERICAN DEMOCRATIC EXPERIMENT

How do we explain capital's accelerating evisceration of the state's social reproduction and strategic planning functions in a moment of intensified global competition? In the past, the state provided a collectivizing and long-term corrective to corporations more individuated and short-term thirst for profit and expansive market share. As state functions—in planning for the larger society's social reproduction needs in, for example, education, or the critical overarching needs of capital in relationship not to a particular sector of the economy, but the larger system of capital accumulation— decay and give way to the onslaught of a more primitive impulse for survival, the individual free-for-all of state plunder intensifies. The plunder is of both the state treasury and its regulatory function.

More and more of the $500 billion of public money dedicated to K–12 education is redistributed to corporations and individual entrepreneurs. The new networks of school systems, like their corporate counterparts, are less accountable to public sector regulatory agencies. As more and more networks of charters are spun off from traditional forms of educational accountability and regulation, what we have is less a system of public education than fiefdoms of charter schooling. Clearly, such a circumstance mirrors the free-for-all in the marketplace, increasingly focused on capitalizing state resources and degrading its regulatory functions.

Comparative studies suggest that current strategies for upgrading public education in the United States are highly flawed. Policy reform in the most competitive economies in Western Europe and Asia, at present, suggests that what works in education includes increased financial investment, centralization of state authority, and emphasis on critical thinking. Why then is US policymaking in the area of education headed in the opposite direction? Is it because the United States is more innovative? We think the answer lies elsewhere. This policy direction is motivated by (1) ever-more fundamentalist commitment to ideology, (2) a state weakened over the course of decades though pitched battle with privateers, and (3) the flood of overaccumulated capital increasingly desperate for new arenas of profit making. The question becomes: Where does this leave the poorest students of color and the larger society? What roles are these students being prepared to fulfill in the new American economy?

THE RHETORIC OF EVIDENCE-BASED REFORM AND
POLICYMAKING DENIAL OF EMPIRICAL FINDINGS

Present policy presumption is that student testing and measures of teacher performance should be the primary strategic intervention for restoring learning cultures and academic performance within public schools. The accumulation of such data is seen as a linchpin for developing effective interventions and improved academic performance. We would be remiss in failing to mention that the reduction of teacher to student classroom ratios, increased strategic investment in the development of teaching capacity, and the length of school day or year are other rational points of departure for the restoration of public education but have largely been ignored. Of course, these policy initiatives would require substantial investment, which to date, has been a third rail in all policy discussion.

If the science of public education and the data it produces are the essential frame for our most recent experiments with schooling, why then are policymakers ignoring the implications of emergent data? In Georgia and Pennsylvania, recent reports indicate large-scale cheating. This phenomenon likely extends beyond these two states, to many others reporting rapid and significant increases in test scores. This new culture of cheating is a predictable outcome and linked to Campbell's law, which suggests when performance and future rides on a single criterion, there is greater likelihood that accommodations of one form or another will occur to ensure positive outcome. Equally important, on the basis of evidence collected over the past decade, the national experiment in charter schooling is failing. Recent studies indicate that there is little difference in test scores between charters and traditional public schools. If anything, public schools are outperforming their charter counterparts. Recent evidence also suggests that exemplary charter performance is less likely traced to innovation than to admission and attrition practices, which disproportionately jettison students who do not test well. This data has been accumulating for over a decade and yet present policies of testing and supplanting traditional schools with charters continues to gather momentum. What explains this paradox?

The "science of testing" and "innovation of charter schooling" as triggers for effective school reform persist, then, despite evidence to the contrary. A profit-making testing industry, along with for-profit online higher education and testing security firms have emerged with many powerful allies. They continue to advocate for more assessment and testing even as their bromide promises of cure quickly evaporate into the ether of limited academic improvement and widespread cheating. Clearly, these interest groups have had a significant influence on the sustained investment in testing by public agencies. These purveyors of quick solutions to complex problems are increasingly supported by politicians who capitulate to wealthy patrons and lobbyists. It is important to, at least briefly, reiterate the policy tradeoff of investing in charters as contrasted with traditional public schooling. The latter requires the significant strategic investment in and outside of the classroom, necessary to create more robust and effective learning environments. The former offers a quicker and cheaper fix of exit and testing as the answer to a failing school system. In a period where new taxes are not being contemplated, progressive social movements are weak, concentrations of wealth grow, and capital is on the prowl for new forms of profit, the answer to this policy question was predetermined.

And so, we must ask: Is evidence a fulcrum for present experimentation or simply artifice for other intention? If artifice and it is erected around other policy intentions, what does it obscure? In our estimation, we need to explore the choices foregone in favor of testing and the context driving it. The capitalization of public education requires sources of legitimization to promote its agenda. Some part of that apparatus is a technology and the science of testing, which is conflated with the only true path to measuring academic performance and the development of structures necessary to improve "achievement." This naturalized landscape and chain of logic regarding reform features science, testing, charter innovation (to improve testing scores), and an ever-more circumscribed curriculum. This apparatus has its merits. It can track student performance in highly specified areas, help build basic competency, and determine what kinds of programming are lifting scores. That said, it is a highly incomplete approach to the complex and daunting project of school reform. Equally important, it is a relatively cheap approach stamped with an ideological power of both market innovation and scientific intervention. The cloak of scientific truth and sense-making has served to conceal a large part of the massive redistribution of public dollars to charter networks, testing services, and, most fundamentally, out of traditional public schooling. It is in the nexus between legitimating discourse, economic redistribution of public resources, and denial of evidence, which refutes claims of success, that demands further interrogation. It is important to reiterate that this dynamic accelerates the movement of underperforming students of color out of traditional schools and public education dollars to entrepreneurial private sector initiatives. In turn, as testing helps to reallocate dollars to the private sector and students to secondary labor markets, it provides a short-term stabilizing ballast for empire and capital. While at the same time, it promotes ever-greater social tinder through the dispossessed bodies of those individuals comprising disposable populations.

WHAT KIND OF FUTURE CAN BE DISCERNED FROM THIS WHOLESALE CAPITALIZATION OF PUBLIC ASSETS AND DEGRADATION OF THE STATE?

We have no crystal ball in which to glimpse the future of public education. The rest of this book will explore a number of the primary policy consequences and trends associated with the rapidly expanding public education marketplace. As empire declines and the forces of capitalization of public assets and degradation of state power gather force, we will be faced with a number of unprecedented choices: What proportion of public dollars should be transferred to the marketplace? To what extent and in what ways should these increasingly private entities be held accountable to public structures? Is accountability possible, in an era during which regulation is politically unpopular? How does capitalism's penetration of public education, along with degraded regulatory functions, and generalized disinvestment in all things public affect the larger democratic project of America? How does present policy reorganize labor? (By driving poor people of color out of schools, on the one hand, and preparing them for little more than the lowest paying jobs through the present testing regimen, we will argue.) How does state investment in policing relate to the ever-greater gap between the very top of the wealth/income pyramid and everyone else? Finally, how is the experience in public education being replicated in every other sector of domestic spending?

The remainder of this book will address the questions that we have sketched here. Their answers construct a still larger question: What kind of future do these trends portend for American society? That future and our stake in helping to shape it are part of the reason for this book. We are committed to more fully understanding the complex forces at work remaking our public education system as well as the likely impact of these trends, in both the short and long term. We want to unpack both the rhetoric of recent reform and the multiplicity of factors that account for its rapid ascendance. We attend, in our work, to the social and political-economic context in which change happens: banks are hoarding money, effectively shutting down prospects for job growth, while dominant economic interests are aggressively hostile to any form of tax increase that would threaten their assets. Simultaneously, these economic interests are increasingly willing to raid the public purse for new forms of profit. We live in a period of economic bubbles, speculation, and efforts to move overaccumulated capital to new profit-making sites. The state represents, perhaps, the last stable market for American capital. All of this of course has powerful implications for policies that might emphasize significant strategic investment in public education. We must also begin to highlight sites of resistance and alternatives to the present naturalized landscape of market reform and plunder of state assets. The development of movements, whether local or national, that resist the present trend is the most compelling and daunting task that progressives can assume. Altering present trends in education reform remains our most pressing challenge. C. L. R. James suggests that some tools are intellectual ideas; others are tools of the imagination and other possible worlds; still others are our human bodies, but most importantly they are social and political organizations for a more humane future. One earns one's freedom and life, as Goethe put it, when one takes them every day by storm (Smith 2009, 64).

FOR FURTHER READING

Bowles, Samuel, and Herbert Gintis. *Schooling in Capitalist America: Educational Reform and the Contradictions of Economic Life.* New York: Basic Books, 1976.

Giroux, Henry. *Stormy Weather: Katrina and the Politics of Disposability.* Boulder, CO: Paradigm Publishers, 2006.

Harvey, David. *The New Imperialism.* Oxford: Oxford University Press, 2005.

Labaree, David. "Targeting Teachers." *Dissent* 58 (3) (2011): 9–14.

Meier, Deborah. "Creating Democratic Schools." *Rethinking Schools* 19 (4) (2005).

Noah, Timothy. *The Great Divergence: America's Growing Inequality Crisis and What We Can Do About It.* New York: Bloomsbury Press, 2012.

Saltman, Kenneth. *Capitalizing on Disaster: Taking and Breaking Public Schools.* Boulder, CO: Paradigm Publishers, 2007.

Chapter 2

Restructuring the Teaching Workforce

Attack Rhetoric and Disinvestment as Effective Education Reform in an Era of Economic Decline

Recently, in a *New York Times* op-ed page editorial, the novelist Dave Eggers and Ninive Clements Calegar (2011) noted, "We have a chance with many teachers near retirement, to prove we are serious about education. The first step is to make the teaching profession more attractive to college graduates.... [They need] better weapons, training and incentives." And yet, over the past few years, we have heaped upon teachers and their unions not the incentives necessary to attract and retain an ever-more able teaching force but scorn. Teaching and public education is a hotly contested political battleground because it is a critical pivot for redistributive justice or a transformative, equitable investment in public education. The reform agenda for public education sketched earlier has been joined to hegemonic understandings that the present crisis of academic accomplishment in the poorest communities of color is not a result of class size, low salaries, lack of teacher support, degraded infrastructure, or resources but rather of teacher failure as measured by the new metrics. Lyn Hancock, an education journalist, decried newspaper reports in LA and NYC announcing every teacher's test or assessment score: "In NYC, schools coverage has been largely tethered to the corporate reformers agenda—mostly to a measuring tool for firing incompetent teachers. Inadequate teachers are without question a serious problem, as are rules and systems that protect them. But it is unwise to think that weeding out the weak will address the other pressing problems facing teachers and schools ... [for example] state budgets that are gutting core services" (Hancock 2011).

As noted earlier, the educational crisis in the United States cannot be about resources, given the desire for austerity. Consequently, it must be about the most visible and influential figures in the classroom: teachers. Therefore the political economy of austerity demands that public school troubles be traced to teacher failure, stripped of context. Teachers are referred to as "overpaid baby sitters," dismissed as incompetent, and unilaterally responsible for the unsatisfactory testing results of students by much of the media and a cross section of politicians. Although the story is complex, what we have been offered as the explanation for public school failure is the easy answer of uncaring, well-paid, satisfactorily supported, and too frequently incompetent teachers committed only to collecting their paychecks and thus neglecting generation after generation of poor students. We learn such teacher neglect and incompetence is protected by unions interested in materially benefitting their members without regard for the welfare of students. Consequently, teacher unions must be weakened if not destroyed, if we are to implement effective public educational reform.

Despite the rational calls by Eggers and Clements (2011), Hancock (2011), Diane Ravitch (2011b), and Linda Darling-Hammond (2012) for strategic investment to promote student academic achievement, present policy momentum is headed in another direction, instead blaming teachers for a "crisis" of public education. This direction has a drastic though predictable impact on the structure of the teaching labor market. Increasingly, the teaching workforce is a temporary workforce—ever-less stable and fungible. Job instability among public school teachers is exacerbated while resultant teacher shortages are simultaneously overcome by cohorts of young instructors in programs such as Teach for America, many of whom use inner-city school experience as a lift-off platform for next stage career development. Other young, committed, but under-supported teachers in these programs too often burn out rapidly. The implicit assumption is that teacher continuity and expertise developed over time matters little, while what matters most is a curricula that proscribes for teachers and students alike, minute by minute, what needs to be taught in order to raise testing performance. Teachers are perceived as easily replaceable in ever-more mechanized and standardized teaching environments. In this regard Chester Finn remarked, "They [teachers] are ... going from a respected profession to a mass workforce in which everyone is treated as if they [*sic*] are interchangeable as in the steel mills of yesteryear" (Gabriel 2011b).

This intensified degradation of the role of teachers and their work environments has been compounded by a political whirlwind of scorn for the productivity of classroom instructors. As Steve Derion, a teacher in Manahawkin, New Jersey, reported: "It's hard to feel good about yourself when your governor and other people are telling you you're doing a lousy job.... I'm sure there were worse times to be a teacher in our history. I know they had very little rights but it feels like we're going back toward that direction" (Gabriel 2011b). Lindsay Vlachakis, a teacher from

Madison, Wisconsin, remarked, "I put my heart and soul into teaching; when people attack teachers, they're attacking me" (Gabriel 2011b).

The profession of public school teaching is being restructured, changing what is taught (teaching to the test), how information is taught (online and ever more proscribed pedagogy), workforce composition (younger, whiter, cheaper, less experienced), and overall workforce stability (less interest in remaining within the profession and increased turnover). These trends, which undercut the status, skill, and stability of the public school teaching workforce, accompany an increasingly explicit and intensified attack on the wages and working conditions of teachers.

Of course, like any other part of the workforce, public school teachers are not pure in intention or capacity. Yes, public unions have missed the boat on building partnerships with the communities they serve and taking a degree of risk in rethinking the meaning of tenure, robust curricula, and the length of a school year. This issue is particularly compelling in very poor communities of color, which have long suffered from both the neglect of policy indifference and decay of fiscal disinvestment. Teachers who are on the front line of school systems battered by such decisionmaking are visible and predictable targets when learning outcomes don't meet the expectations of parents and policymakers. The racial dynamics of this conflict are unmistakable as white teachers and union officials are too often in heated exchanges with parents and students of color. Teacher unions have been insufficiently imaginative and hesitant to make risk-building alliances with parents around their common interest of increased investment in classroom instruction. Instead unions have almost exclusively focused their attention and organizing on membership benefits. That said, a question that remains unasked is whether unions' focus on membership benefits has been the decisive factor in the myriad difficulties of public schooling in poor communities or simply a convenient and popular scapegoat. We wish to posit that the most powerful frames for explaining both the daunting problems of public education and the present simplistic policies of reaction have been rendered invisible.

The attack on public workers has occurred in a context of growing inequality and regressive tax codes that are rarely if ever discussed in relationship to the budget crises of the state. A first line of attack has been ideological, a full throttle campaign to delegitimate the state for its domestic policy failures and as a drain on the ever-more scarce resources of a society experiencing economic contraction. This ideological attack on the state establishes a new front, shifting ever so gradually from the individuals receiving state services (including welfare recipients, young people perceived as potential gang members, affirmative action babies, or substance abusers) to the public sector workers who have worked—for better and worse—in intimate relation within these service sectors. Importantly, this shift sets the stage for an intensified material attack on both the state and the middle class. The restructuring of public services and workers during economic crisis is not accidental but intended. The present policy and media attack on teachers cannot be fully understood outside of these dynamics. The task of this chapter is to excavate the political and economic context and class interests driving present policy decisionmaking.

REFRAMING THE CRISIS OF PUBLIC EDUCATION:
A POSTSCRIPT TO THE MIDTERM STATE ELECTIONS

During the past thirty years, we have witnessed many kinds of political attacks by the Right during election years. Perhaps, the most compelling and effective prior to 2010 was the attack leveled against Michael Dukakis in 1988, for the release of Willie Horton from prison to a community-based transition program during his watch as governor of Massachusetts. Horton's subsequent crimes became the leading edge of a partisan call for tougher leadership than what Dukakis had provided. In effect, he was decried as soft on crime. The image of Horton as a black man released to produce more mayhem and crime was an important subtext to the attack on Dukakis. The threat was not only Dukakis but the black male predator on white communities. The attack ads were largely prepared for and distributed to working-class and middle-class communities. For decades, the leading edge of conservative attack traveled along the tight lines of race. Whether the wedge race issue was "welfare queens," Willie Horton, affirmative action babies, or street violence, the images and narratives always hewed very close to the dangers of the darker races.

We are, however, in a new moment. Although race remains a very powerful source of division and fear, the wedge issues that are being developed and tested have as much to do with class as race. Public workers are increasingly the new Willie Horton, as represented as a menace to the larger electorate. These workers are presented as symptomatic of a state out of control—in its deficit financing, high rates of compensation to public workers, and ultimately in a parasitic relationship to the private sector taxpayer. Blaming public workers is conducive to passing austerity measures. But there still are other reasons for the demonization of public workers at present.

In recent years, the middle class has begun to wage a war against itself. The deserving private sector, middle-class workforce, increasingly experiencing wage and benefit decline, unemployment, and underemployment is directing its resentment at the polls against the middle-class, public workers reconfigured as undeserving. This resentment is being stoked by media reports, right-wing financing of Tea Party candidates, and political speeches about two classes: one the rich, privileged, public sector employees, and the other the middle-class private sector workers, increasingly struggling to survive. Despite the vitriol and visibility of these attacks, their basic premise has been rejected by the electorate. For example, the CBS–*New York Times* poll indicated that a majority of Americans are against weakening the collective bargaining rights of public employee unions and are against cutting the pay or benefits of public workers to reduce state budget deficits (Cooper and Thee-Brennan 2011). It is therefore incumbent that, as politicians and right-wing activists issue reports and impassioned speeches vilifying public workers and their unions, we remind ourselves of what is simultaneously being obscured and omitted.

While legislation in state after state and media attention focus on "dysfunctional unions" and "unproductive" public workers as the frame for explaining the failure of public schools and, more largely, public services, other powerful explanations have been ignored. In New York City, for example, 54 cents of every income dollar earned is collected by the top 1 percent of earners. Yet growing inequality in income and wealth across the United States, not seen since the Great Depression, was at best a backstory. Reducing the tax rates for the wealthy, which exacerbates inequality and restricts state revenues, has been a policy constant. As a result, after the most recent economic downturn, officials in state after state declared their treasury broken and turned to policies that required ever-deeper cuts to essential services. The policy misfit caused by increasingly regressive taxation codes, ever-greater concentrations of wealth, and a desire to balance state budgets is rarely considered and thus at the very least curious. Critically, attacks on public workers intensified at the moment that the larger economy was destabilized and government at every level began to spill red ink.

The irrationality of current policy is particularly vivid when considering the massive turnover of teachers nationally. Turnover can be traced to both the demographics of retirement and the churning of the workforce as a result of working conditions in the poorest districts. Arthur Costigan indicates that the political reality of a scarcity of teachers is particularly acute in poor, urban school systems. It has resulted in an exodus of certified teachers. It is within this context that quality of work life issues may be a contributing factor for most teachers leaving within two years of beginning teaching (Costigan 2005). We are left to deduce that policy attacking teachers is at best misguided and at worst a consequence of a cynical policymaking that circumscribes the problems of public schools to simple frames of scapegoats and a politics of austerity.

Resentment for unemployment, benefit decline, and job instability at present is easily directed toward public workers, including teachers. As a short-term political strategy, this is likely to exacerbate the problems of public schools, creating ever-more unstable and austere teaching and learning environments. Ultimately, the alternate frame of economic disinvestment and regressive tax policy starving public services is a more powerful tool for explaining the troubles of public schools in the poorest communities.

ECONOMIC CRISIS AND RESTRUCTURING OF THE LABOR FORCE

Historically, during periods of economic crisis, dynamics associated with the Doctrine of Less Eligibility disrupt the equilibrium between workers inside and outside the marketplace. Simply stated, the doctrine demands that the lowest paid worker inside of the marketplace be paid more than the highest paid workers outside it. The doctrine is expected to assure an efficient movement of labor to growth sectors of the economy at prevailing market wages. In an earlier historic epoch, such a dynamic accounted for citizens relegated to workhouses, because of the English Poor Laws, earning less than subsistence wages. This meager income can in part be explained by the falling income of peasant farmers and serfs during a period of accelerating industrialization. Workhouse wages had to be set below peasant subsistence income to make certain that economic incentives for rural to urban labor migration existed. If we fast-forward to the present crisis, although the strictures of the doctrine application are less draconian, they remain a powerful force in the restructuring of the public sector workforce. As wages fall in the marketplace, a new equilibrium of economic incentive and disincentive emerges in other sectors of the economy, for example government jobs or entitlements. To achieve such equilibrium means that bottlenecks in the distribution of labor to declining wage sectors of the economy must be cleared. Otherwise, workers will seek options outside of the market, for example unemployment insurance or public employment, to either slow or halt their movement to the lowest wage industries.

This clearing of impediment to the "natural laws" of the marketplace occurs along two fronts. On the one hand, an ideological attack delegitimating public worker salaries is pursued, and on the other, a material attack disinvesting in wages, as well as destabilizing working conditions, is also launched. The present attack on public employees and, more specifically, teachers must at least in part be viewed in this way.

As was suggested, the new equilibrium of lower wages and poorer working conditions in and outside of the marketplace is produced and reproduced by a politics of economic self-interest. A broad cross section of wealthy interest groups including, but not limited to, hedge fund managers, corporate investors, and foundation patrons has cohered around a more or less common political agenda. That agenda joins the following themes: (1) no new taxes on the wealthy, (2) little discussion of substantial strategic investment in critical services, for example public education, (3) acceptance of policies of fiscal austerity, (4) the rendering invisible of rapid turnover problems or instability of the teacher workforce, (5) the singular commitment to using metric standards and student test scores as the basis for evaluating teachers and the ways these patterns have differential impact by race and class.

SCIENTISM, TEACHER ASSESSMENT, AND THE RADICAL RESTRUCTURING OF WORKING CONDITIONS

The lever most directly responsible for applying the pressure reshaping teacher working conditions is the technology of assessment. In the last decade of the twentieth century, initiatives designed to measure the effectiveness of teachers through standardized tests increased in volume. The logic was simple and compelling. Teachers must be held accountable for their performance through forms of measurement that assess growth or change in student academic achievement. For too long, it was argued, students, especially poor students of color, had been the victims of teachers who were not getting the job done in the classroom. Lack of teacher accountability and performance explained the breakdown in public education, and the technology of testing provided a low-cost solution. The relative value of teachers could be assessed and salary and promotion tied to quantifiable achievement. In this way underperforming educators could be weeded out more easily. Policy emphasis on the metrics of teacher performance has only grown during the first decade of the twenty-first century.

Technical, metric-defined teacher evaluations provide a large part of the legitimacy for the current reform agenda. In New York City twelve new tests are being developed whose primary purpose would be to "grade teachers, not the students who take them" (Otterman 2011). Under a new law, 40 percent of a teacher's evaluation will be based on these test scores. Teachers will be subject to firing if they are rated ineffective two years in a row. Daniel Koretz, a professor of education at Harvard and a testing expert, however, has expressed concern with the design of the test, noting that "when you give kids complicated tasks to do, performance tends to be quite inconsistent from one task to the next." Koretz concluded that "Kentucky tried similar tests and abandoned them, partly because they could not compare results from year to year. Teachers were also having their students practice the particular skills they knew would be tested, meaning the exam was measuring test preparation not necessarily broader learning" (Otterman 2011).

The concurrence of economic decline and the ascent of teaching metrics as a primary mechanism for solving the public education crisis is not coincidental. David Labaree suggested "that per student cost is markedly higher as one moves up the system from elementary to secondary school to college. As a result, schools at all levels came under pressure to demonstrate that they were producing learning outcomes that would justify costs" (Labaree 2011, 9). What Labaree failed to take into account, however, is that the intensifying pressure to demonstrate "efficiencies of investment" is largely explained by budget cutbacks in the public sector. Stagnant and declining levels of economic investment in schools, especially in those located in the poorest neighborhoods, are rarely if ever acknowledged. Equally important, the impact of poverty on student academic achievement is considered extraneous and instead dismissed as a convenient and too-oft-used excuse for teacher failure. As Steve Brill explained, "It wasn't that poverty or other factors failed to affect student performance. Instead it was presumed that teacher effectiveness could overcome these disadvantages" (Goldstein 2011a, 17).

A basic assumption underpinning decisions to use instructor metrics is that good teaching can beat back the impacts of poverty, racism, and structural instability on academic achievement. And yet, "the research consensus has been clear and unchanging for more than a decade: at most teaching accounts for 15% of student achievement outcomes, while socioeconomic factors account for 60%" (Goldstein 2011a, 17). The data belie recent policy cant. Teaching metrics are not a substitute for strategic investment.

The most compelling argument for teacher metrics is that they provide a scientific objectivity for analyzing performance. Yet much of the recent discourse regarding testing raises a number of very troubling questions, which we address in Chapter 5. Here we discuss the measures of teacher performance attached to testing. Perhaps the most popular tool currently being used is the student growth percentile (SGP). The SGP has been adopted in several states including, but not limited to, New Jersey, Colorado, and New York. It is rapidly replacing the value added models

(VAM), which attempt to construct a statistical model that "estimates the extent to which a student having a specific teacher or attending a specific school can influence differences in student score from beginning to end of year" (Baker 2011). The goal of the VAM is to determine how a certain teacher alters a child's trajectory while controlling for student background and school characteristics. Because of recent critiques of VAM, however, it is largely being abandoned in favor of what Bruce Baker, an education statistician, describes as a policy shell game. Put simply SGP is worse, not better than VAM. This is largely because SGP was never designed for that purpose. And those who are now suggesting that it is are simply wrong (Baker 2011).

SGP is a descriptive tool for evaluating and comparing student growth. It is not designed to infer the influence of teachers or schools on that growth. The many other factors that might influence student growth, including, but not limited to, background characteristics, mix of students in a class, and student to teacher ratios, are not controlled for in this assessment equation.

Equally important alternate measures such as the VAMs, although more attentive to assessing the share of "the student value added that should be attributed to the teacher as opposed to all that other stuff (a nearly impossible task)," and although less suspect than the SGPs, are also highly flawed (Baker 2011). For example, teachers who serve more difficult students may be systematically disadvantaged. In addition, they produce different results depending on the different tests or scaling of tests; thus the score is not especially reliable or valid. These factors as well as others promoted the shift to the even more flawed SGPs. The evidence regarding the reliability of these measures in assessing teacher contribution to student growth is equally suspect. Jerry Rothstein, a University of California at Berkeley faculty member, performed an analysis of the Gate's Foundation data. In his analysis he notes that "Gate's data show that 40 percent of teachers whose performance placed them in the bottom quartile using the value added measure scored in the top half by using an alternative measure of student achievement" (Labaree 2011, 9).

Importantly, there is not yet a scientifically sound measurement of teacher contribution to student academic advancement. The search for such measurement has a value if it does not deflect from the more compelling need to increase strategic investment addressing the complex learning needs and problems in the poorest communities. This is, however, unlikely as one of the primary intentions in elevating the importance of teacher metrics is to devalue the need for greater strategic investment. It was Bill Gates, for example, who indicated in 2010 that despite stagnant public school budgets for the foreseeable future, test scores must continue to improve.

The search for a magic bullet—in the form of a reliable test—continues unabated while the larger questions of equitable strategic investment, income inequalities, and structural disparities are ignored. The trappings of science to assign individual teacher blame trumps the empirical evidence that has persistently documented the relationship between academic outcomes and differential per capita investment in schooling as well as gaps in family income. The political and economic consequences of assigning greater policy importance to value added measures of teaching than the project of transformative strategic investment in education in the poorest communities are reasonably clear. Focusing on the former creates political distraction from the increasing need for redistributive forms of taxation and more equitable state investment. We all know "people who grew up poor and went onto lead successful, financially remunerative lives" (Goldstein 2011a, 17). But as Dana Goldstein (2011a) asserted, "In the US in 2011, the odds of beating the odds of poverty has [*sic*] become less likely than ever, and teacher quality has less to do with it than does economic inequality" (17).

An important insight of recent research is that income disparity also has significant relationship to academic growth. Data indicate that "kids who begin the school year with decent standardized test scores are the ones who will grow fastest academically; all the advantages such students bring to school—supportive parents, highly verbal home environments, better nutrition—also help them continuously learn more, improving their performance on tests over time" (Goldstein 2011b). Conversely, the disruptions and oppressive life circumstance often experienced by the poorest students, in turn, are more likely to produce fluctuating academic performance from one year to the next. The consequence of this academic advantage of affluence is that teachers working in the poorest communities of color are more likely to be punished for the relatively low growth rates of their students. In turn, school environments that sanctify metric growth, discount empirical findings that indicate affluence influences rates of growth, ignore the relationship between investment and outcome, and exclusively hold teachers accountable for increased achievement create powerful reasons for teachers to avoid or migrate out of the poorest neighborhoods. This migration is perhaps the most detrimental result of intensifying reliance on metrics of student academic growth as a measure of teacher worth.

This point is amplified by the following conversation between a principal and a teacher: "I always felt flattered, Carol, when you gave me the toughest kids to teach. I don't want to worry if they are assigned to me now—but I will. The kids who are hard to motivate and have weak skills will be the kids that no one wants when their jobs are on the line" (Strauss 2011).

The implementation of teaching metrics widens the education opportunity gap between the poorest and most affluent communities. As more and more teachers are forced to teach to tests, the richest learning opportunities will be increasingly skewed by social class. According to Labaree:

> Schools for the disadvantaged are going to be under greater pressure to teach to the test and raise scores on core skills, while schools for the advantaged will be free to pursue a much richer curricula. If your children unlike others are not at risk then the schools they attend will not need to be obsessed with drilling to meet minimum standards. Teachers in these schools will be able to lead their classes in exploring a variety of subjects, experiences and issues that will be excluded from the classrooms further down the social scale. In the effort to raise standards and

close the achievement gap, we will be creating just another form of educational distinction to divide the top from the bottom. (Labaree 2011, 14)

Most telling is the extent to which educational transformation has benefitted the students it claims to better serve. At the very least, a radical shift in classroom focus should improve test scores and, in turn, college graduation rates even if it is at the expense of critical thinking, writing skills, and a deepened understanding of the citizenship role. Sadly, even this basic bar of tangible result has not been hurdled by the "new reformers." To the contrary, "as Paul Tough noted in a recent *New York Times Magazine* piece, at far too many 'miracle' inner city schools the vast majority of students—despite impressive test score growth—continue to score below proficiency in reading and math. These students may graduate from high school but they are unprepared for college or work beyond the service" (Goldstein 2011a, 18). This sad commentary on the impact of the new reform and its instrumental approach to teaching is powerfully conveyed by one of the cofounders of the oft-described exemplar of charter education KIPP (Knowledge Is Power Program). "I'm still failing ... only one third of KIPP networks high school graduates are able to earn bachelor degrees within six years" (Goldstein 2011a, 18).

A series of losses are intimately associated with the testing environments produced by the new reformers: the loss of possibility for incubating enriched curricula and learning environments; the loss of a public recognition of the relationship between investment inequality and degraded classroom instruction in the poorest communities of color; the loss of experienced teachers who with ever-greater frequency migrate out of urban classrooms to other kinds of employment; and the loss of historic belief that public education can animate intellectual growth, robust citizenship, or economic mobility for poor youngsters. Bound to these losses is a steady erosion of public school teacher morale. This crumbling morale may be the most profound loss of present policymaking.

Critically, as teacher morale steadily declines, so, too, do prospects of inventing new and more effective forms of public education. As has been noted across the political spectrum, teachers are the linchpin for reshaping public education. The corrosive effect of the testing culture on learning and teaching conditions, as well as professional morale, will be explored in the next section of this chapter.

Teacher Morale and the Project of Education Reform in Metrics

In 2001, *New York Times* columnist Gail Collins wrote a compelling article on the reasons teachers leave the profession. She noted that low pay was driving teachers out of the classroom. Quickly, however, she shifted focus: "But there is an even more important issue for experienced teachers: professional autonomy. Master teachers are frustrated and angered by the invalid uses of standardized test scores and with the public's acceptance of those who do not teach prescribing for those who do" (Granek Guttell 2001). Collins described low morale, loss of professional autonomy, and ever-greater reliance on testing to circumscribe classroom learning, claiming that these have become more pronounced in the past decade.

In North Carolina, a state widely acknowledged as part of the leading edge of school reform in the 1990s and early part of the next decade, a study was conducted regarding teacher working conditions. The survey revealed that the changes they needed to support their best effort and improve the learning environment included less testing and smaller classes (Dagenhart et al. 2005). More recently a number of other studies has documented the ever-stronger relationship between the intensifying uses of standardized testing to measure teacher success issues and a number of morale-related outcomes.

> "Many smart and motivated potential teachers are turned off by systems that over-rely on standardized lessons worksheets and tests," [said] Christina Jean, a former public school teacher who now works as a field coordinator for the Denver Teacher Residency program, an alternative pathway for career changes. "That is not challenging and stimulating for adults," she [said]. "One of the things I think is really critical is reprofessionalizing and reintellectualizing teaching." (Goldstein 2011b)

A New York City school principal, Carol Corbett Burris, noted in a letter to President Obama:

> The test based evaluation of schools under NCLB has led to teaching to the test. It has also led to a narrowing of the curricula. This approach has stifled engaged teaching and learning as well as creativity. And not withstanding your compliments to me, a sound policy cannot depend on all schools having principals who will successfully push back against the incentives and disincentives created by such a system. (Strauss 2011)

Instructors' sagging relationship to their work and profession is felt daily by students who experience both the alienation and emotional fatigue of their teachers in and outside the classroom. The dulling effect of test-taking curricula demands and the erosion of professional autonomy in combination with inadequate resources further estrange students from their teachers, classes, and more largely the potential of education. The intensifying chain of managerial control exercised through testing and the consequent estrangement of teachers has the effect of loosening relationship to schooling on the part of both teachers and learners. And so in an era of manufactured fiscal crisis and austerity, the technology of testing as a cheap, quick fix for both curricula reform and teacher accountability has served to accelerate the degradation of public schooling. What is largely missed in this reform thrust is the unifying theme, especially for exemplar teachers, that good teachers share one trait: a "strong sense of personal identity with their work" (Schrock 2004, 68). No teaching will ever succeed "unless it connects with the inner living core of students' lives" (69). As testing occupies more and more of instructors' time, teachers become decreasingly likely to identify with their work—not unlike the alienated factory work-ers that Marx described during the Victorian Age. This accounts at least in part for declining morale among teachers and students, as well as exodus from the profession.

The severing of critical thinking, writing skills, and individual identity from the daily instructional exchange between students and teachers is described in the following passages as associated with the phenomenon of an ever-more invasive metrics in and outside of the classroom.

> By utilizing textbooks built around the mandatory state exam, teachers and students have little chance to exercise authority over what might be learned. The traditional rewards of teaching—of fostering relationships with the future generation, of making a difference thinking of creative ways of delivering content, of playing around in the field you love—are still there but barely. They are being pushed aside by layers of regulatory edict and general panic over test scores. (Baines and Kent Stanley 2006)
>
> They [educators] are inescapably political. Why? Because they complicate our vision, pull our cherished notions out by the roots and flay our pieties. Because they grow uncertainty.... Because out of this work of self building might emerge an individual capable of humility in the face of complexity; an individual formed through questioning and therefore unlikely to cede that right; an individual resistant to coercion, to manipulation and demagoguery in all forms....
>
> Our focus however, [alternatively] is on the usual economic indicators. There are no "corresponding civic indicators," no generally agreed upon warning signs of political vulnerability, even though the inability of more than two-thirds of our college graduates to read a text and draw rational inferences could be seen as the political equivalent of runaway inflation or soaring unemployment. (Goldstein 2011b)

These political and instructional outcomes are not a product of chance or accident. To the contrary, they are a consequence of the search for cheap and simple solutions to fix a complex problem. To begin with, the business assumption that technologies of assessment and greater productivity are a substitute for strategic investment in public education is at best specious. Additionally, creating an ever-more docile student body through a standardized, less engaging curricula and mechanistic, nonunionized teaching workforce serves to drown potential dissent in an era of diminished mobility and economic decline. It is within this context that greater reliance on testing and testing curricula in the poorest communities of color prepares students at best for college programs and markets geared to the relatively low-wage service sector and at worst for a life of sustained unemployment.

The radical restructuring of public education is the leading edge of a political crusade to narrow the social contract between citizens and the state. The increasing power of this agenda and the social movements it has birthed has coincided with the most visible markers of American decline: the meltdown of stock markets in 2008 and the ongoing political-economic fallout. The once gradual shift toward privatized forms of education and metrics that took place during the past three decades has given way, since 2008, to reform panic. That panic has cohered around a program of deregulation, disinvestment and standardization of public education, and the marginalization of teacher unions, and it is radically, rapidly restructuring the meaning of both teaching and public schooling. We will return to these points in the concluding chapter.

THE NEW NORMAL: TEACHER REFORM BY THE STICK AND WITHOUT STRATEGIC INVESTMENT

The technologies remaking the teaching profession have been combined with an ideological attack on its unions over the past few years. Recent reforms in Wisconsin are intended to block teachers from negotiating for anything but wages, restrict all settlements to one year, and eliminate unions' automatic deduction from employee paychecks. Similar legislation is being debated in a cross section of states. As Scott Walker of Wisconsin and other governors have acknowledged, the attack on public unions has little to do with the financial health of their states and everything to do with further weakening the primary source of resistance to their policy agenda.

Governors Christie of New Jersey, Daniels of Indiana, Scott of Florida, Perry of Texas, and Kasich of Ohio have proposed sweeping reductions in the levels of health care coverage, pension, and salary for public school teachers. In New Jersey, "there has been a 14 month rhetorical war against teachers and unions, with stepped up pressure to slash their members health and retirement benefits" (Halbfinger 2011). Nationally, teacher salaries are being reduced, either directly through immediate wage cuts or indirectly through collective bargaining reform that limits future salary increases. A recent study noted: "Starting teachers' salaries which now average about $39,000 would have to rise to $65,000 to fill most new teaching positions in high needs schools with graduates from the top third of their classes" (Kristof 2011).

That deficit has created a crisis atmosphere in state capitals causing many politicians to declare bankruptcy. Politicians presume that only one policy option is viable: deep budget cuts across every service sector. It is on this basis that a range of austerity policies are inevitably developed. Wage saving is but one kind of austerity policy. Others include increasing class size, contracting the size of the teaching workforce, expanding online classroom instruction, and stripping teachers of job security, thus reducing their economic leverage and morale.

In Texas, legislators have proposed slashing $4.8 billion or one-sixth of the school budget from 2012 to 2013. John M. Folks, a superintendent of a district near San Antonio, remarked that under these circumstances, "there is no way to avoid laying off teachers and letting classes become larger" (McKinley 2011). Similar trends are being reported in a number of cities and states across the nation. Predictably, teacher layoffs have produced a swelling of class size. As Sam Dillon notes, in an article entitled, "Tight Budgets Mean Squeeze in Classroom" (2011), "Millions of public school students across the nation are seeing their class sizes swell because budget cuts and teacher layoffs are undermining a decades-long push ... to shrink class size. Over the past two years California, Georgia, Nevada, Ohio, Utah and Nevada have loosened legal restrictions on class size. And Idaho and Texas are debating whether to fit more students in classrooms."

Recent policies in Florida offer a vivid example of how cost savings, class size ceilings, and online learning are powerfully linked. "Virtual classrooms called e-learning labs were put in place last August as a result of Florida's Class Size Reduction Amendment passed in 2002. The amendment limits the number of students allowed in classrooms but not in labs. School administrators said they had to find a way to meet class size limits" (Herrera 2011).

Swelling class size, whether masked by e-labs in states that have restrictive legislation, or more visible in states that do not, is an especially troubling trend. Many new reformers are suggesting that increased class size does not affect the academic performance of students. According to Bill Gates and Arne Duncan, successful learning depends not on class size, but on the capacity of an instructor. While it is hard to argue against the importance of the quality and capacity of instructors as a key determinant of academic performance, the independent impact of class size is also powerful. A series of studies, originating in Tennessee and confirmed by the more recent findings of Princeton economist Alan Krueger, indicates that "smaller classes significantly outscored the larger classes on achievement tests" (Dillon 2011).

Today's reformers argue that teachers and the schools have to be torn down, to be rebuilt or not, that is, made virtual. Yet, the present agenda to restructure the teaching workforce and, more generally, public education appears to have an agenda beyond efficiency, productivity, and the best interests of children. We will now turn our attention to that agenda.

ATTACK REFORM: PIT BULL ACCOUNTABILITY AND THE EROSION OF LEARNING CULTURE

As noted earlier, the accountability movement of today holds teachers to new standards of student testing performance, without the systematic, strategic investment necessary to develop teacher capacity or a rich learning culture. Class size may soar, learning environments may decline as a result of budget cuts, and teacher expertise may grow thinner because of accelerating turnover, but faculty must produce increased test scores, or they risk being fired in ever-more insecure work environments.

This harsh, high-stakes environment is but the most recent incarnation of a larger Darwinian policy experiment. Relying upon highly problematic indicators, the logic goes, only the strongest teachers will survive. The most able will produce and the least able will fail and, in turn, be drummed out of the profession. In the absence of substantial investment in teacher development, we are left to deduce that able teachers are born, not developed; that teacher effectiveness is evident in a rise in test scores; that student achievement is a product of individual efforts of individual educators rather than a full school community. Significant investment in capacity development and working conditions for teachers as a part of a program for improved academic performance is seen as both unnecessary and fiscally impossible. Consequently, the new policy order or logic indicates that no matter the conditions, a cohort of teachers will find a way to succeed, and others will flounder. That is the way of biology, the market, and also the way of public school teaching.

The role of technologies such as testing, virtual learning, and standardized curricula in holding budgets constant, reducing the size of the teaching workforce, increasing class size, abandoning any hope of improving teacher capacity, and as a synonym for innovation is described by Joel Klein, former chancellor of the New York City public school system.

> But one of the best things we could do is hire fewer teachers and pay more to the ones we hire. And, as in any other field, technology can help us get there. If you have 5,000 math teachers, many of whom are underperforming, significantly improving overall quality is nearly impossible.... More broadly, we need to foster a funda-mental shift from a top-down, one size fits all culture—mandated class size culture, after school programs and the like to a culture of innovation. (J. Klein 2011, 77)

This reform brew is salted with ideological attacks on the legitimacy of the teaching profession and their unions. It is important to reiterate that what remains largely unaddressed in this discussion is the broader context of economic decline, inequi-table distribution of resources, and the continued starvation of public schools in the poorest districts.

If we enact policy based on the logic that teachers cannot grow and become more effective instructors over time through various kinds of strategic investment, then the very legitimacy of the profession is threatened. Today's policymaking ques-tions the relationship between transmission of knowledge, expertise, and classroom performance. And yet it is precisely at this moment that research indicates that teachers are too often lost at sea in urban settings because of insufficient guidance about what to teach and how to teach it (Kauffman, Johnson, Kardos, Liu, and Peske 2002; Crocco and Costigan 2007). More recently, Douglas Lemov, a founder of the charter network Uncommon Ground, "noticed something about successful teachers that he hadn't expected to find: what looked like natural-born genius was often deliberate technique in disguise. Lemov was not the first educator to come to the conclusion that teachers need better training" (Green 2010).

Deprofessionalizing teaching has significant social and political-economic consequences. A workforce that is ever-more mechanized in its work practices, less expert in what it knows, and lacking discretion that has instead been ceded to central-ized command and control centers defining minute by minute instructional process and testing outcomes is a workforce of automatons. This automation results in a less certified and more fungible workforce that is much cheaper to employ. The radical restructuring of the teaching workforce, away from professionalism, requires both its resocialization and the significant weakening of its collective sources of resistance, union power. As noted earlier, both of these lines of attack are well under way.

The present policy discourse also blinds us to questions of equity of investment across schools. Within states, the average disparity in per pupil spending (adjusted for regional costs) between districts at the fifth and ninety-fifth percentile is $4,286. In forty-three of the forty-nine states for which data are available, districts with higher property values tend to have higher education revenues (state and local combined) than districts with lower property values.

Again, an implicit assumption of present public education policy is that the strongest students in wealthy and poor districts will survive, if not flourish. Those who fail are simply by dint of lack of intelligence, discipline, or inadequate interest rightly relegated to a dead-end life. The theme that runs through this narrative joins an ideology of natural selection with policies of regressive taxation, disinvestment in public services, and growing inequality. A trifecta with political and economic ramifications that align with the short-term class interests of a new American oligarchy who is driving the present public education and teaching reform agenda.

Joel Klein (2011), worried that time is running out, is calling for political leadership willing to take risks and build support for radical reform. The radical reform that Klein would propose, however, is little more than a repackaging of the familiar cant of market reform and the opiate of technology to solve complex learning problems often underpinned by the complex dynamic relationship between instructor and student. We would counter pose that radical solution must be underpinned by an infusion of new resources equitably invested. More specifically, such strategic investment must focus on building teacher capacity, staunching teacher turnover, improving classroom ratios in the poorest communities, developing curricula to stimulate robust learning, creating incentives for the most seasoned and effective teachers to dedicate their careers to the neediest neighborhoods, raising instructor salaries thus attracting more able cohorts to the profession, redistributing a proportion of public resources from central bureaucracies to the classroom, and extending the school day and year.

The investments we describe are being made in Europe and Asia. And this is taking place without parents as the drivers of educational improvement; equitable investments in skillful teaching, challenging curricula, and assessments that encourage ambitious learning are the norm. Additional resources are directed to those schools and students where the needs are greatest and the benefits of such investment show up in international assessments. The Programme for International Student Assessment (PISA) report on equity found, for example, that "while most of the students who perform poorly in PISA are from socio-economically disadvantaged background, some peers from similar background excel in PISA, demonstrating that overcoming socio-economic barriers is possible" (OECD 2010, 25).

The PISA report calls these low socioeconomic, high-achieving students "resilient." They are students who come from households in the bottom quarter of the distribution of socioeconomic backgrounds in their country, but score in the top quarter among students from all countries with similar socioeconomic backgrounds. In Finland, Japan, Canada, and Singapore between 39 and 48 percent of students are resilient. In Hong Kong and Shanghai 72 and 76 percent are resilient respectively. In contrast, in the United States, only 29 percent of disadvantaged students are resilient. Across all countries in the PISA study, resilient students "are more prevalent in those education systems that PISA indicators show to be more equitable" (OECD 2010, 33).

Radical, effective education reform clearly requires the kind of strategic investment the United States is presently unwilling to make. Such investment and new equitable tax structures to finance it are the underpinnings everywhere in the world for increasing the academic performance of poor students. Why would the US experience be any different? Clearly, we have a lack of political will to face the hard facts. Present US policy produces anemic outcomes by definition; only by altering course and investing in approaches proven successful elsewhere will the prospects for effective school reform improve. The source of this resistance, as this chapter has indicated, is both ideological and economic.

THE SHORT-TERM RATIONALITY AND LONG-TERM IRRATIONALITY OF TEACHER ATTACK AS EDUCATION POLICY

As this chapter has made clear, the attack on public school teachers has occurred along two fronts. The first has been an effort to delegitimate the teaching profession. It has resulted in a cohering of proscribed curricula, the scientism of assessment, a reduction of professional discretion, denigration of teaching skill, and elevation of processes of natural selection to evolve a teaching workforce. These trends, in combination with a lack of investment in building capacity, uses of online technology to replace classroom teachers, and policies as well as conditions that promote rapid teacher turnover, produce an increasingly deprofessionalized workforce. These dynamics at least in part explain the falling wages, declining working conditions, and diminished job security of teachers. This first line of attack accompanies an escalating assault on teacher unions. The effort, in a cross section of states to weaken teachers' collective bargaining rights, has served to further erode both the power and autonomy of instructors. This assault on teacher unions contributes to a cascading momentum for wage cuts, benefit rollbacks, and diminished job security. What explains the two-front ambition and radical agenda of the attack? Why is this occurring at precisely the moment when as a nation, we need to build an ever-more competent, stable, and effective teacher workforce?

Diane Ravitch claimed recently, "I am beginning to think we are in a moment of national insanity. . . . We hear pious exhortations about education reform (media, corporate leaders, foundation representatives, and policy makers). Yet, the reality on the ground suggests that the corporate reform movement . . . will set American education back many decades. Sometimes, I think we are hurtling back a century or more to the age of the Robber Barons" (Ravitch 2011a).

Gail Collins, a *New York Times* columnist, recently described how Texas has structured its nineteenth-century reform U-turn around teacher certification.

> Texas has been leading the way in putting for-profit companies in charge of teacher certification.... Some of the programs are slightly more rigorous than those for trainers at neighborhood gyms.... Here is one indicator of how innovative things are getting. Texas is considering, although not with any great intensity, ... a bill that would require that people who go through these programs spend a couple of days practice teaching before they are turned loose in the classrooms. (Collins 2011)

The descendant status of teacher training of any kind, growth of technology that masks increases in student to instructor ratios, and intensifying difficulties of declining wages, benefits, and working conditions for a workforce already in crisis are elemental to a radical restructuring of public school teaching. These are the central inventions of the present corporate makeover of public education. Ultimately, these innovations are an irrational response to the present crisis of American public education particularly in very poor communities. As a result we can expect that the very best teachers will leave urban school systems, capacity development will be at best neglected and at worst grind to a halt, and the general rate of turnover will increase. Equally important, the morale of the remaining instructors will decline and college graduates only prepared for brief teaching stopovers in public schools on the way to other careers will grow. Perhaps, most importantly, the expertise of teachers will atrophy in direct relationship to their declining classroom preparation, and continuity and the status of public school teaching as a profession will be further eroded.

If the goals of the educational reform movement are to minimize investment and maximize private economic gain, current reform practice is both logical and on point. By engaging in such policymaking, taxes are kept low for the wealthiest individuals and corporations as part of their conscious and unconscious decision to withdraw from a collective social responsibility. Lower taxes on the wealthy are reinforced through budget cutting and disinvestment in public agencies. Additionally, reducing the wages and benefits of public employees or teachers creates a new equilibrium between private sector workers, who have for a number of decades experienced unstable working conditions and rapidly declining wages. In effect, the public workers' new normal comports with the conditions that have already become the norm for private sector workers. These wage declines, in combination with low taxes, have contributed to increasing disparities in income and wealth, which increasingly define our political and economic landscape. Finally, the restructuring and degradation of teaching as a profession creates new opportunities for profit making, for example, through new forms of online technology, testing regimens, data analysis demands, teacher certification mills, and for-profit colleges granting education degrees. The capitalization of public schooling represents an increasingly important although obscured driver of present reform as a source of new revenue for the private sector.

And so the restructuring of the teaching workforce is only insane if we have as our goal the improved quality of education for our students, including the neediest of our students. Only if we are interested in the equitable distribution of resources within education, and in producing competitive, creative, and critically thinking members of society in the years to come, does current educational reform appear illogical.

Alternatively, it is entirely rational if the goal is economic gain, ideological hegemony, and withdrawal from a collective life. This chapter posits that it is the latter prism through which we need to interpret recent efforts to reform and restructure the public education workforce. Consequently, this is largely an ideological and economic struggle over the levels of allocation and kinds of strategic investment in public education and teaching. It is not primarily an exercise in technical problem solving through data, online technology, or private sector innovation to improve teaching and learning conditions. Rather, the intention of present corporate reform is to limit investment in public education, cannibalize present public dollars through profit-making ventures, and to finance this agenda through the professional debasement and economic decline of the teaching profession. Make no mistake: this is a political and economic struggle over the distribution of resources to public education, obscured by the rhetoric of innovation, decentralization, marketplace choice, and freedom.

The relationship between equitable investment of resources and effective reform has been established empirically. But evidence does not produce policy, power does. Presently, corporate power is aligned to produce a teaching workforce that is devolved economically and professionally and evolved anew through a process of natural selection or survival of the fittest. Another way exists, but it will require a political contestation of present policy and recognition that effective reform cannot be created on the cheap or on the basis of harsh, ideological attack rhetoric, which scapegoats teachers, or in turn propagates crisis management, draconian reform, and an obfuscation of growing disparity in wealth and income. To alter the direction of present reform will require a power and agenda commensurate with that of the corporate reformers. That power can only be built through a new architecture of partnership between teachers, students, and parents in the poorest communities. Some of that work is already under way. Much more will need to be done in rather short order if the wheels of progress directing us back to the nineteenth century are to be rerouted to create greater equity of investment, strategic development of teacher capacity, and robust learning culture in the poorest neighborhoods.

Only in this way can we address the present peril of both a public education system unable to meet the most basic educational needs of poor students of color and a corporate reform agenda likely to further destabilize and profit from these conditions. No other path to effective public school reform exists. The road must lead to equitable investment and nurturing of our teaching workforce. The alternative is to preside over the steady and accelerating decay of the backbone of our democracy: public education and its teaching workforce.

FOR FURTHER READING

Karp, Stan. "Who's Bashing Teachers and Public Schools and What Can We Do about It?" March 28, 2011. http://www.rethinkingschools.org/archive/25_03/25_03_karp.shtml.

Miner, Barbara. "Looking past the Spin: Teach for America." Spring 2010. http://www.rethinkingschools.org/archive/24_03/24_03_TFA.shtml.

Chapter 3

Charter Schooling and the Deregulation and Capitalization of Public Education Assets

Let us make no mistake, in a fiscal environment that emphasizes structural reform but provides few resources to public schools, social neglect on a massive scale multiplies. These conditions are driven by ideology, rage at a failed public school system, despair, and profit making. At the center of this reform storm are charter schools, sold to the public as less bureaucratically encumbered and a more innovative marketlike alternative to the failed policies of traditional public education. Critically, expansive investments of increasingly scarce public resources are being directed to this reform project and away from traditional public schools with no discernible public evaluation to assess its effectiveness. This redirection of dollars is most evident in the poorest communities of color where traditional schools are being closed at an accelerated rate and replaced by charters.

Some part of the drive to reinvent public schooling through charters has been fueled by the sense of deepening failure and crisis in traditional educational institutions. This failure is widely accepted on the basis of aggregated empirical evidence that indicates declining international standing of US students on a cross section of standardized tests. Consistent with Naomi Klein's analysis in *The Shock Doctrine,* the frame of crisis legitimates demands for radical reform, producing rapidly imposed interventions. The interventions in public education today are expected to, simultaneously, shock and marketize public institutions (Klein 2007).

Importantly, a number of academics have contested the belief regarding pervasive crisis within public education as measured by standardized tests. Gene Glass (2008), a noted education statistician, and Yong Zhao (2006) dispute the notion that

US scores have fallen during the past five decades. Equally important, they question the relationship between economic development/dominance and the performance of public schools. The data marshaled by Glass is especially compelling in raising serious doubts about the logic and empirical support for the failures of the American public education system.

Reform advocacy has largely focused on mapping charters onto the grid of public schooling to foster competition and, in turn, presumably improve performance. It is within this context that the charter school movement was born. Choice, competition, and effectiveness underpin government and the business sector's agenda for public schools. We will return to this point later in the chapter.

THE PRESENT LANDSCAPE FOR
REORGANIZING PUBLIC EDUCATION

During the past forty years, a large part of the debate about the reorganization of public education has pivoted around school vouchers. Milton Friedman and other conservative advocates long argued that public schools were best served by offering the purest forms of choice to consumers through vouchers. These cash vouchers, it was suggested, would enable parents to intensify competition for entrée to the best schools and conversely create the freedom to stimulate an exodus or out-migration from the worst schools. The public school system would be repaired through vouchering because of heightened competition and the consequent flow of public and private money out of dysfunctional settings and to the highest performing sites.

For an extended period in the 1990s and through the turn of the twenty-first century, vouchers had little if any policy cachet. More and more decisionmakers agreed that vouchers were most likely to subsidize educations of the middle and already affluent classes looking to place their children in high-performing private schools as opposed to public schools. Thus vouchers provided exit from underperforming public schools to private schools. Left out of the exodus, however, were the majority of very poor parents and students of color. As a result, in the 1990s charter schools were increasingly seen as a more rational midpoint between choice and the status quo. Therefore the focus in reorganizing public education, for the twenty years following, was not on vouchers but charter schooling.

Since the electoral ascent of the Tea Party in 2010, however, the reform momentum has shifted focus.

Early in May [2011], Indiana Governor Mitch Daniels signed what is probably the broadest voucher law ever enacted in this country. A few days later Oklahoma approved tax credits for those who contribute to a privately funded private "opportunity scholarship" program. In New Jersey, on May 13 a voucher bill was approved by a Senate committee with bipartisan support. In Washington DC, the voucher program which was killed by Democratic majorities in the last Congress is all but certain to be restored. In Wisconsin Governor Scott Walker ... is pushing hard to broaden Milwaukee's voucher program to other cities and many more children. (Schrag 2011, 25)

Peter Schrag (2011) claimed that thirty-six states were contemplating privatization measures that would reintroduce vouchers as a viable policy option. These states included Arizona, Florida, Ohio, Oregon, and Pennsylvania—each of which intend to provide "funding for vouchers, tax credits or other tax funded benefits for private education. No year in recent memory, said Foundation for Education Choice President Robert Enlow, has provided better opportunity for the cause" (25).

Milwaukee has developed the most richly funded, comprehensive, and publicized voucher program over the past twenty years, creating essentially two different school systems within the city. As Milwaukee journalist Bob Peterson noted,

> They are different systems yet both receive public dollars. While fewer than two percent of voucher school students have special needs, nearly twenty percent of the Milwaukee public school students do. Private voucher schools can choose their students by counseling out the hard to educate. They can expel students who have no right to due process. Milwaukee schools must serve all students. Private voucher schools have virtually no accountability or transparency. Within MPS by contrast all salaries, qualifications of teachers, content of curricula, disaggregated test scores are public. The suspension and expulsion figures are public. Finally, public schools honor the state's open meeting and record laws. None of this is the case with voucher schools. (Peterson 2011)

Barbara Miner, a Milwaukee journalist, indicated voucher advocates in Milwaukee have made clear for twenty years their goal is to replace public education with a system of universal vouchers that includes private and religious schools (Miner 2011). Importantly, in a year in which Wisconsin governor Wilson is cutting $834 million from public education, he is simultaneously advocating for vouchers that will total $131 million that will come straight out of the public school budgets. That money will provide tuition for 21,000 students, making vouchers, in essence, one of the largest school districts (Miner 2011). In 2012 vouchers were available to any Milwaukee family, no matter how rich. So while some poor benefit, this new legislative initiative also will allow the wealthiest residents access to 6,442 vouchers to defray costs at elite private schools in the area. Again, vouchers as a policy instrument are widening the opportunity and economic gap between poor children of color and their more affluent and frequently white suburban counterparts. The outflow of tax dollars from public to private schools further degrades the fiscal base and educational potential of neighborhood schools that disproportionately serve the poorest children of color. Simultaneously, the rich spend less on their elite educations.

But what of the promise that vouchers would yield not only choice and heightened competition but increased academic achievement? Students in the voucher schools did no better than those enrolled in Milwaukee public schools. The findings, however, are unreliable because more than half of the students had dropped out of voucher schools before the data was tabulated (Miner 2011). The record of vouchers is discouraging. Yet, paradoxically, policymakers are preparing to unleash similar initiatives across the country. The public relations promotion of charter schooling and vouchers as marketlike devices facilitating choice, competition, and, in turn, improved academic performance is very powerful. What separates these two experiments, however, is the relative breadth of the charter experiment as contrasted to vouchering. The available data on charter schooling is both more abundant and comprehensive. And although we are witnessing a reemergence of vouchering as a primary tool in public education reform, the charter experiment has been the most publicized, politically acceptable, and well-funded tool for reinventing the organizational base of public education for two decades. Given the enduring centrality of charter schools in education reform, they will be our focus for the remainder of this chapter. It is important to keep in mind, however, that the preliminary data emerging from vouchering suggests that there is a very wide gap between the promise of advocates and the empirical reality. Some part of what we will explore in this chapter is the extent to which chartering replicates or reverses this trend.

WHAT ARE CHARTER SCHOOLS?

Charters, although they receive state funding, stand outside traditional public school systems. The contractual relationship is between founders of the school and government authorizer(s). This contractual authorization is critical to the development of standards, types, and quantity of schools. Increasingly, charter authorization and accountability are conducted not with single "mom and pop charters" but with networks of charters that are organized through education or charter management organizations (EMOs/CMOs). A local charter in New York City might be affiliated with a national or regional charter network such as KIPP (Knowledge Is Power Program) or Common Ground. It is argued by advocates that EMOs have many advantages, including economies or efficiencies of scale, potential to disseminate innovation from one region to another, and entrepreneurial drive to build robust networks and establish uniform standards, providing ever-more powerful competitive counterpoints to established bureaucratic public education.

Despite this, the growth rate of EMOs has increased rapidly during the past decade. In 1999 a total of 61 charter schools were managed, for example, by nonprofit as contrasted to for-profit EMOs nationally (Molnar and Garcia 2007). From 2004 to 2009, the percentage of charters operated by EMOs increased from 17 percent to 74. Equally important, by 2009 the total number of charter schools nationally was estimated to be 4,900. That number doubled over an approximate five-year period (Miron and Dingerson 2009).

The rapid expansion of EMOs as a management umbrella for charters occurred in a cross section of states. In Michigan, for example, instances where operators of "mom and pop" charters turned their school over to an EMO because their work was experienced as "a burn out" situation were reported (Schnaiberg 1997, 1).

Similar findings were reported in a number of other states (Bracey 2004). The irony, Bracey suggests, is that schools run by EMOs often offer no curricular freedom or building-level decisionmaking. Indeed, evaluators of the charter schools in Michigan referred to charters as "cookie-cutter schools" (5). The convergence of centralized managerial control of an increasing number of charter schools and the more general phenomenon of the explosion of charters nationally is a fact. As was noted earlier, however, what needs to be explored is the tension between new forms of centralized management and the promise of both innovation and increased student achievement. Many of the people involved in educational reform are arguing that the increased use of umbrella organizations to manage charter schools limits individual school autonomy, flexibility to innovate, and overall student achievement.

Alex Molnar has noted that one of the most important differences between charter school laws in different states is the degree of autonomy granted. A number of states have been guided by the precept that charter success depends on freedom from public bureaucracy and thus a high degree of autonomy. Other states concerned with accountability have developed more restrictive legislation. In Arizona, California, Colorado, Massachusetts, and Michigan, laws regarding charter schools "allow ... schools to operate as independent legal entities with a high degree of autonomy." Conversely, charter school laws passed in Hawaii, Georgia, Kansas, New Mexico, and Wyoming are described by charter advocates as weak because "they grant charters little more autonomy than public schools" (Molnar 1996, 1).

Effective monitoring is critical to holding charters accountable to their promise of increasing academic achievement, maximizing responsible fiscal management of resources, and promoting dissemination of their innovations to public schools. Such oversight and enforcement of standards, however, has been very difficult to accomplish.

Paul Hill and colleagues noted: "Conventional public schools are considered accountable because they must follow all the rules set by local and state boards, and abide by all of the provisions of contracts that these boards enter into with unions and other organizations. Charter schools are exempted from many of these rules, and instead, are required to demonstrate student learning" (Bracey 2005, 5).

Jeffrey Henig adds, "The state and local leaders who are pushing most aggressively for ... charters and ... choice have not made it a priority to link their initiatives to requirements for public dissemination of data, and staged implementation. In an environment of low information and exaggerated claims, the risks of doing damage are as important to consider as the problematic advantages of precipitous and undigested reform" (Bracey 2005, 6).

An accelerant for charter reform has been the deepening budget deficits faced by states as they struggle with the general depression of the economy since 2008 and the attendant decline in tax revenues and increase in economic instability. Importantly, as the sea of red ink rises, one of the few fiscal lifeboats being offered by the federal government is tied to charter reform. Federal public education money is increasingly tethered to charter expansion. For example, during the Obama administration, the number of charters has continued to increase. The breakneck pace of charter expansion, however, worries advocates and critics. Charter school leaders are increasingly expressing doubts about the wisdom of rapidly expanding. Ben Lindquist, executive director of the Charter School Growth Fund, noted:

> There just aren't that many charter school operators that are well positioned to expand with quality and efficiency. The risk right now is that we will drastically over-estimate the capacity of the national charter sector to deliver new high quality seats for underserved families at a sustainable cost to taxpayers. At this juncture, it is very important not to open the floodgates too wide (through federal funding). If we are not careful we will get a large market segment that is littered with mediocrity. (Toch 2009, 35)

THE PROMISE OF CHARTER REFORM

Historically, competition has been described as the primary force for change within market environments. Capitalism is, as Friedrich Hayek (1944) suggested, dependent on an ongoing process of creative destruction. Those businesses unable to compete on the basis of the quality of their product, pricing, or profits will ultimately be destroyed as more efficient and innovative corporations displace them because their heightened productivity or more effective products prevail in the marketplace. Market competition is seen as unleashing the creative or innovative forces that ultimately benefit consumers. Competition is seen as the vital stimulant for efficiency, innovation, and effectiveness in the development of any marketplace good or service. Heretofore, these competitive forces have been singularly associated with the for-profit sector of the economy, but these boundaries have been redrawn over the last three decades.

For market advocates, the failure of public education is largely a consequence of the lack of competition between schools. Public school systems are often characterized as monopolies that fend off competition and experimentation because of their insular bureaucratic structures, regulations, and practices. Charter advocates argue that only by introducing school choice, and in turn, competition, can public education be transformed. As long as monopolistic control is ceded to a public education establishment, the kinds of innovation that will bury failing schools and birth the new forms of education necessary to transform the system can't occur.

This logic has certain merit. Clearly, we cannot expect public education to transform itself. The impetus for change must come largely through various forms of external pressure. Equally important, some part of that external pressure will likely emerge from new forms of schooling having the autonomy, belief, and imagination necessary to create approaches that are ever-more effective in educating students. Historically, public school systems in the poorest urban areas have not been able to introduce practices or structures to transform learning conditions or academic outcomes.

Charters are especially appealing to the private sector and business leaders, because their logic of choice, competition, and transformative change is resonant with both the ideology and experience of the corporate sector. New investments in charter schools, along with praise for making such investments, by hedge fund managers confirm that appeal:

> The schools are exactly the kind of investment people in our industry spend our days trying to stumble on.... With incredible cash flow even if in this case we don't ourselves get any of it.
>
> It's the most important cause in the nation, obviously, and with the state providing so much of the money outside contributions are insanely well leveraged. (Haas 2009)

Eva Moscowitz, manager of a network of charters in Harlem and a former New York City councilwoman, noted, "These guys get it, they aren't afraid of competition or upsetting the system, they thrive on it" (Hass 2009).

Charter reform assumes that transformative educational change can be stimulated through freedom from encrusted bureaucracy. This freedom is expected to produce innovative practice and, in turn, effective classroom practice. Although freedom to innovate is a necessary ingredient for effective classroom practice, it is not sufficient. A series of questions therefore need to be raised about the character of reform most likely to transform public education. Can we rely on free market forces to remake education, or do we need to apply a multilayered theory of change that is consistent with the complexity and dynamism of the public education project? Is innovation only produced by competition or does collaborative culture also trigger innovative practices, and if so under what conditions? What kinds of innovation are being spawned by charter schools and to what extent are they being disseminated more widely? Can innovation be better disseminated? Can innovation flourish in environments that are resource starved? These questions will be addressed in this chapter and then again at the book's conclusion.

Anticipated Innovation as the Primary Currency of Charter Reform

It is important to pause for a moment and consider the charter movement's promise of innovation. Critically, there simply is no state or national educational innovation bank that collects information on school curriculum and teaching practices and then disseminates it to public schools.

Importantly, intensified competition regarding test scores has seriously impaired the willingness of successful charters to share their experiences or practices with other schools whether charter or public, if they are out of network. In effect these organizations are functioning in a competitive marketplace that rewards performance. Would Google share its technology or innovative startup work with Microsoft to protect American interests? Alternatively, can we expect Toyota to share its hybrid technology to shore up the American economy or more largely to protect the environment? The answer to both of these questions is an unequivocal no. Intensified competition for resources diminishes the probability of organizations sharing their competitive advantage or new forms of innovation. Yet part of the promise of the charter leadership was that innovation would bubble up from the rich soil of choice. A basic understanding was that it would disseminate its innovative practices to public schools to improve their performance.

The testing culture of charters and increasingly public schools is not conducive to experimentation in educational practice. What has passed for innovation is the development of structures that drill students to produce better test results. Clearly, such attention to improving basic test-taking skills and academic capacity is necessary for poor youth of color who continue to lag in their reading and math scores. The most effective approaches have indicated that an extended school year and day as well as highly structured curricula consistently focused on the transmission of specific information or knowledge can produce increased test scores. These understandings are not new but rather part of an extended discussion in public education and also inflected in many public school practices over the past decades. What the best of charters have done is to reintroduce the relationship between increased learning time, highly structured proscribed curricula, and testing results. Such an approach, however, does not constitute the kind of deep innovation that will be necessary to equip poor students of color with the range of skills necessary to compete in the new global market place.

The limits of such an approach must also be considered in relationship to the larger collective project of public education to develop critical thinkers and effective citizens in a democracy. Again, it is important to reiterate that available data suggest in aggregate charters are not outperforming public schools. In other words, charters, even on their own terms, are not as successful as originally envisioned by movement leaders and policymakers. We will return to this point later in the chapter.

Justice for the Poor

The efforts of individual parents to secure a quality education for their children through charter schooling are rational and on the rise. Charters provide parents hope that their children will have better opportunities than past generations. Isn't that the hope that drives and explains the daily sacrifices of many parents? It is not surprising, as Pauline Lipman notes, that new educational options such as charters resonate with a swelling number of families, as well as educators (Lipman 2009, 389). The "good sense" in these policies (Gramsci 1971) is that they mandate decisive action to "turn around" a system that has failed to educate students—especially students of color (Lipman 2009; Orfield 2010). This "sense making" is derived both from the parents' experiences and the language utilized by advocates. The agenda for choice is often infused with a language of equity and justice. As Lipman (2004b) notes, school reform is often framed as a choice between justice, equity, innovation, and accountability and the "failed policies of the past"(39).

This powerful interlock between the frustration of parents and language of hope and accountability offered by charter leaders has created a cascading demand to exit public schools for charters. Most concretely, parents are voting for charters with their feet as they leave public schools. The attraction of smaller classes, better test scores, committed teachers, private and public funding, as well as safe learning environments have been a magnet for parents, and as a result, the lottery systems used to select children into charters have been overwhelmed by elevating levels of demand. Importantly, it is this demand, currently surpassing supply, that provides charter advocates one of their most powerful arguments for expanding the number of charter schools nationally.

Although the choice for charters makes sense within this context of failed public education, a number of critical policy questions remain unanswered. How do we imagine that charters will be able to yield greater equity and justice for poor children of color? What is the record of privatization or social policy structured around market principles in promoting greater equality and justice? What kind of fiscal investment is necessary to fix public education for the largest number of students in the poorest communities? Perhaps, most critically, what has been the record of charters to date in improving the academic performance of poor students of color?

In general, charters have targeted the poorest communities of color as sites for their schools. As noted, that choice can in part be attributed to profound need for effective schooling and frustration with the public system. Consequently, these communities have the enormous pent-up demand for new forms of education. Such decisionmaking therefore makes both policy and practical sense. New education products like charter schools, however, must be sold to parents/consumers if they are to channel that demand into an exit choice from public education. More specifically, the product has to be branded in ways that make it both immediately recognizable on the one hand and define it as more effective on the other. Like SUVs that are represented as the most rugged or coffee characterized as having the best taste and greatest caffeine kick, charter schools have to both identify and then create the magnetic field of "market" allure for their targeted consumers.

The branding of charter schools as preferred and elite because of limited seats was described in a recent issue of *US News and World Report* entirely devoted to choice and school reform. "A waiting list is not the worst thing. 'It's like driving past a truck stop with no trucks,' says Nida. 'You want to go where everybody wants to be'" (Rettig 2009). The creation of an image of an elite product seduces poor parents into both desiring and striving for admission to the sanctified world of a charter education. When parents learn that they can't enter because of an insufficient number of seats, they often become angry, blame teachers, and organize to close schools and open charters. An especially powerful example of this dynamic has occurred in both Detroit and Los Angeles. Parent frustration at not being able to enter the "lifeboat" of charter education is understandable. How would any of us react to the social reality of limited seats blocking our child's access to a quality education? Parental activation to ensure a quality education through charters and choice in large part represents a continued willingness to fight the inequity raining down on their children.

This packaging of charters as an elite institution is no accident; to the contrary it is part of a conscious advertising campaign that brands charters as the preferred choice for knowledgeable consumers or parents. Like a BMW, Armani suit, or Jameson whiskey, the charter school is a choice for the best and the brightest, those interested in the "good life." But that good life promised by charters is highly suspect as the following passage by Pauline Lipman (2004a) suggests:

> The construction and consumption of images of "good education" through high stakes testing … obscures the complex socio-cultural and historically situated nature of actual teaching and learning, privileging how the school looks on standardized measures over what is really going on there. Nevertheless, a system of ranking and sorting was a necessary condition to identify schools to be closed and to turn them over to private operators. (479)

THE EMPIRICAL RECORD

Standardized Testing Results

Gary Miron and Leigh Dingerson (2009), on the basis of the findings of a Stanford survey of charter school performance, indicate that there is an inverse relationship between the rapid proliferation of charters and rates of student achievement. They report that "states with positive student-achievement growth had only 61.6 charter schools on average, while those with negative growth had an average of 275 charter schools" (30, 36). Although the rapid expansion of charters produces clear benefits in meeting some of the pent-up demand, this phenomenon produces simultaneous and paradoxical costs as it erodes the charter movement's capacity to either stimulate innovation or increase student achievement. Miron and Dingerson also indicate that in "the poorly performing states" a much higher proportion of charters are run by for-profit EMOs. These preliminary findings suggest that the rapid expansion of charters and their association with ever-larger EMOs may produce a series of dilemmas that undermine performance. A central dilemma is that the rapid pace of charter development may undermine capacity to ensure quality. Additionally, large or medium-sized EMOs may structurally undermine innovation. Finally, the difficulties of scaling up effective charter experiments through ever-larger EMOs and a proliferating number of schools are increasingly being experienced as a daunting challenge (Toch 2009). These findings, however, are at odds with a large part of the prevailing wisdom regarding charter reform.

For example, Secretary of Education Arne Duncan's response to the data was to reassert his commitment to charter reform and demand that unsuccessful charters be closed and successful ones replicated. More specifically the *New York Times* reported that Duncan obfuscated the sweeping implications of the aggregated data by indicating "that low quality institutions are giving their movement a black eye" (Dillon 2009). Duncan was quoted as stating in the aftermath of this national study that "the charter movement is putting itself at risk by allowing too many second-rate and third-rate [charter] schools to exist.… Charter authorizers need to do a better job of holding schools accountable.... [We must] get in the business of turning our lowest performing charter schools around."

Perhaps most importantly a number of national studies over the past five years indicate that on the basis of standardized testing results, aggregated charter performance is no better than that of public schools and often worse. In August 2004 the *New York Times* reported that data collected by the federal Department of Education "dealt a blow to supporters of the charter school movement." The data indicated that fourth graders attending charter schools were lagging a half year behind their counterparts in public schools in both reading and math (Schemo 2004). As well-known advocate for charter reform Chester Finn noted, "These scores are dismayingly low.... A little more tough love is needed for these schools. Somebody needs to be watching over their shoulders" (as quoted in Schemo 2004). The results were based on the 2003 National Assessment of Educational Progress, commonly known as the nation's report card. The *New York Times* noted that the math and reading tests were distributed to a nationally representative sample of 6,000 fourth graders in 167 charter schools across the nation and were consistent with the findings of a cross section of local and state studies.

A more recent survey conducted by the Center for Research on Education Outcomes (CREDO) of Stanford University produced similar findings in 2009. CREDO partnered with fifteen states and the District of Columbia "to consolidate longitudinal data on student level achievement for the purposes of creating a pooled analysis of the impact of charter schooling on student learning gains" (CREDO 2009, 1). The authors note that "virtual twins" were created for 84 percent of the students in charter schools. Perhaps, most critically, the report documents impacts for 70 percent of the students attending charter schools in the United States. It is generally acknowledged that the CREDO study is the first comprehensive national analysis of charter school impact on student achievement. In its summary of findings, the authors suggest that the report shows wide variation in performance. That said, however, the data reveals charters are less effective than public schools in delivering learning results. More specifically, 17 percent of charters produce outcomes on standardized tests superior to public schools. However, nearly half of the charter schools nationwide have results that are no different than public schools, while over a third or 37 percent of charters deliver testing results that are significantly worse than if the student had remained in public schools (CREDO 2009, 1). Over three-quarters or 87 percent of charter schools nationally produce the same or worse outcomes than public schools on standardized tests. Again, this data has not produced a series of editorials questioning either the basic direction of charter reform or asking for a systematic review and refinement of the strategy. Perhaps more importantly, it has not slowed the growth of charter expansion; to the contrary, in the midst of these findings growth has accelerated.

Ben Lindquist, the executive director of the Charter School Growth Fund, recently indicated

> that only 6 percent of the 340 organizations that have sought support have met the organization's academic and financial standards for funding. There just aren't that

many charter school operators that are well positioned to expand with quality and efficiency. The risk right now is that we drastically overestimate the capacity of the national charter sector to deliver new high quality seats for underserved families at a sustainable cost to the taxpayer.... It is very important not to open the floodgates too wide [through federal funding]. If we are not careful, we will get a large market segment that is littered with mediocrity. (Toch 2009, 35)

The development of effective schools is largely a product of targeted investment, capable teachers, and a robust curriculum. Clearly, attention to testing and basic skill development is critical to the work of both public schools and charters. But if this goal is the principle, if not exclusive, concern of a school because of the testing environment's powerful sway in determining the direction of rewards and penalties to staff and organization, then the objectives of charter schooling, and more largely public schooling, are likely to shift. All eyes are on the test scores and attention is simultaneously deflected from large parts of the purposes of public education. Critically, one such perversion of purpose has been the widespread cheating on testing to artificially raise test scores in Atlanta, Washington, DC, and Pennsylvania.

Access, Dropouts, and Graduation

Recent evidence indicates that the most academically challenged students are least likely to be enrolled in charter schools. ESL and learning disabled students—who are more expensive to educate—find few spaces available to them in charters and as a result are increasingly concentrated in traditional public schools. Thus, as public schools experience various forms of disinvestment, their costs per student are rising. This paradox is not accidental, but instead a predictable outcome of market-driven charter reform. In an environment of intensifying competition and scarce resources, academically challenged students are an increasingly inefficient, unproductive charter investment. Meanwhile, traditional public schools have legal requirements to offer access and programming to all students. This distinction raises a number of questions: First, how can charters be called public schools if access is limited for academically at-risk students? Second, if relatively able students are disproportionately migrating to charters and the most academically challenged remain outside of charters, does this transform public schools to a "dumping ground" for the most troubled or difficult-to-educate children? The reduction of resources and the number of high-performing student role models assure that traditional public schools will be less and less able to demonstrate improved academic performance for the poorest students of color. In turn, such outcomes are likely to lead to even louder calls for further slashing and redirecting the budgets of traditional public schools.

Further, academically weak students who transfer to a charter are more likely to be counseled out, removed, or voluntarily leave. The consequence is that public schools are obligated to readmit charter schools' most difficult students. This selective out-migration further concentrates students with the greatest academic and social needs in public schools. Clearly, public schools have no comparable safety valve to other systems. Charles Payne has noted, for example, that at KIPP, an exemplar CMO:

> Nearly all students believed that their school would help them get to college, all thought their teachers held high expectations of them. However, there were significant problems, including attrition. Of the students who entered fifth grade in 2003, 60 percent left before the eighth grade.... The portrait here seems to be one of schools having valuable social and academic impacts for a select subgroup of vulnerable children, but not reaching the toughest kids. (Payne and Knowles 2009, 232)

Zein El-Amine and Lee Glazer (2008) reached similar conclusions about the exemplar charter program SEED in Washington, DC. "Although SEED sends its graduates to college, it has a significant rate of expulsions and suspensions, and its practice of often retaining students at the lower grades results in a high rate of voluntary withdrawal. The school maintains an entering class of 40 students, but has never graduated more than 21 in a year. In 2007, only 12 students graduated" (59).

Critically, attrition through expulsion or voluntary student withdrawal stimulated by disincentives for remaining are not an aberrant charter experience. To the contrary, a number of recent reports from across the country have begun to question the migration of students out of charters and back to traditional public schools. Equally important, the relationship between testing performance and the exit of students is an issue receiving increased attention both because of its impact on equity and test scores. More concretely, if the most challenged test takers are leaving and the most able remaining as a result of both overt and tacit charter practices, the outcome on testing results is clear. Test scores will indicate exemplary performance while rendering invisible the more salient reality: charters have done little more than hold on to their most able performers while cutting loose in one way or another their most troubled. This is the present-day version of "creaming," or cherry-picking students, for best outcomes.

Charter school practices that return academically weak or troubled students to public schools have a cost. If student withdrawal occurs after the annual enrollment audit, funding to cover the costs of the students' education remains with the charter school. After the head count, no matter the migratory pattern of students on the basis of expulsion or active efforts on the part of administrators to push students out, the money stays with the charter school. In turn, there is a clear fiscal penalty to public schools as they are expending resources for especially difficult students without public reimbursement.

Disinvestment in traditional inner-city public schools because of student exit choice to or from charters produces further declines in programming, instruction, and building maintenance, which cumulatively diminishes traditional public school students' hopes that education can make a discernible difference in their lives. The experience of those left behind or returned as surplus and unworthy of investment is a powerful daily reminder of their marginalized relationship to the rest of the culture.

This intensifying dispossession is tethered to their splintering hope of using education as a bridge to the larger society and a different life. As the charter movement and the market are increasingly offered not as an experiment to stimulate change within traditional neighborhood schools but as an alternative to public education, the collateral damage associated with market dynamics, in this instance, the heightened dispossession of the most disadvantaged students because of increasingly unequal investments in inner-city public schooling, is increased.

IDEOLOGICAL FAITH, CAPITALIZATION OF PUBLIC ASSETS, INTERLOCKING POWER, AND CHARTER REFORM

It is curious indeed that despite a growing body of evidence suggesting charter schools do not produce desired outcomes, there has been a growing political commitment to their expansion. What explains the dissonance between the record of charter reform and this swelling demand for growth? How does political ideology in combination with economic and social forces dictate reform agenda and contribute momentum despite the modest achievements of charters in aggregate? Of particular importance is how economic gain and capitalization of this public asset is a growing impetus for charter reform.

The powerful relationship between business interests, education reform, and charter schooling is increasingly evident in a number of large urban centers. The business community's involvement in public education policymaking has been well documented. For example, in June 2009 the Civic Committee of the Commercial Club of Chicago, an influential group founded by and with strong links to the business community, issued a report that extolled charter schools. They concluded their report by indicating school choices in Chicago must be aggressively pursued—including expanding the number of charter and contract schools. Secretary of Education Arne Duncan's market-based reform initiatives in Chicago were inspired and supported by such business groups (Lipman 2009). In Washington, DC, a hotbed of charter reform, Mayor Anthony Williams (who was mayor from 1999 to 2007) partnered with the business group Federal City Council to embark on a program of privatization that included the promotion of charters and vouchers. Mayor Williams's stewardship of Washington, DC, witnessed the number of charter schools expanding from three to sixty-six between the late 1990s and 2006 (El-Amine and Glazer 2008).

The interlocking of political and business interests is not confined to local or city decisionmaking. Federal policymaking circles include a number of key Gates Foundation officials; Duncan's inner circle, for example, consists of two former Gates employees. His chief of staff is Margot Rogers who was special assistant to Gates's education director. James Shelton, assistant deputy secretary, was a program director for Gates's education division. Importantly, the Gates Foundation has been one of the leading proponents of, and private investors in, charter reform. Relationships between business, policymaking, and political decisionmakers are neither new nor surprising. What distinguishes these relationships is their intense focus over an extended period of time on charter reform. There is a shared understanding among a cross section of very powerful actors that charter reform is the mechanism of choice for transforming public education. Choice and competition are seen as the only basis for the regeneration of public schools.

The reform frame of business leaders pairs an unwavering belief in market reform with little complementary understanding of the unique role and purposes of public goods. For some politicians greater ideological skepticism may exist but their choices are to some extent determined by patrons and although they may resist the direction of policy reform, they are less and less able stop it. For other politicians, however, there is a tight fit between their political ideology and charter expansion. They believe often uncritically in the ultimate problem-solving authority of the market. The recent decision by the Obama administration regarding the linking of federal stimulus money and charter expansion has eroded the basis for even the modest forms of resistance that have existed to date and offers yet another example of the erosion of state and corporate boundaries in policymaking. This point is vividly illustrated by the influential roles former Gates employees have had in shaping and driving federal reform.

The nexus of ideology, power, and reform extends to the distribution of foundation resources in an era of public institution starvation. A cross section of foundations with close ties to business interests has helped to spearhead and enlarge charter reform by extending financial support to targeted schools and districts. The Bill and Melinda Gates Foundation embraced CMOs in its pursuit of alternatives to dysfunctional school systems. The Walton Family Foundation, a creation of the Wal-Mart empire, saw charter networks as a way of expanding its commitment to school choice. The Walton and Gates foundations were joined by three other foundations established by wealthy entrepreneurs: the Doris and Donald Fisher Fund, founders of Gap; the Eli and Edythe Broad Foundation, founded with money from homebuilding; and the Michael and Susan Dell Foundation, funded by Dell's computer fortune (Toch 2009, 4).

Foundations and wealthy patrons championing charter schooling were characterized as the entrepreneurial reformers. The language of entrepreneurial reform tightly aligned with the "creative forces of the market" directed at transforming public education. Social entrepreneurs were presumed to be largely drawn from business leaders or those trained in business practices. Critically, little attention has been paid to social entrepreneurs trained as teachers or principals, like Deborah Meier, who have created effective and innovative learning environments but not used market principles.

As Miron and Dingerson (2009) argued, once dedicated to educational quality, today's charter school movement is increasingly dominated by a harder ideological edge of lobbying groups advancing an agenda of expansion. For example, groups like the Center for Education Reform and the National Alliance for Public Charter Schools have indicated that unlimited charter growth is one of four indicators of a strong charter law. The position of these national organizations has been reproduced by local lobbying groups dedicated to pushing for the increased growth of charters in a cross section of state capitals. Importantly, many of these advocacy organizations are supported by the same foundations cited earlier.

This point is underscored by the Hoover Institute when it notes:

> Here in short is one roadmap for chartering's way forward: First commit to drastically increasing the charter market share in a few select communities until it is the dominant system and the district is reduced to a secondary provider. The target should be 75%. Second choose the targeted communities wisely. Each should begin with a solid charter base (at least 5% of market share), a policy environment that will enable growth (fair funding, non district authorizers, and no legislated caps), and a favorable political environment (friendly elected officials, editorial boards, a positive experience with charters to date and unorganized opposition). This solution isn't an improved traditional district; it's an entirely different delivery system.... Charter advocates should strive to have every urban public school be a charter. (Libby 2009, 26)

Charter Schools and the Maximization of Economic Gain

The rapid expansion of charter schooling is a strategic linchpin for significantly increasing the private sector's share of the education market along with consequent profit margins. The "business of public education" spends $500 billion annually. Recent reports on for-profit charter schooling in a cross section of states, including, but not limited to, Texas, Ohio, and Florida, indicate that there is a fundamental relationship between for-profit charter schooling and the diverting of public resources away from students. This should not be surprising. The principal commitment of managers is to increase the value of stock and dividends to owners. This is accomplished by extracting profit from reduced overhead associated with labor, programming, and facilities. As with other private sector companies, however, practices of cutting labor costs do not extend to first-tier managers who make substantial salaries and enjoy a range of perks.

Importantly, for-profit charter companies' search for new contracts is ongoing. Their network of support, as with other corporations, includes politicians, important business leaders, and foundations. Therefore, despite the blatancy of profit taking, underinvestment in student learning, questionable accounting practices, and the falsification of testing results, for-profit companies remain important players in the contested terrain of public education policy and practice. Failure is ascribed not to the structure and predictable dynamics associated with for-profit education but rather the deficiencies of a particular company. In effect, the individual company, not the larger policy, is questioned. The political choice to look the other way and not face the fatal flaws of for-profit enterprises as a mechanism for providing public education is in great part a consequence of the powerful forces aligned in support and the lubricant of channeling profits to lobbying for contracts and special advantage.

Since 2002, however, the expansion of for-profit EMOs has slowed while the growth of nonprofit EMOs has accelerated. One might therefore conclude that the dynamics of profit making have largely been replaced by the purer aspirations of nonprofit management agencies. Unfortunately, that has not been the case. Education, as was pointed out earlier, represents a very large market for entrepreneurs. The potential areas of profit making are not limited to the provision of education services. Other sectors of the economy are also profiting from the chartering of public education.

For example, real estate interests stand to make potentially large profits by leasing and building facilities for charter schools. This market has particular importance for charter schools because, as a matter of policy, they are not eligible in most states for capital construction money. Consequently, charter schools frequently have to rely on churches, public schools, and a range of other makeshift arrangements for space. Clearly, these makeshift, often unstable arrangements are not conducive to creating satisfactory learning environments. Over time, a number of for-profit companies have come to both recognize and profit from this situation. One venture capital investment company, Entertainment Properties Trust (EPR), has entered this market. EPR has developed what it describes as triple net leases. EPR is the landlord, buying buildings, leasing them to charters, and "filling a need." The tenant pays for maintaining the buildings and running the classrooms. The tenant, according to Daniel Wolff (2009), is in this instance charter school operator Imagine, founded in 2004 and serving 36,000 children from New York to Arizona (2). The result has been a first-rate investment because the tenant has been a dependable source of revenue through school taxes. Unfortunately, the cost of the lease accounts for half of the per-student revenue received by a number of the schools. Clearly, as one administrator remarked, "that is an enormous percentage of your budget to pay for classrooms." The benefit of stable classroom space provided by the leasing and venture capital firm has been offset by the educational cost of redirecting public money from the classroom to for-profit real estate entrepreneurs. Again, this is not an isolated example of real estate interests and leasing companies profiting from charter schools' intensifying need for building space. The misfit between charter programming and available building space can only be expected to become more acute as charters rapidly expand because of federal policy. In turn, the tradeoff between leasing space and investing in classroom instruction is likely to become an ever-more defining feature of education practice and policy in the next decade.

Potential profit making for the real estate industry, however, is not limited to leasing arrangements. Equally important is the relationship between charter schools and the construction industry. In New York City, for example, approximately $220 million of tax levy dollars has been allocated to the construction of charter facilities. Clearly, this is an emergent and significant area of profit making for a construction industry that has been wounded by the collapse of both the housing market and the curtailment of mortgage lending by the banking industry. Such expenditure was expected to produce intensified competition between companies and the efficient allocation of scarce public resources. This expectation, however, is being questioned by public school advocates who are documenting the relationship between school construction decisionmaking and political networks. Perhaps the most vivid example of this possible interplay of political power and economic investment is the allocation of $26 million to the PAVE charter school, in Brooklyn, New York, to build a private facility for 350 children. The allocation represents 12 percent of the capital budget while the children who will benefit represent a much smaller fraction of the students attending charter schools in New York City. Equally important, it has been suggested that the building will be constructed in an isolated area with two underutilized school buildings. An inquiry is presently being conducted by journalists and advocates on the extent of interpenetration of real estate interests that have a relationship to the mayor, the charter movement, and the awarding of contracts. This much is clear: public money earmarked for charter school construction will grow in the next decade. This growth will be accompanied by the prospect of substantial profits for private companies increasingly unable to sustain profit margins in commercial and residential housing markets. Consequently, these contracts will be highly prized and the construction industry will become yet another actor lobbying for the expansion of charter schools.

Other profit centers are also associated with charter schooling. These include, but are not limited to, vendors supplying needed infrastructural fiscal and managerial support. Equally important, a range of services traditionally provided by public workers from janitorial maintenance to curricula development are likely to be outsourced to private sector companies. An especially fertile area, however, of profit making increasingly aligns charter schooling with virtual learning technology.

Virtual Learning and the Shifting Landscape of Charter Reform Profit Making

The cascading crescendo of charter school investment is accented by its increased attention to virtual or online learning. About "45,000 K–12 students in the US took online courses in 2000; in 2009 that number had grown to 3 million" (Waters 2009). The benefits of virtual learning are clear and undeniable, reaching students who have dropped out or were chronically truant, reinventing sites of learning, introducing learners to speakers who would otherwise be unavailable, and producing efficiencies of scale. Online technology has the innovative potential to stimulate new forms of learning in a cross section of schools. That said, like any other form of technology that is neutral in the laboratory, its purpose and structure is reshaped by real-world conditions or context.

Online learning has been introduced into public education during a period of fierce contestation regarding the levels of investment and capitalization of neighborhood schools. Importantly, the intensified competition for public education dollars is especially vivid around online dollars. Many marketplace entrepreneurs in and outside of charter schools have emerged to both define and fill this profit-making opportunity. For traditional public schools the intensified competition for public dollars in a period of both economic decline and disinvestment has been exacerbated by the growth of online learning. At a recent online conference, a former teacher and television producer noted in his presentation "Build It or They Will Go: Community vs. Enrollment Erosion":

> Online learning lies at the heart of serious competition between traditional brick and mortar schools and entrepreneurial proprietary schools that are taking advantage of the charter movement.
>
> Districts must recognize the phenomenon of proprietary innovation [as] essentially the same disruptive technological change that has rocked newspapers, the photo processing industry and the music business. They must find a way to own the online learning and technology space and aggressively identify and move forward with the benefits of educational technology. If they don't the for profit schools will and enrollment erosion will begin a hollowing out of K–12 district populations that will be difficult to reverse. (Waters 2011)

The rush to penetrate public education sector assets in large part through online learning technology is not limited to either relatively small companies or for-profit charter networks. For example, Rupert Murdoch acquired 90 percent of Wireless Generation, a high-tech company specializing in data processing, information collection, and online learning. At the time of the acquisition Murdoch said he saw "K–12 education as a $500 billion sector" (Resmovits 2011). The $500 billion that Murdoch was referring to was the entire budget in the United States for K–12 education. In his statement he identifies all of public education as a private sector market. At a conference in Arizona, Michael Moe, an investment banker who has worked for over a decade at converting K–12 into a source of significant profit for Wall Street, noted that, like health care in an earlier era, education was the next "undercapitalized sector of the economy" (Fang 2011, 12). "It was within this context that he read through a list of venture investment firms such as Sequoia, Benchmark Capital and Kleiner Perkins that had invested in the education technology or virtual learning sector of the economy" (12).

The growth of online learning has occurred despite a cautionary review of research in the Department of Education in 2009 that found "that few rigorous studies have been done at the K–12 level, and policymakers lack scientific evidence of the effectiveness of online learning (Gabriel 2011a). An inquiry of virtual schooling in Pennsylvania conducted by the Center for Research on Education Outcomes indicated that "students in online school performed significantly worse than their traditional counterparts" (Fang 2011, 14). A study conducted by the University of Colorado in late 2010 found that 30 percent of virtual schools run by profit organizations met minimum education outcome standards as compared with 55 percent of brick and mortar schools (Fang 2011, 14). Larry Cuban, an education professor at Stanford, indicated that the research "did not justify big investments by districts in online learning. There is insufficient evidence to spend that kind of money period, period, period" (Richtel 2012, A1).

In an article on virtual learning designed by the for-profit K12 Inc., the *New York Times* reported, "By almost every educational measure, the Agora Cyber Charter School is failing" (Saul 2011). Around 50 percent of its students are behind grade level in reading and math. There is no body of evidence that shows an upward trend. Liz Pape, president of the Virtual High School Global Consortium, noted: "'I think many people see online courses as a way of being able to remove a pain point, and that is, how are they going to increase the graduation rate?' If credit recovery were working, she said, the need for remedial classes in college would be declining—but the opposite is true" (Gabriel 2011a).

Despite the evidence, the momentum for online learning continues to build. This momentum is largely about the profit-making potential of virtual learning. In Florida, for example, "virtual schools cost nearly $2,500 less per capita than at traditional schools" (Fang 2011), not only allowing states to reduce budget spending, but drastically increase the amount of money that can be earned by private investors off each individual student. The earlier cited Agora Cyber Charter School expected income of $72 million in 2011–2012, a figure that represents 10 percent of the total anticipated revenue of the parent company K12 Inc., "which is the biggest player in the online school business" (Saul 2011). The second-largest company, Connections Education, with revenues estimated at $190 million, was recently bought by the global education and publishing corporation Pearson. Charter virtual learning as an economic motor of profit making has been joined to a phalanx of lobbying initiatives richly financed by right-leaning patrons such as Koch Industries, Eli Broad, Home Depot founder Ken Ragone, and Rupert Murdoch. Less politically active but equally wealthy patrons such as Bill Gates have directly and indirectly supported the drive to rapidly expand virtual learning. Two conservative organizations, the State Policy Network (SPN) and the American Legislative Exchange Council (ALEC), have taken a lead role in devising tactics to rapidly expand the financing and political support for online learning. Special task forces composed of corporate lobbyists and state legislators have written model legislation. ALEC, for example, has offered template legislation entitled "The Virtual Public Schools ACT" (Fang 2011, 15). From Idaho to Indiana to Florida, new laws are being developed that will radically restructure public education, shifting the responsibility from brick and mortar public schools to online education businesses with little if any record of academic accomplishment.

The push for spending on online learning is in large part driven by schools facing tougher financial choices. More specifically, draconian cutbacks in traditional public schools are forcing very difficult choices. For example in Florida, virtual classrooms have become a way of enlarging class size and reducing per-student cost despite its Class Reduction Amendment passed in 2002. The amendment limits the number of students in a classroom, to between twenty-two and twenty-five, but not in a virtual lab. Administrators were effectively placed in a straitjacket, trapped between class-size limits and fiscal austerity. They recognized that there was no way to beat the class-size mandate without virtual labs (Herrera 2011).

Online learning's contribution to "efficiencies" or reduction of costs in a period of public education disinvestment takes other forms. For example, Alex Molnar, a professor of education at Arizona State University, indicates "what they want is to substitute technology for teachers" (Gabriel 2011a). This point is illustrated in Memphis where teachers supplement their incomes by contracting to work ten hours a week with 150 students. That is one-quarter of the time they would devote to teaching the same students face to face (2011a). In Idaho, a virtual learning initiative may result in a shift of tens of millions of dollars "away from salaries and teachers" (Richtel 2012). Teachers indicated that state legislators responded to heavy lobbying by "technology companies such as Apple and Intel." In response, teachers and parents "gathered 75,000 verified signatures ... to put a referendum on the ballot next November that could overturn the law" (2012).

Charter schools, small to midsize independent online companies, and global corporations are the primary centers of profit making in virtual learning. Questions that have surfaced regarding improved academic performance, the role of teachers, and economic austerity in relationship to online learning echo concerns about charter education. However, the data and legitimate reservations about the escalating investment in unproven forms of "innovation" have been trumped by larger forces that on the one hand are capitalizing education and on the other reducing public investment in neighborhood or traditional schooling. Those forces contradictorily threaten to radically restructure public schooling in ways that may make it not more but less effective. This point is illustrated by the tendency to target students who are not committed to this new learning medium. Alix, a high school student in Florida, explained in the *New York Times*: "'None of them [other students] want to be there,' Alix said, 'and for virtual education you have to be really self-motivated. This was not something they chose to do, and it's really a bad situation to [be] put in because it is not your choice'" (Herrera 2011).

The present intentions of the charter movement and momentum of federal policy are to replace large sectors of traditional public schooling with alternate forms of education. As noted in Chapter 1 the redistribution of a substantial proportion of public education dollars to an expansive education marketplace represents a wholesale and accelerating capitalization of public assets. Politicians increasingly dependent on the capital of dominant economic interests to run for office are more willing to cede this area of policymaking to donor influence, foundation expertise, and/or media pressure. The consequent legislation promulgated by legislative bodies leaves policymakers with less and less autonomy to invent and reinvent policy on the basis of data, changing conditions, best practices, or experimental strategic investment. Instead the ongoing, legislated starvation of the state in combination with capitalization/privatization of public assets leaves policymakers with few options outside of the education marketplace. These dynamics predictably serve to intensify a shedding of state responsibility and redirection of its resources.

The multiheaded profit-making hydra of charter schooling must be situated within the context of overaccumulated capital in finance centers, which must be moved to places where it can earn profit. An approach increasingly being employed is the capitalization of public assets outside the marketplace. In this way new wealth and profit can be created, through public assets and taxes largely financed by the working or middle classes. This upward redistribution of wealth and capitalization of public assets is a short-term strategy to produce new profit centers that cannot solve the longer-term crisis of American empire. Critically, this short-term strategy has profound implications for the social reproduction functions of the state, democracy, and more largely the longer-term legitimation of the social order.

THE SOCIAL AND POLITICAL CONSEQUENCES OF CHARTERING PUBLIC EDUCATION

Historically, charter schools have not been the only choice option for parents of public school children. To the contrary, in New York City and other major urban areas, public school choice has been afforded parents for decades through enriched, magnet sites provided by traditional forms of public education. Choice no matter its form does result in an ever-greater emphasis on parent commitment to the individual achievement of a child and less and less attention to the collective fate of a neighborhood and its students. I don't want to romanticize the present or historic commitment of individual parents to the collective of students at a neighborhood school. However, a primary link between urban residents and their community has been and continues to be their local neighborhood schools. Those linkages are quite weak as is evidenced by the relatively few parents in the poorest communities who visit local schools to meet with a teacher or principal. That said, traditional local schools are an institution with the potential to integrate individuals and groups into communities and the neighborhood.

This potential has not been achieved. By removing schools from neighborhoods and situating them on the basis of a lottery or an academic criteria across a city or district, the capacity of public education to function as a collectivizing and democratizing institution for neighborhood residents is further minimized. The counter argument advanced by a racially and economically diverse cross section of parents has been that choice will raise standards, heighten accountability, and ensure the more effective education of students. These claims have had merit for a limited number of individual students offered public school choice districtwide. It is within this context that Norm Fruchter (2007) indicates, "I now think that broad public school choice programs, carefully structured and implemented to ensure equity of access and outcomes, can contribute to improving academic achievement, particularly for students of color in urban settings." He adds a cautionary note by further suggesting "the persistent pressure from advantaged parents and complicit districts to transform choice programs into clusters of privilege and inequality requires constant resistance" (80).

Dispossession from Geographic Community

Present education policy committed to expanding choice draws together students from larger and larger geographic areas by stimulating their out-migration from neighborhoods and into stronger nonlocal schools. In addition, it further rewards already advantaged citizens, and ultimately ensures an ever-more anemic (and sometimes hostile) connection between local schools and low-income community members. Alternatively, it is argued that the costs of geographic dislocation are more than offset by heightened achievement, particularly for students of color. Much of this shift is occurring despite the, at best, mixed academic record of charters, which indicates that more often than not traditional public schools outperform charters.

The policy inclination to selectively sever student and parent ties to neighborhoods is joined to a series of important assumptions about the restructuring of public education. To begin with, it assumes that satisfactory targeted investment and improved achievement cannot be accomplished through neighborhood schools. Secondly, it presupposes that the engine of innovation is consumer demand (made possible by the expansion of choice) and not local principals, teachers, and parents committed to improving and changing the learning and instruction conditions for students. Finally, it cedes place or neighborhood in part to the pain and frustration of local public schools' historic record of underperformance.

Rarely assessed are the losses associated with the out-migration of students from local schools to charters. What is the cost, for example, of locating a charter in a neighborhood that draws its student population from other parts of the city? If individual academic achievement or a lottery is systematically used to determine admission, how does such an approach decollectivize the project of public education? Equally important, how does it promote dispossession for both parents and students? For students, the costs can be subtle and complex. It is likely that place-based friendships among neighborhood children are weakened as a result of out-migration to charter schools. And the social cleavage between those who leave and those who stay behind is likely to grow because of ever-more vivid differences in academic resources available in varying institutions, in addition to the status conferred by charter attendance.

These dynamics may mirror the experience of upwardly mobile immigrants as they take physical and psychological leave from their communities of origin, family, culture, and history, in turn erasing their past to shape their future. The dislocation associated with the choice for individual achievement is both economically rational and a reaction to the interlocking influences of market forces and social policy. For those students who take flight on the basis of parent choice, the costs of dislocation from place is rarely measured or mentioned. And yet, the ever-more tenuous relationship to the communities in which they live, the neighbors with whom they share space, and the friends who were part of their early development does create experiences of dispossession. Clearly, we need to more fully explore this phenomenon. However, this much we do know: The growing disconnect between citizens and the places where they live does have an impact on local participatory democracy and the formation of local, place-based identity.

If an individual's time is increasingly invested in institutions outside his or her neighborhood, such as in nonlocal charters, then the degree to which the individual (and his or her parents) identifies with local issues, groups, or organizations is also likely to be diminished. A fight for better neighborhood schools is no longer understood as a fight relevant to one's daily life—or even the future. This distance between those who continue to struggle against declining neighborhood schools and those who have exited the local system ultimately weakens grassroots resistance efforts by undermining community solidarity. Fruchter (2007) warned that "the choice argument substitutes the expansion of individual options for the transformations of societal institutions. Choice subordinates efforts to achieve collective justice to the extension of individual and familial capacity" (77).

Parents' public voice on matters of collective or communal concern has been muted in other ways by the choice for a charter education. For example, the accountability of charter schools to parents is unclear. Their governance structures are constituted by and large by board members drawn not from parent groups but funding sources, education experts, and administrators. Equally important, charter boards do not have a legal obligation, unlike their public counterparts, to have collective meetings with parents to discuss policy or practice issues.

The loss of communal voice as a result of both public officials' rush to charter reform and charters schools' greater insulation from parent influence is illustrated by a letter written by New York State Assemblyman Daniel O'Donnell to Chancellor Joel Klein:

> I write to express my outrage at the disrespect exhibited yesterday in its handling of proposal to house Harlem Success Academy at M241.... Yesterday's treatment of the parents and leaders of District 3 completely refutes any assertion by DOE that it wishes to meaningfully involve parents in decision making at any level. I have learned that no advance notice was given to the public parent leaders or District 3 staff.... I also learned that [the] charter school had time to arrange for two busloads of advocates to attend and testify and outfit their speakers with the school's apparel. Yesterday's true message could not be clearer: DOE has made its decision about PS 241's future and will proceed regardless of the hearing's outcome. No other meaning could be derived from failing to give notice of a public hearing, or from the brief, inconvenient window during which stakeholders could sign up to testify. (O'Donnell 2009)

Policymaking Embedded in the Marketing of Charters

The fantasy of charters as a magic bullet for what ails public schools has grown and with it the public clamor to replace larger and larger parts of the education system. As we have shown above, the popular understandings of charters are not only simplistic but inaccurate. A system as complex, underresourced, and overburdened as public schools is immune to a single transformative magic bullet. As has been noted, without additional targeted investment, capacity development of staff, and stakeholder involvement, public schools will continue to flounder.

The increasingly lethal fantasy that market forces alone can meet the challenge of providing a quality education to a nation's citizens depends on a misreading of out-migration to charters and a lack of appreciation for the fundamental value and makeup of a public good. Albert Hirshman argues that one cannot really exit from a public good like education. "A private citizen can get out of public education by sending his children to private schools, but at the same time, he cannot get out, in the sense that he and his children's life will be affected by the quality of education" (Fruchter 2007, 78). Present initiatives regarding charters are part of a larger discourse and policymaking direction regarding the substitution of all things public or collective in favor of private forms of market exchange. The unique attributes of a public good as contrasted to market commodities are rarely noted—for example, the intention to affect collective outcomes of social good rather than measures of individual accomplishment; the pursuit of social and economic equity, creating exchanges based on collaboration, rather than competition; and an emphasis on developing a critical understanding of one's relationship to a larger world are but a few of its potentially distinctive qualities. These outcomes are highly intertwined with the processes that create them.

In the marketplace less attention is paid to the qualitative, relational, participatory, collaborative, and noneconomic nature of exchanges that are key to the overall quality of our public goods as well as our democracy. Rather the exchange is more quantitative (profit), circumscribed (production processes necessary to create profit margins), and individuated on the basis of targeting consumers and constructing measures of monetary success. Molnar remarks,

> Charter schools, like private school vouchers and for profit schools, are built on the illusion that our society can be held together solely on the pursuit of self-interested individual purposes. Considered in this light, the charter movement represents a radical rejection of not only the possibility of the common school but of common purposes outside the school as well. The struggle is not between market based reforms and the educational status quo. It is about whether the democratic ideal of a common good can survive the onslaught of a market mentality that threatens to turn every human relationship into a market transaction. (Molnar 1996, 15)

Charter Schools as the Trojan Horse Concealing an Absence of Strategic Investment

As indicated throughout this volume, effective schools are largely a product of targeted investment, capable teachers, and a robust curriculum. It is therefore important to return to the question of investment in public education reform. In large part, charter reform has been financed not by new public dollars, but rather a redirection of money away from public schools. Resources have been "freed up" by closing "failing public schools." Additionally, money has followed students from one school to another. In other words, the choice for exit or closure has meant that traditional school budgets are slashed while the investment in charters grows.

Any discussion regarding disinvestment from traditional public schools must begin with a description of the original Faustian-like bargain that charter reformers made with the state. An economic incentive proffered by advocates to shift education funding was that charters would cost less to run than traditional schools. The fundamental flaw in the structure of this financial arrangement has been addressed by a number of charter movement leaders, most notably Nelson Smith, the chief executive of the National Alliance for Charter Schools, who admitted: "We made some bad bargains to get the laws on the books" (Toch 2009, 5). This point is reinforced by data collected in 2002 and 2003 that indicate "charter schools in 16 states received an average of 78 percent of the funding of traditional public schools" (Toch 2009, 5). More recently Debra Viadero reported,

> Charter schools typically receive less public funding per pupil each year than regular public schools do, and in many states are forced to pay for their own facilities. Only 10 states and the District of Columbia … give charters annual per-pupil funding for facilities, and only three provide them with more than $1,000 per student. The report also documents the schools' heavy reliance on philanthropies, which have provided over $600 million over the last decade. (Viadero 2009)

The differential investment between charters and traditional public schools is part of a larger government disinvestment in public education. Lower expenditures on students in charter schools paired with increased state investment in charters means that state investment in education per student has declined rapidly. Additionally, the state's unwillingness to invest in facilities and transportation for charter schools suggest that charters have become little more than an excuse for the state to pull out of its commitment to educating the citizenry.

The "efficiencies of charter cost reduction" are interwoven with basic practices of its reform. An especially important tenet of most charter schools is a deep distrust and opposition to unionization. Unions are perceived as disinterested in student need and resistant to the new "outcome-based" measurements of teacher effectiveness. This association of unions and teachers with school performance problems works to undermine the collective influence of educators within schools, consolidating power and authority among public school administrators and CMOs' executives. Some critics have argued that one of the most important goals of charter reform is to reduce the power and reach of public unions. The argument that unions represent members while charter reformers are singularly interested in the academic development of students is at best flawed and at worst disingenuous. To begin with, charter school movement leaders are advancing an agenda that extends well beyond student need. Equally important, teachers' unions, although interested in membership welfare, are increasingly waging battles to increase investments in both public education and student performance.

The use of the present crisis to break unions is again not accidental, while at the same time the critique of the union role is not entirely without merit. Most relevant to this discussion, however, is the relationship between unions and the rates of pay for classroom teachers. Few would disagree that the single most important issue for teachers unions has been salary scale. Much of their fight over the past thirty years has been to move teachers up the economic ladder. Clearly unions such as the United Federation of Teachers (UFT) have had some success in advancing this economic agenda, although often it has come at the expense of a longer workday. One of the regulations that charters have been able to sidestep because of their agreement with the state is that guiding the relationship between teachers unions and public schools. Consequently, charter schools have been able to pay their teachers less and demand longer school days and academic years. This, in turn, has allowed charter schools to reduce their costs for personnel relative to traditional public schools and simultaneously squeeze more work out of their labor force. Similar labor savings and disinvestment occurred in both social services and health care when policies of privatization were initiated in those sectors of the welfare state. Importantly, personnel or labor savings more than make up for the differences between public and charter schools regarding per-student reimbursements. Labor cutting permitted by charter legislation that allows circumvention of union contractual agreements when combined with lower rates of public reimbursement per student have made charters an especially "efficient" and "fiscally viable" education policy option.

THE BOTTOM LINE

As students choose to exit public schools, the composition of the population remaining also changes. As Ted Sizer and George Wood noted:

> The United States seems to have acquiesced to the notion that good schools are to be treated as a scarce resource, and those with the highest income levels or the ability to seek out best choices are provided with the best schools. Lacking either the resources or personal capital to find such schools, everyone else is shuffled off to what is left. This has led to a concentration of our most needy students and challenged families in schools that are under-resourced and lack a drawing card. (2008, 10)

The ever-greater competition between public schools and charters over an essentially fixed pot of money has produced bitter squabbling in New York City, for example, over the distribution of space within neighborhood schools. The *New York Times* reported:

> "It's not fair to our students," she said of the decision, which gives the charter students access to the room for most of the day. "It's depriving them of a fully functioning library, something they deserve." ... Even determining how many rooms are free is contentious—most schools use open space for activities like dance, tutoring and computers—but the Education Department officials often treat those rooms as "underutilized space" to allow another school to come in. (Medina 2009)

The stark differences between public schools and charter schools often sharing the same space is illustrated in the same article: "In some cases as in Harlem and

Brownsville, the regular public school has not performed well and has seen enrollments shrink while parents flock to the charter on the other side of the building. Charter schools that have had success raising private donations have new desks and computers to show for it" (Medina 2009).

Erica Frankenberg and Genevieve Siegel-Hawley (2009) elaborate on the charters' role in creating a separate but increasingly unequal form of public education. They note that the "year 2000 marked the last annual US Education Department report on charter schools, a key federal overview on charter trends in enrollment, implementation and accountability" (12). Data in this report were disaggregated, however, on the basis of race and receipt of free and reduced-price lunches—an indicator of family income—English-language learner (ELL) status, and disability. Over time, even with equalizing correctives such as lotteries, charters continue to have difficulty achieving an enrollment that is diverse. Frankenberg and Siegel-Hawley note that charter reform simply reinforces unequal education opportunity. The factors affecting such outcome are partially identified below:

> Without necessary safeguards against the segregating effects of charter schools— already documented by the government in their own charter school evaluations, in addition to research by other scholars—families are left to comprehend and cope individually with the complicated landscape of school choice. This is challenging for families with limited resources, time or knowledge of the variety of educational options—even more for families that are disadvantaged by mainstream society, such as having limited English proficiency or who dropped out themselves. A recent study of the Institute for Race and Poverty notes: "if parents do not act to move children from failing schools then expanded choice will not lead to improved performance in traditional or failing schools." ... The authors provide evidence that few parents or families actually opt out of failing public schools.... Limited or unequal access to charter schools renders irrelevant the theory suggesting that increased choice will improve the quality of all schools. (Frankenberg and Siegel-Hawley 2009, 3)

CONCLUSION

Charter schooling, to the extent that it could increase school choice, was hailed as a way of leveling the playing field between poor communities of color and their wealthier neighbors. But imagining that choice alone could produce an egalitarian educational system did not properly acknowledge the range of social forces that sustain the inequalities in public education. As Norm Fruchter (2007) notes: "Choice seems unlikely to disrupt or transform the interlocking of power and racism that have imposed inferior education on children of color for decades. Choice is at best, only a tactic and a limited one in the ongoing struggle to achieve effective education" (76).

In the meantime, the downward spiral of American public education continues as basic economic issues of teacher to student ratio, infrastructural decline, outdated or inadequate supplies, antique technologies, and the underdevelopment of classroom supports are ignored especially in the poorest communities. The creative destruction of public education, however, continues unabated. New forms of public schooling, most prominently charters and virtual learning environments, are created. Old forms of public schools are closed. In that transaction huge percentages of poor students of color continue to be neglected, while the current reform, nevertheless, sustains its allure and continues to be both promoted and expanded. The consequent deepening dispossession—affecting parents, children, educators, and neighbors—will be discussed more fully in the final chapter.

FOR FURTHER READING

CREDO. "Multiple Choice: Charter School Performance in 16 States." Stanford: CREDO, 2009. http://credo.stanford.edu/reports/MULTIPLE_CHOICE_CREDO.pdf.

Fabricant, Michael, and Michelle Fine. *Charter Schools and the Corporate Makeover of Public Education*. New York: Teachers College Press, 2012.

Fang, Lee. "Selling Schools Out: The Scam of Virtual Education Reform." *The Nation* (December 5, 2011): 11–18.

Payne, Charles, and Tim Knowles. "Promise and Peril: Charter Schools, Urban School Reform, and the Obama Administration." *Harvard Educational Review* 79(2) (2009): 227–239.

Chapter 4

Dispossession Stories

In the shadow of empire, as the US public sector is strategically refashioned—fiscally, morally, and racially—our curiosity turns to the strategic role of public schools in the redesign. Perched at a precarious intersection of fiscal disinvestment, on the one hand, and policy hyperattention, on the other, public schools and test-based accountability occupy a peculiar role in the highly contested theater of crisis, accountability, and privatization.

In an economy in which unemployment rates are on the rise for educated people, and shockingly high for low-income black and Latino—immigrant and otherwise—marginalized youth, we are surrounded by and suspect of a language of crisis and accountability pinned onto the bodies of urban youth of color, as we witness national, state, and local policy committed to:

- massive disinvestments in public K–12 schools, public higher education, and public educators, strategic investment in private "solutions" to educational (and other public) troubles;
- dedicated and sustained commitment to testing, policing, closing schools, and charter conversion as technologies for improving urban public schools; and
- a relentless refusal to address how income inequality, housing insecurity, rising unemployment rates, racism, mass incarceration, and anti-immigrant policies affect academic outcomes.

The Economic Policy Institute (2011) tells us that since 2001 the income of the top 1 percent has risen by 18 percent while that of blue-collar male workers has fallen by 12 percent. Forty-one percent of single mothers in the United States live below the poverty line. White median wealth is now 44.5 times higher than black median wealth. In this context of swelling inequality gaps, federal policy and resources are being channeled away from the public classroom and toward privatized strategies for "accountability" and "security." Teachers are being vilified, school budgets cut, curricula narrowed, schools more segregated and stratified than in recent history, and yet funding for testing and school policing remains intact. As music and art disappear, history and science are trivialized, after-school programs are well funded by No Child Left Behind (NCLB) and supplemented by Race to the Top for drilling test prep into the minds of black and brown youth—despite the absence of evidence that such pedagogical strategies are effective.

As if Michael Foucault produced an ironic tragedy, federal, state, and local policymakers' calls for "evidence-based practice" ring hollow as prevailing policies advance, for poor youth of color, aggressive high-stakes testing, expansion of charters, and drive-by educators with little experience—strategies with little evidence to justify their implementation. Indeed, available data confirm that these three strategies bundle as a package of reform that stretches equality gaps; heightens segregation and selectivity; produces no discernible academic gains over time; and weakens the equity, sustainability, and democratic base of the public education system. Indeed we are witnessing a fiscal and educational taxing of the poor. By fiscally undermining, centralizing, and corporatizing control over the very institution that sits at the heart of American democracy, the collateral effects of privatizing public education are enormous, most intimately in low-income communities but ultimately for the fate of our fragile, multiracial, multiethnic democracy. And as we will argue in this chapter, disinvestment in teaching and learning and substantial investments in testing and policing lay at the heart of the privatization process.

When national, state, and local policies sever supports by capitalizing services, starving public sector institutions such as public schools, evolving ever cheaper, mechanized forms of service, and in turn bolster punishment and containment as the only viable place for investment in poor communities, the consequences are by now predictable. Inequality gaps grow; trust in the public sphere takes a nosedive; profits swell for industry and elites; and low-income and immigrant families are ever-more disposable as they grow more alienated from, and fearful of, the very institution presumably designed to welcome them into the economy, into the country, into democratic fabric. It is this last point that we will explore in the following chapters. As inequality grows, a clear outcome is that increasing numbers of poor and working-class people are declared disposable and dispossessed from public institutions and over time from the larger social order. The dynamic between the crisis of capital and growing inequality is clear. What is less visible are the consequences of these policies. The impact of the present ideological and fiscal assault on teachers and public schools was discussed in Chapters 2 and 3. What remains largely unaddressed, however, is how these economic and political forces render as disposable the poorest communities of color caught in the crosshairs of austerity policies, deepening poverty, and the intensifying call for testing accountability. It is within a larger political-economic context, described earlier, that policies of public education disinvestment and budget-neutral reform of testing accountability, charter schools, and virtual technology grows. These conditions have a very powerful and particular impact on poor communities of color, which have the most complex and demanding academic learning needs. These budget-neutral policies, when combined with the costs of intensifying policing for schools with insufficient resources and concentrations of poor youngsters of color, have led to multiple strands of student experience of disposability and dispossession.

Therefore, in the second half of the volume we review the contemporary *technologies* of dispossession—to understand how global capital has set its sights not only on faraway lands but on dispossessed communities in the United States, their public schools, services, and workers, right here at home. We begin by theorizing dispossession stories, how private interests are being insinuated into public life. We begin our analysis of dispossession through an ethnography over time, of a single school, the former Brandeis High School, and offer a short biography of the building, as it has been transformed over twenty years from a site for "disposable" children, to a site for intensive testing and policing, to a school in declared "crisis" and in need of being closed and reopened, to a site for the children of the newly gentrifying neighbors. By bearing witness to these banal and seemingly inevitable shifts in a building located in a "changing community," we can understand how dispossession unfolds. Elites reclaim, and seemingly clean up, those parts of the public sphere that once served poor youngsters of color, as if their best interests were a synonym for the larger collective interest.

After we visit with Brandeis High School, we'll focus more explicitly on what we are calling two technologies of dispossession: the strategies funded as responses to crises actually borne of economic and racial oppression. That is, we will investigate how *high-stakes testing* has become the well-funded science of dispossession and privatization, providing a veneer of objectivity, dispassion, and truth to the powerful political momentum for racialized land grabs, centralization of power and control, and the systematic denial of educational opportunity to the poorest youth of color. We then turn to the deep public investment in *discipline*—suspension, expulsion, and criminalization—as the braided strategy of disenfranchisement, in schools and on the streets, for youth of color and poverty. Finally, we analyze how dispossession moves under the skin of poor and working-class youth of color, influencing their behavior and interior lives in a city where inequality gaps swell through the design and structure of social policy.

DISPOSSESSION STORIES: HOW PUBLIC SPACE BECOMES A PRIVATE COMMODITY

Over the past twenty years, Michelle Fine, with colleagues at the Public Science Project, has been gathering dispossession stories: empirical accounts of how public opportunities, institutions, and resources are being redesigned in law, policy, and academic practices that further tip educational advantage in the direction of children of privileged families, while an array of equally expensive public policies—testing, policing, and surveillance—are being unleashed within low-income communities, reinforcing and extending inequality gaps that already characterize urban America.

Across a variety of communities and public sectors, Michelle and other researchers at the Public Science Project have been tracking what we call *circuits of dispossession and privilege* (Fine and Ruglis 2008)—how changes in law, policy, and institutional practices on the ground are realigning educational goods once considered "public" toward limited access primarily for the children of elites and a few token working-class children of color. We are interested in the social-psychological circuits through which economic and political shifts circulate and find their way under the affective and cognitive skin of parents and youth living in privileged and marginalized communities.

Theoretically, our work on dispossession draws on critical race theory (Du Bois 1899), the epidemiology of inequality gaps (Wilkinson and Pickett 2009), political theory on neoliberalism (Harvey 2004), and critical psychology focusing on how injustice penetrates the ways in which young people make meaning, make protest, and make do (Sirin and Fine 2008; Fine and Ruglis 2008; Fox et al. 2010). Critically, these dispossession stories are situated within a political economy, producing swelling inequality gaps.

In *The Spirit Level: Why Greater Equality Makes Societies Strong* (2009), British epidemiologists Richard Wilkinson and Kate Pickett demonstrate that more unequal societies, with larger income/wealth disparities between top- and bottom-class fractions, experience higher rates of "social pain" across a variety of indicators including school dropout rates, teen pregnancy, mental health problems, lack of social trust, high mortality rates, violence and crime, and low social participation. Their book challenges the belief that the extent of poverty in a community predicts negative outcomes, and they assert instead that the size of the *inequality gap* is associated with various forms of social suffering.

Wilkinson and Pickett document how place matters. The inequality gap of the United States ranks among the highest in their international comparisons and New York State has the highest incidence of such differences in the nation. The Congressional Budget Office provides evidence that time matters, too. In 2011 the richest 1 percent of households captured 20 percent of the nation's pretax income, up from 10 percent in 1979. During the same period, everyone else's share—the 99 percent—went down. At the intersection of place and time, in 2011 New York City is, according to the US Census Bureau, the least equal city in the nation. Thus, New York City dispossession stories chronicle a very particular history, documenting the redesigned landscape of educational opportunities and trajectories in a city already saturated in stratified educational options (Wilkinson and Pickett 2009).

Layered atop and sewn into a nation, a state, and a city with extraordinary and compacted inequality gaps, New York City educational policy over the last three decades has been shaped by federal, state, and local neoliberal policy initiatives, ranging from the Reagan era through to NCLB, Race to the Top, and New York City mayoral control. Neoliberalism (Harvey 2004) is a political, economic, and ideological system that privileges the market as the most efficient platform for distributing social goods, minimizes the role of government responsibility in assuring collective well-being, and highlights instead personal responsibility for assuring individual well-being. By facilitating market-driven reform to determine how and for whom opportunities and burdens are redistributed, neoliberal policies tend to facilitate the upward flow and control of resources, opportunities, and power toward wealthy communities and corporate interests. Simultaneously, a downward drip of surveillance in the form of testing, policing, and restricted access to quality institutions for working-class and poor youth is stimulated.

Neoliberalism operates through various mechanisms of material and power consolidation. It is important to reiterate that Harvey (2004) distinguishes *capital accumulation,* the processes by which elites and corporations generate, sustain, and consolidate power from *accumulation by dispossession,* a set of practices by which elites and corporations repossess formerly public goods or services and convert them into individually held private goods. Critically, there is a dynamic relationship between these processes. As capital accumulates and is distributed to fewer and fewer in a period such as this one of growing inequality, the consequent misery for those locked out and simultaneously witnessing the degradation of their public institutions grows. More to the point, as concentrations of capital grow for elites through accumulation, so, too, does the bitterness of dispossession course more rapidly through the lives of the poor. Once these processes are unleashed and inscribed in law or policy, Harvey argues, those who are dispossessed are typically left to fend for themselves, policymakers implicitly assuming their misfortune is self-induced.

New York City public education, under Michael R. Bloomberg's mayoral control, is often lauded as the cutting edge of the "new reform and reformers" in public education. It is thus an especially powerful case example for demonstrating how seemingly neutral policies produce vastly differential outcomes by race, ethnicity, class, neighborhood, and immigration status.

REFORM AND "CHOICE"

As you will see in great detail in the following chapters, New York City public schools, under mayoral control, have become the laboratories for a significant and highly consequential line of neoliberal policy—an expansive system of what is called school "choice," but who gets to "choose" remains a topic of heated debate in the city. New York City has been a champion of school choice, once a commitment of progressive communities, but "choice" has been converted into a tool that stratifies, rather than equalizes, educational opportunity.

Historically, in New York and nationally, school choice has long been heralded as a progressive measure, endorsed by the early small schools movement (Meier 2005), advocates of racial integration and magnet schools (Orfield 2008), and those supporting rigorous vocational education. While "choice" has always had significant critics, particularly within long-betrayed communities of color, calls for "choice" have historically been modulated by rigorous attention to equity. Thus in Cambridge, Massachusetts; Shaker Heights, Ohio; Berkeley, California; Montclair, New Jersey; and the early small schools movement in District 4 of New York City, "choice" was a strategy by which educators and communities collaborated to create high-quality, integrated educational settings that strove to be fundamentally equitable—never perfect, of course, but the vision was a radical blend of choice and equity.

Today, most prominently under New York City's mayoral control but throughout the nation, the language and policies associated with "choice" have been systematically decoupled from equity and linked to "freedom" deployed through choice, enacted as a loss of equity. No longer tethered to a collective notion of equity, "choice" has become a proxy for *exit from*, not integration within, the public sector. This occurs via vouchers and charters or exit from the diverse masses of students to selective admissions schools. "Choice" in New York City has been torqued to serve the interests of elite parents and a relatively small number of families of color through "lotteries," leaving behind huge concentrations of low-income students, largely students of color and immigrant students, who have been subjected to two extremely well-supported public policies—high-stakes testing and zero-tolerance discipline policies that rely upon suspensions, expulsions, and in-school policing.

While all three streams of policy—choice, testing, and policing—have been underwritten as measures of educational flexibility, accountability, and security, the consequences have bifurcated by race/ethnicity and class. The best-informed families and highest-achieving students indeed enjoy "choice." However, students of poverty, students of color, and immigrant youth disproportionately attend segregated schools flooded with school safety officers who work for the NYPD. With increasing options for school "choice," large comprehensive high schools, in particular, have become "dumping grounds" for low-achieving, academically struggling students. These students disproportionately are not yet fluent in English or designated as in need of special education. These schools are, by national law, increasingly designated as "failed," a designation that prompts a set of interventions including school closings. Even if the testing and the policing were intended to improve student outcome and school climate, the overwhelming evidence suggests that they provoke just the opposite, particularly for students most in need. What will become increasingly clear is that in schools with high concentrations of poverty, the testing and the policing have adversely affected student engagement and have lubricated the school-to-prison pipeline.

With little regard for histories or structures of oppression, and often enacted in the name of reform or progress, neoliberal policies of systemwide "choice" that do not take into account race, class, or linguistic equity tend to benefit, or widen options for, those already privileged and deny access to, or burden, those already limited. Such policymaking is a powerful agent that both reinforces and legitimates growing disparities in income and wealth that pockmark the economic landscape.

Across twenty years we have been gathering dispossession stories to track, contest, and interrupt the enactment, justification, and racial/class consequences of public policies that have explicitly or more subtly facilitated an upward redistribution of educational resources and a diminution of opportunities and resources to those most in need.

It may be useful to distinguish three strategies of dispossession:

- *Dispossession by categorical denial* is perhaps the most straightforward strategy by which specific groups are denied educational access because of a contested or "suspect" status (e.g., unauthorized students denied federal aid via the Dream Act; Latino immigrants in Alabama who fear expulsion from their schools; incarcerated or formerly incarcerated students in college denied Pell Grants; see Fine et al. 2001).
- *Dispossession by cumulative, cross-sector disinvestment* has been studied by documenting the differential impact of citywide policies of disinvestment and surveillance (high-stakes graduation requirements, policing in schools, stop-and-frisk policies) on distinct groups of youth. Polling for Justice (see Fox and Fine 2012), a large-scale youth participatory action research survey of 1,100 young people in New York City, has catalogued how various education, health care, housing, and criminal justice policies in New York City differentially affect youth by race/ethnicity, class, immigration status, sexuality, and gender. It investigated the swelling precariousness of urban youth, the extent to which young people as a generational cohort, and by race and class, are now situated in "risky" relation to education, economics, health care, and housing, with social contracts for mobility and possibility broken most systematically for poor and working-class youth.
- *Accumulation by dispossession* involves an elaborate process by which public buildings, opportunities, and resources once generally available, or specifically dedicated to a working-class or poor community, are being repossessed by and for elite interests, private profits, or selected children.

We offer below a glimpse of a critical ethnography of a school that once served poor and working-class youth of color. It was closed and reopened for a new class of students in the rapidly gentrifying Upper West Side of Manhattan as a structural response to class anxiety. Importantly, this narrative of accumulation by dispossession reveals a sense of human (in)security felt even by the upper middle class and elites of Manhattan. The Brandeis-McCourt ethnography reveals how parts of the public sector are being made over to serve the children of elites, and simultaneously dislodge or dispossess the children of the poor and working class in a language of neutrality and educational accountability.

Through the biography of a single school, Brandeis High School, we can eavesdrop on an intimate struggle over public space, real estate, whiteness, and precious (versus disposable) children. We can see how two technologies of dispossession—testing and policing—pave the way for colonization of public space. In addition, this narrative reveals how banal dispossession comes to seem natural, perhaps terrible, but necessary.

OUT OF "CRISIS" AND ON THE "RISE": THE
BIOGRAPHY OF A SCHOOL BEING DISPOSSESSED

Framing Dropouts (Fine 1991) tells an ethnographic story of a school building serving low-income black and Latino youth; the book was published long ago about students deemed "disposable"—worthy only of state warehousing and neglect. Fast-forward by a quarter century and this community of Manhattan has whitened, private schools are viewed as "kind of pricey," condominium prices soar, and local families decide they need and deserve a local high school. Set in the lap of a rapidly gentrifying Upper West Side community, the Brandeis story offers us orchestra seats for viewing how real estate struggles bleed into a refashioning of public goods as the forces that swell inequality gaps devour Brandeis.

The school and its students were historically neglected by, or viewed as a nuisance to, the wealthier neighbors. But the community now sells itself on the Internet:

> With a median income significantly above that of Manhattan as a whole, New York City's Upper West Side is a residential neighborhood with great diversity. Extending South to North from 59th Street to 110th Street with Central Park and the Hudson River forming the East and West boundaries, the Upper West Side is home to multiple cultural attractions and parks.
>
> The American Museum of Natural History is a favorite family attraction with the Children's Museum of Manhattan running a close second. The Upper West Side is home to the New York Historical Society, Lincoln Center for the Performing Arts, the Metropolitan Opera House, and shopping and restaurants at Time Warner Center. The famed Dakota Apartments, where John Lennon was killed, are located across the street from the Strawberry Fields memorial in Central Park. For gourmet shopping, the Upper West Side offers Fairway Market, Citarella and Zabar's. The playground and walkway through Riverside Park are favorites for outdoor recreation. For outdoor dining, the UWS has several options including the Boatbasin Cafe and the Cafe at the 70th Street Pier.
>
> Due to the residential feel, higher median income, and desirable architecture, Upper West Side housing prices are higher than many other New York City neighborhoods. (Real Direct 2011)

Brandeis, like so many other comprehensive high schools in New York City, morphed for a transitional moment into a site of heavy surveillance, via testing and policing. By 2009 the Department of Education in New York City determined that Brandeis would unfortunately have to close, only to be reopened as a selective high school for local youth and their families. The faces would whiten, the scores would rise, the community would relax, parental engagement would be enhanced, educators would seek positions here, and the metal detectors would come down. The colonization process would be complete and appears meritorious; victory declared.

Caveat: this story can be told in two voices—the historically pernicious story of whiteness, capitalism, and colonization stealing yet another building from black and brown youth and their families. That story, although well documented in other places and times, will be told again here. The other voice tells the story on the ground, where a terrible school that has long betrayed the hopes and dreams of youth of color is finally closed, improved, held accountable, reclaimed. Both renditions of the Brandeis biography are true, if partial. One is a story of structural neglect and the other about the structural abandonment of black and brown youth. Switch the bodies and declare success.

But in the midst of this "redemptive project," the haunting question must be asked: Where are the missing bodies?

BLEACHING PUBLIC BUILDINGS: DISPOSSESSION AS EDUCATIONAL ACCOUNTABILITY?

We can have democracy in this country, or we can have great wealth concentrated in the hands of a few, but we can't have both.
Louis D. Brandeis

In 2009, the *New York Times* broke the story that Brandeis High School would be slated to close that year.

> Brandeis, with 2,251 students, is an increasingly endangered species of school—a large general-curriculum institution rich in course offerings but short on personal interaction. These big high schools, once staples of the city's educational map, have been overhauled by the Bloomberg administration, and other urban education reformers who promote more intimate learning environments as an antidote to poor performance.
>
> Opened in 1965, Brandeis is the 15th school to be marked for closing this year; others include the Bayard Rustin High School for the Humanities in Chelsea, another large high school. Since Mayor Michael R. Bloomberg took over control of the city school system in 2002, 96 schools have been ordered to close, including more than two dozen large high schools.

Brandeis was the school where I (Michelle Fine) had conducted an ethnography over twenty years ago of dropouts and those students pushed out, when I published *Framing Dropouts* (1991). I never used the official name of the school because of respect for the hard work of the educators and youth struggling in a building structurally doomed to fail because of wide-ranging underinvestment. But in 2009, reading the institutional obituary, I knew that Louis Brandeis would be buried and a complex of small schools resurrected in its place. I pulled *Framing Dropouts* off the shelf to remember the effect and thoughts circulating within me almost a quarter century ago.

It was 1988 when I sat in the back of what I called Comprehensive High School auditorium and cried. Salty tears of joy and rage. Two hundred and fifty young people walked across the stage, with flowers and corsages, to cheers and the rapid lights of cameras flickering for the survivors. Mothers, aunts, fathers, siblings, grandparents gathered from the Bronx and Harlem, Puerto Rico and the Dominican Republic to celebrate their babies graduating high school.

My field notes read, "I just want a moment of silence for the 500 missing." In a school of 3,000, barely one-twelfth graduated. Where are the disappeared? If this were a school with middle-class white students, everyone would be outraged; it would be closed. What we tolerate for the poor is unthinkable for elites. At Brandeis, in the 1980s and certainly since, I learned that it was normative for black and brown bodies to drain out of public institutions, without diplomas, with few alarmed about the disposability of a substantial majority of students of color. Progressives and conservatives may explain the leakage differently—racism or capitalism vs. poor motivation, inadequate intelligence, and bad mothering—but too many agreed that it's inevitable.

Little did I know that in the late 1980s, mass incarceration was being infused into the darkest neighborhoods of New York State. State coffers were quietly realigning budgets, migrating monies, and bodies of color from schools to prisons. In 1973 the state's prison population was 10,000; by 1980 it doubled to 20,000. By 1992 it more than tripled to almost 62,000.

As I sat in that gymnasium, I didn't realize that the state had other bids on their bodies. Only later would I learn that "since 1989, there have been more blacks entering the prison system for drug offenses each year than there were graduating from SUNY with undergraduate, masters, and doctoral degrees—combined" (Gangi, Schiraldi, and Ziedenberg 1999, 7).

Almost twenty-five years later, after generations of disinvestment and disproportionate placement of difficult-to-teach, over-age, under-credit students into the building, in the midst of a swelling inequality gap in wealth, income, real estate, and human security, the *New York Times* reports that a "crisis" is finally declared. The solution was to close the school and reopen it for "better" students who live in, and beyond, the district.

New York 1 reports some tension between the Department of Education and Gail Brewer, the local city councilwoman (NY1 News 2009):

> The Department of Education says the biggest problem is that students just do not choose to enroll in the school, which currently has 2,200 students and 200 teachers.
>
> City Councilwoman Gail Brewer, who represents the district, accused the DOE of making a snap decision based on poor information.
>
> "They have no history of being in the building. They don't know the neighborhood," said Brewer. "I don't think this is the right approach."
>
> The majority of students at Brandeis, which opened in 1965, are black and Latino and reside outside the school district. Many are special education students or speak English as a Second Language.
>
> Brewer said the school's principal faces adversity like few others.
>
> "The problem is that she gets many, many students reading way below level," she said. "It's very hard to get a student who may not speak English or who writes

in another language, to be able to graduate Regents [five content-based examinations students must take and pass in order to graduate] in four years."

The councilwoman believes that giving students more years to graduate would make the school's rating increase. However, the DOE says that even when incorporating those who graduate in six years, the graduation rate is still only slightly more than 50 percent.

Based on test scores, graduation rates, and cumulative disregard, the New York City Department of Education decided in 2009 that Brandeis, like so many other comprehensive high schools serving black and Latino youth, would be closed. The new building is a complex of four small schools—two "non-selective" high schools, one "second chance" school, and the new Frank McCourt High School for journalism and writing, sponsored by many neighborhood organizations including Symphony Space, adorned with the ample support of local parents and community. Ironically, in the name of Frank McCourt, who grew up poor in Ireland, the school was designed for the newly gentrifying families of the Upper West Side.

Community activists and educators were deeply engaged in challenging Brandeis's makeover. Most of the community meetings were cordial and seasoned with public commitments to "diversity." But the slippery discourse of white deservingness was leaking through the doors. "I guess this school will be for 3s and 4s?" asked one parent, referencing high test score signifiers burned into the consciousness and identity of New York City youth. "If we are serious about getting these kinds of students into that building, we'll have to remove the metal detectors," explained another parent, a father of color. And a woman facilitating the discussion elaborated, "If the other schools want to keep the metal detectors, or need them, we might want to use a different entrance."

And soon, the discursive architecture of separate and unequal was flooding the room, being spoken by white and African American prospective parents. A number of community members spoke: "This school has betrayed central and East Harlem for at least 30 years. It would be a cruel joke to clean it up, invest in transforming the school and then opening it for local elite children. That would, of course, constitute just another betrayal of Black and Brown students in New York." The DOE representative explained that "any child would be welcome to the school.... They will submit attendance, grades and test scores and the computer will choose those who are eligible. Then we'll interview."

"But how about a preference for the siblings—or the children—of Brandeis' graduates?" someone asked.

"No, the building will be open to children city wide, using criteria that are demographically neutral."

Here's how it works: students who satisfy the published criteria (score as a 3 or 4 on standardized tests, submit a writing sample in English, and have good attendance and a grade-point average of 3.0 in middle school) are eligible to have a parent submit their names into a lottery. The actual conduct of the lottery itself is fair. But all of the preconditions are coated in relative privilege. Test scores in New York are highly correlated with race and class; writing samples in English are often coached by privately paid tutors; regular attendance and GPA are of course correlated with stable homes and hard work. The most profound imbalance, unfortunately, skews the process to favor parents who are savvy, informed, and entitled enough to submit their child's name into a lottery. And therein lies a piece of the makeover, couched in a language of open access and justice, even as the evidence suggests that students in the lottery vastly underrepresent the poorest of the poor, English-language learners, and students in need of special education. Like color-blind ideology (Neville et al. 2010), the language of demographic neutrality shrouds economic and cultural inequality and consequent experiences of dispossession.

It is within a context of generations of cumulative inequalities (in terms of finance equity, facilities, resources, teacher experience, distribution of high-need students, graduation rates, rigorous curriculum, science equipment, and technology) and the consequent reliance on empirical indices of "deficient" testing results and expanding police surveillance that reasonably justifies the designation "failure," unleashing processes that are likely to result in a school closing. This strategy of educational reform—segregate children by race, ethnicity, class, and academic history into varying strata of schools; police their behavior ever-more intensely; measure and publicize differential outcome data; declare crisis, close school, and reopen for more selective public or charter students—is a national trend built into federal, state, and local policy. And while the intervention is presumably designed to improve education for the children who were attending the failing schools, the scant evidence available on school closings suggests something quite different.

In January 2011, Ana Kiona (a pseudonym adopted by an educator from Brandeis) chronicled the next chapter, "The Chronology of Takeover," of Brandeis on her blog, *Brandeis High School: Diary of a School Designed for Closure*:

> While local intelligence always believed that [McCourt] and perhaps other similar schools would "inherit" the building, it now appears that another plan may be underway.
>
> On November 18, 2010 it was announced that BHS would most probably be the site for Eva Moskowitz's Upper Westside Success Academy. [Moskowitz is perhaps the most iconic figure leading the charge of the charter invasion of public schools in NYC.] The mere mention of two initial sites, PS 145 and PS 165, engendered forceful protests from parents, teachers and community leaders. However, there is nobody to protesting the "redesign" of the BHS site. The students, parents and teachers of the disappearing BHS have been silenced over time by the momentum and apparent inevitability of the change. The leadership of the first three schools has always known that they were probably in their current location on borrowed time.... The neighborhood activists and local merchants would love nothing more than for them all to go. Only the fourth school has local political support as well as active parents.... Equally important, the momentum for change has grown in part as a result of a recent expansion of luxury housing and a desire among some affluent Westsiders to make the public school system work for them.

Currently there is a shortage of prize elementary school seats in the affluent portion of the district. Enter Eva Moskowitz who has advertised that she will offer a private school—quality education for free. While she states that priority will be given to ELLs, siblings of students in her other Success Academics, and students citywide slated to enter failing schools, her information and recruitment sessions have been held in English in the richest and whitest section of the UWS. These sessions have occurred at the Jewish Community Center, the Westside YMCA, and in the homes of wealthy Westside residents who support charter schools. Her bus shelter ads and literature are only in English and imprint the image and impression that charter schools aren't just for poor children of color. (Education Notes Online 2011)

The effort to radically restructure BHS and other schools on the Upper West Side has in turn produced push back. Resistance was mounting from a variety of quarters—legislators, community organizers, educators, and parents. As "Anna" was blogging, the Upper West Side and Harlem activist communities were organizing the "Stop the Squeeze!" Rally to reject the Success Charter and other co-locations in public school space.

On May 3, 2011, parents of students from various BHS schools—largely, but not only, Frank McCourt—filed a petition against the Board of Education of the City of New York also known as the Panel for Educational Policy to halt the co-location of the Success Academy Charter School within the Brandeis Campus. Parents were joined by Public Advocate Bill DeBlasio. The petition argues that the co-location plan represents a violation of policy requiring that co-location be considered if there is evidence of "under-utilization," after an educational impact statement has been produced and there has been an extensive process of public review, at least forty-five days in advance of any city board vote, with public assessment of all public comments. The petition contests the co-location on the basis of fact and procedure. Within a few days, the United Federation of Teachers and the NAACP filed an additional lawsuit, challenging the list of school closings and seeking to halt the co-location practice as a policy that endorses "separate and unequal" education.

On June 1, a New York City judge ordered that construction be halted (Finnegan 2011). By July, "the Bloomberg administration scored a major victory in court late Thursday when a New York State Supreme Court justice ruled against the United Federation of Teachers' efforts to keep troubled schools open and prevent charter schools from moving into public buildings. The widely watched case means that the closure of 22 schools can go forward and that 15 charter schools can move into public buildings" (Martinez 2011).

The biography of this building enters yet another chapter as more schools are closed throughout the city, and the mayor demands the opening of more charters.

* * *

In November 1910, W. E. B. Du Bois published the first issue of *The Crisis: A Record of the Darker Races,* insisting that a record be kept of the ongoing crisis of "the darker races." Du Bois recognized that crisis, for poor people and people of color in the United States, had been woven deeply into the fabric of our nation's history, that public schools had served as an institution through which crisis festered and was washed over, structured primarily in ways that reproduce class and racial stratifications (Anyon 1997; Bell 1992; Bowles and Gintis 1976; Delpit 2006; Fine 1991; Kozol 1972; Woodson 2010). Like his colleague Carter Woodson, Du Bois wrote on the searing capillaries through which systemic miseducation of children of color stains our national history (Woodson 2010). Most significant for our purposes, Du Bois noted the structural and historic educational cries of the "darker race" would be routinely ignored *until they are not.* Today we hear the calls of "crisis," and the wise echo of Du Bois's body of work asks us to be suspect.

Framing Dropouts, along with scores of other texts on urban schools, documents the deep and sustained inequities that have historically characterized the struggle in poor communities of color for quality education. These public education crises of the recent past and present have been produced by structural disinvestment in low-income communities, the global flows of capital, and the racial stratifications that define our inequality gaps. The ideological and cultural declaration of crisis paves a path for the dispossession and privatization to roll into, and over, poor communities of color (Fabricant 2010; Fine 1991).

There is, then, a doubled crisis at the heart of this analysis. The structurally induced crisis in education recognizes the deep historic neglect and miseducation of the poor, the immigrants, and children of color. This crisis has long been festering within the Brandeis building. The ideological crisis references those moments in history when failure is strategically announced, policymakers decide to attend to the problem not by resolving the problem but by closing and building, reopening schools for a new, "cleaner" breed of student. Working-class and poor communities lose access to a precious community resource.

With the tools of critical theory, history, and design, the Brandeis-McCourt-Moskowitz analysis is, by now, a remarkably familiar urban cautionary dance circulating in New York City and around the country, particularly in schools historically attended by low-income African American, Latino, and immigrant youth. Each move in this dance is laminated in color—that is, the colors of race and class. These are the moves of dispossession: twinning a density of very poor youngsters of color with significant learning needs to underfinanced neighborhood schools; the original miseducation that circulated in the building; the cumulative generations of students pushed out; the introduction of metal detectors and police to control concentrations of students considered, labeled, and produced to be dangerous and uneducable; and the closing of the building, only to be cleansed and reopened for the deserving. These are circuits of privilege and dispossession, power lines that meet dangerously in gentrifying neighborhoods.

The narrative of progress and a new beginning for Brandeis makes a kind of sense to those parents, students, and educators yearning for a good public school that feels safe, smart and engaging, respectful and intellectually exciting. We have no judgments about parents seeking the best school they can get for their children.

One might worry, however, that public policies framed as educational progress and accountability are actually widening inequality gaps and exacerbating the cumulative segregation and exclusion of children already plagued by rising poverty, destabilized lives, and disrupted families and housing situations.

Public policies, which systematically facilitate dispossession through building displacement, dropouts, and pushouts, are instituted as if demographically neutral. Young bodies of color have been exiled, and no one is tracking where they go—or don't go—after eighth grade. More than twenty years after *Framing Dropouts,* I am still asking, "Where are the missing bodies?"

Nationally we find ourselves in a contradictory moment: politically struggling to sustain public education dedicated to racial, ethnic, and class justice without romanticizing or justifying the oppressive miseducation that has bled through communities of color for generations. In this brief dystopic journey since 1988, we see the scratches on the soul of public education etched by technologies of dispossession such as testing, police surveillance, and building closings. Indeed the Brandeis/McCourt struggle offers a biography of neoliberalism and containment strategies, fused to reconsolidate public education for the development of elites. It also illustrates the fierce and aggressive containment strategy of slotting and redistributing students by test scores to prized public education options and in turn denying access to most poor youth of color, allowing a few to slip in. At the same time, we witness the mobilization of parents, civil rights groups, legislators, educators, youth, and unions in New York as in Cleveland, Chicago, Los Angeles, Philadelphia....

We turn now to isolate and interrogate the consequences of a single strand of public policy, testing, that has circuited through "failing" schools. Testing scores represent the most legitimate social signifier for identifying a failing school, declaring crisis, and promoting a closing. While high-stakes testing doesn't necessarily cause these buildings to fail (although test-obsessed schools often sacrifice quality teaching for emphasis on test prep), the well-funded technology of testing systematically diverts policy attention away from the structural conditions imposed on youth, communities, and schools, which produces inadequate outcomes and naturalizes racial and class hierarchies, foreclosing educational opportunities for most youth of color.

FOR FURTHER READING

Fine, Michelle, and Jessica Ruglis. "Circuits of Dispossession: The Racialized and Classed Realignment of the Public Sphere for Youth in the U.S." *Transforming Anthropology* 17(1) (2008): 20–33.

Chapter 5

High-Stakes Testing and the Racialized Science of Dispossession

The Bloomberg administration, which has made accountability the watchword of its overhaul of public education, is asking elementary school principals across the city to give standardized tests in English and math to children as young as kindergartners.

(Gootman 2008)

Half a century ago, in 1959, Horace Mann Bond, psychologist, educator, and father of Julian Bond, suggested to Thurgood Marshall that the government could save money on testing of all children by simply counting the number of toilets in a household to determine so-called "talent"—more toilets, more talent; fewer toilets, less talent. He recommended that instead of administering IQ tests to youngsters, the government should "subsidize the building of two-holers, three-holers or even eight-holers" (Bond 1959, 9). That's when Marshall started calling him "Mr. Toilets."

In 1975, Donald Campbell, a leader in the field of experimental design and quantitative social sciences, offered a similar, if less clever, warning about the tyranny of single indicators of talent: "The more any quantitative social indicator is used for social decision making, the more subject it will be to corruption pressures and the more apt it will be to distort and corrupt the social processes it is intended to monitor" (Campbell 1975). The lineage of educational testing, classification, and segregation in the United States and globally is long and bloody, profitable and highly consequential (Barkan 2011). Whether scientists were measuring the cranial capacity of Negroes, assessing the IQ of immigrants at Ellis Island, or classifying aboriginal peoples by skin color, classificatory systems have been foundational to racialized stratification of humankind.

Even if Campbell did not integrate Bond's concern about the racialized and classed deployment of these single indicator regimes, both men indeed predicted the disfigurement of teaching, learning, and the larger legal and educational corruption that would ensue if high-stakes testing became normative.

These men are neglected prophets—clearly Bloomberg wasn't reading their finest works. The science of stratification is today naturalized by a massive investment in high-stakes testing, in drag as accountability, in public schools.

Within the past decade, since the 2002 birth of No Child Left Behind (NCLB), we as a nation have perfected an entirely imperfect system of testing students, teachers, and now schools; these scores have been central to decisions about students' promotion, graduation, admission into or rejection from a selective public school or charter; educators' tenure, salary, or dismissal; districts' federal and state funding; and the conditions under which a school might be closed, turned around, or threatened with the dismissal of principal and staff. This massive transfer of public finances and power to testing companies has been shrouded in a veil of science and accountability. But fugitive suspicions have pierced the veil. Michael Winerip of the *New York Times* has been tracking the biography of the New York State achievement gain miracle, and its fall from grace:

June 2008. Newly released state test scores show another record year for New York children. Math scores for grades three through eight indicate that 80.7 percent are proficient, up from 72.7 in 2007....

June 2009.... The national assessment's fourth-grade reading scores have been stagnant for four years, and the eighth-grade scores are their lowest in a decade. But somehow, state test scores again soar to record levels. In New York City, 81 percent of students are deemed proficient in math, and 68.8 percent are proficient in English. "This is a big victory for the city," the school's chancellor, Joel I. Klein, says, "and we should bask in it." In November the mayor is elected to a third term, again riding the coattails of sweet city scores.

July 2010.... Dr. Tisch, the chancellor of the Board of Regents ... stand[s] up at a news conference and say[s] that the state test scores are so ridiculously inflated that only a fool would take them seriously, thereby unmasking the mayor, the chancellor and the former state commissioner. State scores are to be scaled down immediately, so that the 68.8 percent English proficiency rate at the start of the news conference becomes a 42.4 proficiency rate by the end of the news conference....

February 2011. The city's 64 percent graduation rate is called into question. The state announces a new accountability measure: the percentage of high school seniors graduating who are ready for college or a career. By this standard, the graduation rate for New York City in 2009 was 23 percent.

Many would argue, and we wouldn't disagree, that the contemporary commitment to *testing as accountability* may have been well intentioned, by some, as a strategy to hold schools' feet to the fire, particularly in low-income communities. The legislated mandate for accountability burned into the language of NCLB spoke responsively to many low-income parents as a check on low expectations and racial bias, a tool for parents' rights. But by all empirical accounts, the testing/accountability regime of the past decade has not heightened achievement or graduation rates, has not reduced racial/ethnic achievement gaps, and in low-income communities of color, the presumed target of the reform, the adverse consequences have been devastating.

Even if test-based accountability initiatives were not *intended* to disadvantage youth based on race or class, we now have ample evidence of their disparate impact on low-income students, schools, and communities of color. Enacted through massive investment in the testing industry and deep penetration of testing into the body of public schools, test-based accountability initiatives have fundamentally refashioned public education, producing profit, privilege, dispossession, and a policy environment that naturalizes class and race stratification; eroding learning as a practice of inquiry, passion, and curiosity; undermining art, music, physical education, and writing; judging and threatening to dismiss educators; narrowing the streams of skills children are expected to develop; and preparing children in "test factories" toward rote memorization and compliance and away from critical engagement with the world.

Test-based accountability initiatives not only affect individual students and communities; they are now central to state policy. Educational "reforms," including charter development, school closings, and the opening of selective admissions public schools, have relied heavily upon testing as the race and class passbook to admissions that determines who, where, and how far any child can travel educationally. Accountability regimes have been the triggering mechanism for school closings and charter openings, removing educational and democratic power from the hands of local communities and educators, presumably "for their own good," and placing it into the hands of corporate and philanthropic leadership and their bureaucratic collaborators.

Like the sophisticated suburban transportation systems connecting elite communities to centers of employment, travel, and entertainment, with heavy navigational reliance on test scores, urban school districts are now being spatially and academically redesigned. Elite children enjoy an enriched array of educational opportunities. A slice of "deserving" children of poverty are being recruited selectively to enroll beyond their neighborhood schools. And the most "difficult"-to-educate youth—largely students of color, poverty, and immigrants—are being increasingly measured, segregated, and concentrated in buildings where they are over-tested and over-policed, leaving most ill-equipped to pursue higher education or compete effectively for living-wage jobs in the labor market. It is important to note that with all of these reforms, framed as progress, a meager 13 percent of children of color graduating from New York City high schools have been "tested" as college ready.

Something is terribly wrong with this picture—and the most vulnerable fall prey to policy experiments designed to get politicians elected.

In the remainder of this chapter we explore how high-stakes testing has become the scientific justification for this radical redrafting of public education, dispossessing youth of poverty, of color, and immigrant students, and cultivating opportunities for youth of privilege. We bear witness as high-stakes testing enables a dramatic makeover of public education, providing scientific justification for the gentrification of educational opportunity.

A Note on High Stakes

Our concern here is with the term *high stakes*. Important and honest debates can be had about testing as an assessment strategy; that is not a debate we have the time or inclination to engage. Our concern in this chapter addresses the race and class consequences of the stakes associated with standardized tests, the money invested in testing regimes, and the use of testing evidence to strip power away from educators, parents, communities, and students.

A testing system becomes *high stakes* when the results of the exam trigger significant life-altering decisions: to be promoted or not; to graduate or not; to be tenured or receive a salary increase; or to close a school. This statistical legitimation of severely differential opportunities makes the radically unequal outcomes associated with race-, class-, and immigration-based segregation appear to be natural and deserved. We examine the evidence on the accountability initiatives launched across the country on their own terms, reviewing the extent to which such policies increase achievement and decrease racialized gaps in achievement, promote higher graduation rates or spikes in dropout/pushout rates. We trace the degree to which public monies are being transferred to private hands, often through no-bid contracts, for testing, professional development, tutoring services, and most recently test security assurance. We then turn to consider the larger "ed reform" design: the use of high-stakes testing as the seemingly neutral technology for renovating a deeply stratified architecture of public education opportunities. That is, we follow the evidence, trace the disparate impact, investigate who is making money, assess the racialized and classed redesign of educational architecture, and chart the circuits of resistance mobilized nationally for educational justice. We study how the project of public education is being torqued by public policy away from development of all children and toward investment in a worthy few.

We worry, throughout, about the ways in which the science of testing naturalizes, as if inevitable, racial and class stratification sold as coterminous with the "progress of the city." To make this all possible, we excavate the media and research-based artifice legitimating the "science" of measuring "success" through testing and discover the cultural fingerprints of some of the most conservative foundations in the nation, harnessed to equally muscular public relations offices designed to squash dissent and humiliate critics (Barkan 2011; Goldstein 2011b).

FOLLOW THE EVIDENCE: HIGH-STAKES TESTING IN AN AUDIT CULTURE

In an article published in *Accounting, Auditing and Accountability Journal*, Jesse Dillard and Linda Richula (2005) critique the mass proliferation of accountability systems that trigger moral decisions based on technical evidence. Accountants by profession, Dillard and Richula warn readers about the rapid-fire spread of accountability systems that sever moral and technical decisions, logic models that overdetermine human welfare as if objective, and metrics for which no one is personally accountable when "innocent human beings" are thereby deprived of their humanity. Dillard and Richula are concerned that technical systems of accountability have been adopted without challenge, exiling human wisdom, deliberation, and complex judgment from organizational decisionmaking, unleashing a flood of decisions based on "evidence" while ignoring concerns of humanity, equity, and democracy. At their most dystopic, they write that rigid and unmediated accountability regimes can cultivate "administrative evil" that permeates and undermines organizational health while no one is officially responsible for the devastating results and no one can intervene to staunch the bleeding.

With this perspective on critical accountability, we examine below how various departments and boards of education have invested in high-stakes testing infrastructure as a strategic technology that produces and justifies a science of stratification, swelling inequality gaps, dispossessing children of poverty, and privileging children who already enjoy privilege. Tautologically, when evidence suggests that the system is in failure, the response has been more testing—a true, if ironic, sign of how organizational disease can rage out of control even as specific forms of "accountability" have developed a deep-root system in the schools.

THE SCIENTIFIC CONSENSUS ON HIGH-STAKES TESTING

There is a vast professional consensus that high-stakes testing should never be a sole criterion for significant educational decisions. Major professional and scientific organizations, including the National Research Council, the American Psychological Association, the American Educational Research Association, and the National Council on Measurement in Education, concur that no single test should be used to make major decisions like who receives a high school diploma. The American Psychological Association has posted a position paper on its website refuting the use of test results as a single measure of performance:

> Measuring what and how well students learn is an important building block in the process of strengthening and improving our nation's schools. Tests, along with student grades and teacher evaluations, can provide critical measures of students' skills, knowledge, and abilities. Therefore, tests should be part of a system in

which broad and equitable access to educational opportunity and advancement is provided to all students. Tests, when used properly, are among the most sound and objective ways to measure student performance. But, when test results are used inappropriately or as a single measure of performance, they can have unintended adverse consequences. (American Psychological Association 2010)

Writing for the Committee on Incentive and Test-Based Accountability in Public Education for the National Research Council of the National Academies of Science (2011), Michael Hout and Stuart Elliot offer three evidence-based conclusions relevant to our concerns:

- Test-based incentive programs, as designed and implemented in the programs that have been carefully studied, have not increased student achievement enough to bring the United States close to the levels of the highest achieving countries. (4)
- The evidence ... reviewed suggests that high school exit exam programs, as currently implemented in the United States, decrease the rate of high school graduation without increasing achievement. (4)
- When incentives encourage teachers to focus narrowly on the material included on a particular test, scores on the tested portion of the content standards may increase while understanding of the untested portion of the content standards may stay the same or decrease. (3)

The National Academies find that high-stakes testing policies *do not* sufficiently increase student achievement, *decrease* high school graduation rates, and *narrow* the curricular band for educators.

These conclusions echo the findings of Laura Hamilton, Brian Stecher, and Kun Yuan (2008) of the Rand Corporation who add a set of statistical concerns to the high-stakes testing controversy. Hamilton, Stecher, and Yuan explain that "the process of creating performance standards, setting cut scores (for minimum grade level achievement and or access to relatively enriched learning environments) and attaching labels indicating the student's level of performance is fraught with technical difficulties and political controversies" (12). They document disturbing patterns beyond obsessions with "test prep": dedicating disproportionate amounts of instructional energies to boost the scores of those students near the cut score, overassigning low-performing students to special education, overretaining students in nontested grades, encouraging absences on test days, granting substantial exemptions from participating in testing, and increased dropout rates (GAO 2009).

Yet another line of research investigates the oft-discovered relationship between miraculous spikes on local achievement measures and a simultaneous stagnation on national indicators of academic progress including the National Assessment of Educational Progress (NAEP). Dana Goldstein, in "The Test Generation" (2011b), finds that a number of state and city level studies from the No Child Left Behind era found that swiftly rising scores on high stakes state tests were accompanied by appalling stagnation in students' actual knowledge as measured by the National Assessment of Educational Progress, the gold standard exam administered to a sample set of students each year by the federal Department of Education. In 2005, for example, Alabama reported that 83 percent of its fourth graders were proficient in reading even though the NAEP found that only 22 percent of these children were proficient readers. The harsh punishments associated with NCLB had encouraged Alabama and most other students to dumb down their tests and then teach directly to them.

Education policy analysts John Robert Warren and Eric Grodsky (2009) have conducted longitudinal comparisons of state-specific achievement trends on local exit examinations and state-specific achievement trends on national assessments. Drawing from three decades of data, they conclude:

> After evaluating the effects of high school exit exams using nationally representative data spanning nearly 30 years, we conclude that exit exams hurt students who fail them without benefiting students who pass them—or the taxpayers who pay for developing, implementing, and scoring them. Exit exams are just challenging enough to reduce the graduation rate but not challenging enough to have measurable consequences for how much students learn or for how prepared they are for life after high school.

ON DISPARATE IMPACT: FOLLOW THE
FAULT LINES OF RACE AND CLASS

National professional organizations have consistently argued against a singular reliance on high-stakes tests for critical educational decisions. This caution has been raised repeatedly about student decisionmaking. Policy analysts and meta-analytic scholars have reliably documented the absence of positive learning gains. Even more damning, perhaps, are the critiques posed by another set of policy analysts and scholars who provide evidence of the disproportionate and adverse impact of high-stakes testing on students of color, students of poverty, immigrant students, and students in need of special education. A vast and highly reliable portfolio of studies has accumulated on the racialized impact of high-stakes testing, cohering around a set of central points about disparate impact.

These studies converge around a core set of findings:

- Disparate racial, ethnic, and class impact on achievement outcomes:
  - Students of color and poverty (including immigrant students) are more likely to attend schools highly focused on testing to the exclusion of other areas of study;

o Students of color and poverty are disproportionately likely to be held back a grade because of low test scores and to fail state or local high school graduation exams;

- Disparate racial, ethnic, and class impact on graduation and dropout rates, particularly in high-minority districts.

From 1998 until 2002, sixty-eight of the largest urban districts had rising graduation rates, with twenty-four of those districts reporting double-digit increases in graduation rates. Since 2002, when NCLB became law, the number of states using high school exit tests has more than doubled from ten to twenty-six. During this same time, seventy-three of the largest hundred districts in the United States have seen their graduation rates decline—often precipitously. Of those hundred districts, which serve 40 percent of all students of color in the United States, sixty-seven districts failed to graduate two-thirds of their students. According to both the Center for Education Policy and the Advancement Project, since 2002, many students with high academic needs have been pushed out, encouraged to exit high school prior to graduation. And as we know from New York City data, many of those who do graduate and move into higher education, having "passed" the tests, are unable to satisfy requirements for entry and must pursue remedial courses.

- Systematic reliance on high-stakes test scores is associated with a dramatic drop in students of color gaining access to enriched learning environments.

Consider, for instance, the shifting entrance criteria, and then racial and ethnic distributions of gifted and talented programs in New York City. In the early days of mayoral control, Mayor Bloomberg promised to expand access, particularly in underserved areas, to elementary school gifted and talented programs, long criticized for racial imbalance. Once Bloomberg's accountability initiative was implemented, the Department of Education (DOE) enforced an admissions policy based solely on standardized test scores, with a strict cutoff at the ninetieth percentile (Avitia et al. 2009, 4). With this policy shift,

> the number of children entering New York City public school gifted programs dropped by half [from 2008 to 2009] under a new policy intended to equalize access, with 28 schools lacking enough students to open planned gifted classes, and 13 others proceeding with fewer than a dozen children.... But the most profound change is the overall shrinkage of the gifted program, with 1,305 kindergartners and first graders starting new classes this fall, down from 2,678 last year, according to the Education Department. That drop comes despite the fact that 16,324 students applied for entry-level slots this year, up from 6,246 in 2007. (Gootman and Gebeloff 2008, B1)

In several primarily black and Hispanic districts, so few children were eligible that the classed were suspended. Almost 40 percent of students who satisfied the eligibility criteria live in the city's four most affluent districts.

Given this compendium of research studies, substantial professional and scientific consensus about the lack of positive impact and the consistently affirming evidence of adverse impact on racial and ethnic disparities, it is stunning that Secretary of Education Arne Duncan with President Obama decided, in late 2011, to use their authority to grant NCLB waivers to states on the condition that they agree to *adopt an intensified regimen of test-based accountability provisions.*

Commenting on Duncan's (and Obama's) 2011 offer to "waive" some of the provisions of NCLB pending states' dedicated pursuit of test-based accountability, Economic Policy Institute analyst Richard Rothstein writes:

> States will be excused from making all children proficient by 2014 if they agree instead to make all children "college ready" by 2020.... Mr. Duncan will now use his waiver authority to demand, in effect, even more test-prep, more drill, more unbalanced curricula, more misidentification of success and failure, more demoralization of good teachers and more needless stress for young children. (Rothstein 2011)

The relentless commitment to testing regimes as platforms for accountability is, in our estimation, wrongheaded, racially unjust, and educationally disastrous for individual students and communities. As troubling, however, and perhaps more structurally damaging, is the proliferation of "ed reform" policies premised, without reservation, on high-stakes testing to navigate the redesign of education systems in ways that widen achievement and opportunity gaps. Policymakers have deployed testing as the trigger *and* the justification for the race/class stratification of education opportunities, accomplished in the language of "choice" and authorized in the name of accountability.

TESTING AS THE INK OF "CHOICE"

Stratification and Denial of Equal Educational Opportunities

In 2004, in an attempt to create a landscape of educational options beyond the large, failing neighborhood high schools considered last resorts in New York City, the Department of Education expanded its portfolio of "school choice," particularly for high school admissions. All eighth graders are invited to apply to no more than twelve high schools for which they seek admission. High schools then rank their applicants. In a culminating moment, this policy shift produced the following headline: "More Than 80 Percent of Students Admitted to a Top Choice High School for Fourth Consecutive Year" (NYC Department of Education 2009).

In the world of New York City high school admissions, however, the "objects of desire" are not the larger band of programs referred to in the headline but rather two tiers of elite high schools with quite selective admissions policies. The eight most highly selective high schools do not even participate in the standard "choice process." These schools administer the Specialized High Schools Admissions Test (SHSAT). And in these schools the racial and ethnic disparities are glaring.

Jennifer Medina reported in the *New York Times* (2010) that a lack of diversity persists: "Just seven black students were admitted to Stuyvesant High School's incoming freshman class, down from a dozen last year.... The number of Hispanics also dropped ... with 17 being admitted this year, compared with 24 last year. A total of 958 students were admitted."

In order to qualify for admission to Stuyvesant, considered the "crown jewel" of the city's schools, and other top-tier schools in the city, youth have to sit for the SHSAT. Medina reports that in the city district that is 80 percent black and Latino, 5,261 eighth graders were admitted to the top eight schools: 7 percent black, 8 percent Hispanic, 57 percent Asian, and 28 percent white.

In the next tier of high school rankings, almost a third of the city's high schools screen applicants based on test scores, grades, attendance, interviews, essays, or other forms of examination. In the last several years a number of these schools of choice have decided to rely upon the SHSAT. Those schools are more diverse than the top eight, but only by a bit. Highly competitive schools, like Baruch College Campus High School, can receive more than 7,600 applications for 120 seats. Liz Robbins writes in the *New York Times* (2011), "A computer then compares the two rankings, using the same algorithm developed to match medical residents with hospitals." In 2011, 78,747 students applied and the computer matched 83 percent to one of their top five choices. "Over the past three years, officials said, there has been a slight but steady increase in the number of unmatched students, up from 8 percent last year and 7 percent in 2009." These are students who have been admitted to none of their top twelve choices.

It will surprise no reader to learn that "choice" works most effectively for more privileged parents and students, and least well for low-income, hard (more costly) to educate students. Educational researcher Madeline Perez (2009) studied families' experience of "choice" as their children graduate from one of two middle schools, separated by thirty blocks, worlds apart. One school is on the Upper East Side and caters to wealthy white families and the other is thirty blocks north, serving low-income Latino immigrant families. While the wealthier families expressed considerable doubt about the efficacy of "choice" and the lottery, they knew how to make the system work for them. At the same time, the immigrant families expressed more trust in the system, even as it failed to produce rigorous educational options for their children. As Perez notes, "Basing the applications process on the medical school model which is similar to college admissions is generally a 'set up' for low-income families. This creates the conditions in which families who already have experience with this kind of system are better equipped to both understand and manage the process" (12).

After a year of intensive ethnography, tracking families through the maze of "choice," Perez concludes:

> Unfortunately, the system of "choice" originally espoused to eradicate segregation ends up being a sham and has only reinforced and reproduced segregation by race and class. This ends up hurting the most vulnerable families—families that need

quality public schools the most because they cannot afford other options. This also results in prioritizing families who are viewed as more desirable to the DOE.... Perhaps the most damaging result of this process is that because poor parents are not aware that the high school admissions process is a competitive game that has specific rules, they blame themselves for undesirable results. Unfortunately, they are not aware of the dynamics of the political economy that allows wealthy and middle class families to benefit from the public system. (2011, 445–446)

WHEN CHOICE WAS BRAIDED WITH EQUITY

The system of "choice" that Perez documents is so wildly distinct from "choice" as originally conceived in small schools of District 4 in Harlem in the 1980s, that it is almost unethical to use the same language.

Michelle Fine remembers visiting District 4 in the late 1980s, at the beginning of the New York City small schools "choice" movement in East Harlem. Anthony Alvarado was the District Superintendent and Debbie Meier the director of Central Park East. "Choice" filled the progressive educational imagination as integral to a vision of educational justice, inquiry, equity, and deep democratic participation by parents, educators, and students. Meier and the other directors of new small schools in District 4 gathered around small wooden tables, discussing students, families, and educational possibilities, delicately navigating "choices" and placements within a broad, generous, and deliberative framework of equity. While each school had individually carved a sweet pedagogical niche of distinction, the schools cooperatively allocated seats across many parts of the community. More to the point, seats were distributed with a sense of fairness to struggling students, highly motivated students, and needy students and with educational resources to match the particular theme of the school. Educators worked with community members and administrators pooling wisdom and resources, inventing clever strategies to offer foreign languages, taught by community members, before the official school day would begin, within the constraints of the union contract. They creatively generated a curriculum for "advisories" so that every child across schools would enjoy an adult mentor—over time—and every adult in the building, including janitors, coaches, and secretaries, had a group of children for whom they were responsible for support, development, and nurturance. These educators generated rich, inquiry-based performance assessment strategies so that they could track, through student work, collaboration with community, and collegial conversation, the learning needs, developmental challenges, and cultural gifts of their students. These were heady times when "choice" was deliberately situated within an equity frame.

Beyond New York City, experiments with "controlled choice" and detracking sprang up in Cambridge, Massachusetts; Shaker Heights, Ohio; Raleigh, North Carolina; Charlotte-Mecklenburg, North Carolina; Montclair, New Jersey; Berkeley, California; and numerous other communities throughout the nation, blending commitments to educational options with visions of racial and ethnic justice. In each context, policies, institutional design, programs, and practices were recalibrated to approach, if unevenly and never quite enough, racial and class justice within and between schools (Anand et al. 2002; Bell 1992; Galletta and Cross 2007; Meier 2005; Mickelson and Smith 1998; Orfield 2008).

In the 1950s, before and after *Brown v. Board of Education*, "choice" rode on the coattails of protests, litigation, and legislation fighting segregation and mandating integration. Activists put their lives on the line for educational justice, when "choice" was an alternative to separate and unequal.

In the 1980s, "choice" emerged in more local settings, tied to a vision of racial, ethnic, and class justice, cobbled together by dozens of educators and community members working deliberately across schools and communities to open up pedagogical possibilities while cultivating democratic engagement and equitable access.

In the early 2000s (fast-forwarding through struggles against vouchers; e.g., in Milwaukee), we learn from the fine ethnographic eye of Perez that choice has metastasized into an overdetermined competition for survival, as if quality education were a limited resource, a scarce commodity available primarily via exclusion: where wealthy parents game the system, poor Latino parents pray for a safe school on the No. 6 subway line, and too many eighth graders find themselves without any choice for ninth-grade admission.

Historically braided with uneven and contentious commitments of equity for all, in neoliberal America, "choice" has been decoupled from concerns of educational justice. Radically renovated as a policy initiative to enable freedom, exit, and wide-open access for some, "choice" has been deployed in ways that dismantle the fraying fabric of democracy and public education for most. Thus today, in the name of "choice" we watch as many of the most vulnerable children have no choices at all, as many of the most vulnerable schools are designated failures and closed only to be reopened for a different group of students and families. Meanwhile, elite schools enjoy enormous choice.

The passbook for navigating the system is stamped with test scores—often a proxy for class, poverty, privilege, race, and ethnicity. In times of extreme inequality, even seemingly "neutral" criteria are loaded with inequities and power differentials.

SCHOOL CLOSINGS: THE PERVERSE TWIN OF "CHOICE"

Today, under mayoral control and neoliberal flourish, as in Chicago, Los Angeles, and many other cities, the language of school choice has been disfigured by district mandates for school closings and the proliferation of selective charters. Inspired now by the neoliberal vision of educational options as a marketplace where autonomous individuals shop for educational quality, these education policies have been triggered and then legitimated by heavy reliance on test scores as the arbiter of school failure, evidence of "crisis," and (once the bodies are washed and switched), proof of the miracle of "reform."

Mark Simon of the Economic Policy Institute and education analyst Leigh Dingerson (2011) have researched the national rash of school closings propelled across Newark, New York City, Los Angeles, Chicago, and Philadelphia. They open "Dismantling Schools—Disrespecting Communities" with a tragic but familiar urban icon:

> The sight of a shuttered school building—its playground gathering litter—is increasingly common. In school districts across the nation, public schools are being shut down.
>
> In some cases, school closings are inevitable due to declining enrollment or population shifts within a district. But over the past decade, school closings have been promoted as an educational strategy. Indeed, federal money specifically intended to support disadvantaged students, is now offered to districts that agree to close schools with poor academic outcomes. Does this qualify as support for disadvantaged children?
>
> There is no research that links school closings to improved student achievement. There is research that suggests that student achievement—at least initially—drops when a school is targeted for closure, and that most students who are uprooted by closing a school, and forced into other, nearby schools, fare no better academically.
>
> So why the rush—even the mandate—to close public, community institutions rather than provide them with the supports they need to better serve their students?
>
> The trend towards closing schools as a "school improvement" strategy has gathered speed over the past decade, sparked by a well-documented movement towards the privatization of public education and the break-up of centralized public school systems. It is no accident that these efforts have centered on schools that serve low-income students of color. Waving the banners of "crisis" and "focusing on the students," and seemingly determined to avoid discussions of funding disparities and the impacts of poverty on student performance, corporate education activists have pursued policies at the local, state and national level that encourage school closure. The theory is that these schools—these community institutions—are too broken to be fixed. What message is being sent to the students, parents, teachers and principals who form the souls of those buildings?
>
> This implosion model has swept through many of the nation's largest school systems, from New York to Washington, DC to Chicago, Los Angeles, Newark and New Orleans. After nearly a decade, there is little academic change to show for it. Instead, early community warnings that the reforms were harming neighborhoods, demoralizing teachers and eroding public will for public education have been unheeded.

The story line of school closings epitomizes national trends: centralized accountability systems—the very ones that Dillard and Richula (2005) worried could propagate "administrative evil" with no one to blame—identify a set of historically underinvested schools in low-income communities of color as "failures," or "underenrolled."

In an act of administrative responsibility, policymakers move to close the schools. Public meetings and protests are choreographed but the music of protest seems only a front-stage distraction from deals already cut behind closed doors. Within days or weeks or months, the failures are closed and new schools of "choice"—selective traditional schools or charters—open. Very different student bodies walk through the front door (or the back door). The schools' relationship with the local community is severed. In a simple declaration of failure, the building gets a makeover, the community loses a precious resource, and democratic participation in public education degenerates to twentieth-century nostalgia. However, as Economic Policy Institute writer Josh Bevins argues about federal interventions allegedly designed to rescue the economy, we are witnessing "failure by design."

Since the implementation of mayoral control in New York City, almost 100 public schools have been closed and then reopened—usually with more competitive entrance criteria. The original schools registered consistently low test scores, high dropout rates, and sometimes high rates of violence, thereby rendering them eligible to be designated as "not achieving adequate yearly progress" and eventually closed. In other cities, large numbers of public schools are being closed for inadequate student enrollment or poor performance—almost all in the poorest, blackest parts of town.

Anne Galletta and Vanessa Jones describe the situation in Cleveland, Ohio, where they work with a group of youth researchers documenting the demography, geography, economics, politics, and the racialized educational consequences of school closings (Galletta, 2011, personal communication).

- In June 2010, fifteen school buildings were closed, fourteen of which were on the district's east side, with predominantly black and high poverty neighborhoods. This involved approximately 2,904 elementary and 1,613 high school students.
- In June 2011, seven facilities were closed, all on the district's east side. This affected 1,392 students.
- Combining figures from 2010 and 2011, the affected total students for all schools for which we have enrollment figures is 5,909.

In Cleveland, as in Detroit, when schools are closed there are scores of collateral consequences. From the point of view of the students, the most urgent question concerns the financing of bus passes—How am I going to get to my new school?—followed closely by educational disruption, crossing gang lines, and academic loss. Along with: Does this mean I am a failure? How am I going to compete in this new school? Is my diploma worthless? And who is going to pick up my baby brother/sister from school?

Despite the popularity of school closings as a reform de jure, in our presumably data-driven policy environment, there has been very little empirical analysis of its impact. An exceptional piece of research was undertaken in 2009 by the Consortium on Chicago School Research to document the academic and social consequences of school closings on urban elementary school students in Chicago (Gwynne and de la Torre 2009).

Tracking 5,445 K–8 students who had attended eighteen Chicago public schools closed for poor academic performance or underutilization between 2001 and 2006, consortium researchers found that most displaced students were transferred to equally weak schools—public, charters, and for-profit contract schools. One year after closing, no significant improvements in math or reading scores could be determined for the displaced students. In fact, the greatest loss in mathematics and reading achievement occurred during the chaotic year prior to the school closing, when plans were just announced and when the schools were filled with the angst of institutional death and displacement.

The achievement levels (as measured by test scores) of a small group of displaced students did, however, improve. Students who transferred to schools with high academic strength and high levels of teacher trust and efficacy showed marked improvements in math and reading. However, only 6 percent of students transferred into such schools. A full 42 percent of students transferred into schools with low levels of trust or efficacy. Overall, then, in terms of academic improvement, these researchers "found few effects, either positive or negative, of school closings on the achievement of displaced students" (Gwynne and de la Torre 2009).

Two disturbing findings, however, deserve mention. First, many of the closed neighborhood schools were later reopened as charters but not accessible to neighborhood students. Second, students from closing schools were significantly less likely to participate in Summer Bridge programs and had higher transfer rates across schools, from their first receiving school, than their Chicago public school peers.

The interaction of high-stakes testing, declaration of school failure, school closings, charter expansion, and displacement reflects a straightforward enactment of policy initiatives intended to transport Hayek's marketplace supposition, regarding the need to destroy prior institutional arrangements to create more effective and efficient arrangements to public education. While Chicago has enjoyed a rich resistance movement, "the schools that are being closed ... are almost entirely in African American communities experiencing gentrification" (Lipman and Hursch 2007, 170). The renaissance of Chicago is being hosted in "an increasingly dual city" where as a matter of policy, the poorest students of color are increasingly likely to experience the dislocation and dispossession of replacing traditional neighborhood schools with charters.

COMMUNITY PROTESTS IN RESPONSE TO THE RASH OF SCHOOL CLOSINGS

While the rationale for school closings may appear reasonable, responsible, and fiscally efficient, it is important to examine whether school closing actually remedies the original problem, and essential that we explore the collateral damage of closing a school for students, communities, and educators and for the messy democratic processes we engage in public education. Thus, it is no surprise that threatened or actual school closings are mobilizing parents, educators, and youth across urban communities.

On January 27, 2010, at 3:30 a.m., the New York City Mayor's Panel for Educational Policy voted to close nineteen schools for poor performance. By all accounts, Brooklyn Technical High School filled with hundreds, some say thousands, of parents, educators, and youth who testified for close to nine hours, protesting the school closings, many of which are large comprehensive high schools including Christopher Columbus in the Bronx, Norman Thomas in Manhattan, Paul Robeson and WH Maxwell in Brooklyn, and Jamaica High in Queens. Jamaica High School has 17 percent students who are English-language learners, 11 percent in special education with half of those classified as needing the "most restrictive environment." At Queens Collegiate, a new small school recently created *within the same building*, fewer than 4 percent of students are English-language learners and none is in the most restricted category of special education.

Parents complained there had been no community consultation on the school closings (e.g., Jamaica High) or designs for new schools of choice (e.g., Queens Collegiate). Advocates for Children released a statement noting that the schools slated for closing were disproportionately serving homeless youth: the number of New York City students who were classified as homeless rose by 21 percent citywide from 2007 to 2009 but increased by an average of 580 percent at the schools slated to be closed. Educators noted that the schools designated for closing had been assigned disproportionately high numbers of youth with special needs, without the appropriate supports (Gonzalez 2010).

On January 28, the day after an evening of frustration, anger, defeat, and disappointment at democracy denied, Mayor Bloomberg told the press, "Last night we listened very carefully, and nobody made a good convincing case why we should let any student go one more day than we absolutely have to with a bad education" (Otterman 2010).

As in New York, throughout the nation, school closing has become an increasingly popular "reform" strategy and the mobilized push back from parents, educators, and community members has been loud and collective. Mark Simon and Leigh Dingerson (2011) report:

> Community, student and parent voices are getting louder. In Chicago, hundreds of parents camped overnight in front of the Chicago Public Schools building, waiting for a chance to testify against school closings in their neighborhood. In September 2011, organized parent and community groups in New York City hosted a day-long conference that brought together teachers, district officials and others from around the country to share school improvement strategies that produce student gains, in sharp contrast to Mayor Bloomberg's school closing agenda. In Oakland, parents demanded and won the right to develop a reform strategy for several neighborhood schools that improved student academic performance without closing schools.

Like smoke and fire, where there are closings, there is mobilized resistance—what Herbert Marcuse might call national embers of the Great Refusal.

Elena Herrada, school board member in Detroit, Michigan, spoke recently at an organizing meeting where parents, educators, policymakers, lawyers, advocates, and youth gathered to mobilize against the dismantling of public schools in Detroit and against the imposition of an Emergency Manager for "failing schools" in Detroit. Responding to a parent who asked, "Why should we defend keeping bad schools open? We should have fought for them to improve, not only to resist their closure." Herrada stood to remind the group:

> We blamed ourselves when they closed the factories; we blamed ourselves when they closed the churches; we blamed ourselves when they closed our schools.
>
> We can no longer blame ourselves! They are stealing our schools, our economy and the next generation. It's time to organize … again. This is our city. (Herrada, personal communication, 2011; see also Herrada 2012)

MAKING DISPOSABLES: THE UNHOLY ALLIANCE OF OVER-TESTING AND OVER-POLICING IN LOW-INCOME SCHOOLS

In reviewing the literature on high-stakes testing, it has been disturbing to discover the nasty co-incidence of policies that mandate over-testing and over-policing of children of color in schools of high poverty. If testing is the most widely apparent transformative force in the restructuring of public schools over the past decade, a shadow policy and infrastructure deserves equal attention. Well-funded, hyper-concentrated in communities of poverty and color, and deeply reproductive with respect to inequality gaps, there has been a dramatic state investment in discipline, suspension, expulsion, and criminalization of youth of color in and around their schools. These twinned technologies must be understood as pivotal policies of dispossession and containment of youth of color and poverty.

Testing regimes mark some bodies as worthy and others as disposable, cast in a language of accountability. School policing/zero-tolerance/surveillance regimes capture and inscribe young bodies of color as dangerous, in need of containment, potentially or actually criminal, cast in a language of human security and safety. While both policies—high-stakes testing and policing in and around poor schools—have been cast as essential to educational progress, and justified as particularly necessary in communities of color, the perverse consequences of both fall well below the popular radar.

Many have written on the school-to-prison pipeline, the strategic overlap of testing and policing in schools that serve low-income communities of color (Advancement Project 2010; Ayers, Dohrn, and Ayers 2001). There have been significant exposés of zero-tolerance policies and their ironic production of more student removal and not necessarily safer school buildings. We won't repeat the findings of those reports, books, and scholarly and activist materials but recommend some key working documents such as those published by the Advancement Project (2010) and the New York Civil Liberties Union (2011). We will, however, raise the troubling specter that testing and policing have a set of shared, racialized dynamics that induce the early exile of students of color with high needs and high costs, truncating their educational careers, undermining their economic prospects, and effectively removing them from the pool of living-wage labor force participants.

Youth who attend large, unsafe, underfunded testing and dropout factories disproportionately end up without a diploma. Many of them end up suspended, expelled, and entangled with the criminal justice system. Especially salient to this discussion is the dynamic relationship between policing, testing, and the disappearance of the low-achieving, poor students. Most disheartening, Daniel Losen (2011) writes: "There is research supporting the possibility that frequent suspensions are used to avoid accountability for the test scores of lower achievers" (15). This is most disquieting given the wildly differential rates of suspensions and expulsions that exist across schools.

Racial Disparities in Suspension Rates

In September 2010, the US Department of Education Office for Civil Rights reported that more than 28 percent of black male middle-school children, nationwide, had been suspended at least once, compared to 10 percent for white males, 18 percent for black females, and 4 percent for white females (Losen 2011).

In 2011, Daniel Losen of the Civil Rights Project of the National Education Policy Center published a policy brief on racial disparities in school discipline, documenting four dynamics:

> Racial, gender, and disability-related disproportionality in suspension data;
> Dramatic increases over time (especially since 2002);
> Adverse academic and, therefore, economic and civic consequences;
> Suspensions targeted particularly for low-level or discretionary infractions.

The policy brief documents high levels of out-of-school suspensions for blacks compared to all other racial groups. This outcome is part of a larger trend that has been on the rise over the past three decades. In 1988, 10 percent of blacks, 4 percent of whites, 5 percent of Latinos and Native Americans, and 3 percent of Asian/Pacific Islander students were suspended. By 2006, 15 percent of blacks, 8 percent of Native Americans, 7 percent of Hispanics, 5 percent of whites, and 3 percent of Asian/Pacific Islander students were suspended out of school for a day or more.

Students with disabilities are disproportionately likely to be suspended. The cumulative impact of the relationship between specific characteristics (race and physical impairment) and increased likelihood of suspension is underscored by the fact that 22 percent of black students with disabilities experienced out-of-school suspension for a day or more in 2008.

The Policy Intersect of Testing and Suspension

The particular overlay of high-stakes testing and zero tolerance has been investigated by a few skilled analysts who have been interested in the cumulative racial impact of policies that layer educational dispossession onto communities of color. This research, summarized below, suggests that high-stakes testing contributes to academic environments conducive to harsh and racially biased discipline policy.

According to data cited in the volume *Test, Punish and Push Out: How Zero Tolerance and High-Stakes Testing Funnel Youth into the School to Prison Pipeline,* between 2002 and 2007, national school expulsion rates decreased for white students by 2 percent but increased for blacks by 33 percent and Latinos by 6 percent (Advancement Project 2010). Black and Latino youth were more likely (than whites) to be enrolled in testing-intensive schools, more likely to be suspended, be expelled, and drop out; and, according to Western and Pettit (2010), black and Latino high school dropouts are six times more likely than white dropouts to end up in the criminal justice system. High-stakes testing contributes to an academic environment conducive to harsh and racially biased discipline policy, facilitating in some schools a rise in youth involvement with the criminal justice system.

The Advancement Project (2010) has been studying the relationship between high-stakes testing environments, "dropout factories," and schools' reliance upon zero-tolerance disciplinary policies. In their investigation, they document a patterned and racialized commitment to high-stakes testing and rigid enforcement of zero-tolerance discipline policies. The research suggests that testing-intensive urban schools serving black and Latino students are more likely to use disciplinary mechanisms—in- or out-of-school suspension policies—than are schools that are less focused on high-stakes testing. Further, schools they classify as "test-prep factories" register higher than average racial disparities in suspension rates. This tangled relationship between high-stakes testing and school suspension policy is important to track over time—particularly since 2002 when NCLB became law.

Longitudinal research suggests that suspension and expulsion rates spiked after the implementation of NCLB, which mandated high-stakes testing.

The Rise of "Discretionary" Suspensions for "Ambiguous" Charges

It is interesting to note that most suspensions, since 2002, occur for reasons deemed "ambiguous" or "discretionary." Studies of zero-tolerance suspensions in North Carolina, Texas, Philadelphia, and New York City converge on three findings:

> Most suspensions are for minor and discretionary offenses.
> Racial disparities peak in these ambiguous categories.

School cultures characterized by over-testing and over-policing are more likely to report higher rates of suspension than schools with more relaxed testing and disciplinary policies.

"Discretionary" suspensions reflect a particularly racialized pattern. Losen describes a North Carolina study of black/white suspension rates for the same minor infractions that demonstrates that black first-time offenders were suspended at substantially higher rates than whites for: cell phone use (31 percent blacks vs. 4 percent whites), dress code (26 percent blacks vs. 5 percent white), disruptive behaviors (38 percent black vs. 22 percent white), and displays of affection (42 percent black vs. 3 percent white).

In a systematic analysis of Texas state disciplinary records tracking all Texas seventh graders over at least three years, the Council of State Governments reported that a full 31 percent of students were suspended off campus or expelled at least once during their years in middle and high school. Each of these students was suspended on average four times. Consistent with other analyses, first-offense punishments were significantly harsher for minority students than white students, receiving out-of-school suspension and alternative classroom placements at higher rates. A full 97 percent of the suspensions were considered discretionary, with wide variations between schools serving similar demographic groups.

Documenting Cultures of Punishment and Exile

Youth United for Change, in collaboration with the Advancement Project, undertook a systematic investigation of "Zero Tolerance in Philadelphia" (2011) and open the report with the observation, "There may be no other large, urban school system that matches the District in its promotion of zero tolerance and in the heavy use of out-of-school suspensions, expulsions, disciplinary transfers to alternative schools, referrals to law enforcement, and school based arrests" (2).

In Philadelphia, most of the students expelled between 2008 and 2009 ranged in age from eight to fourteen, with the mean age for expelled students between eleven and twelve. During this same time period, 417 out-of-school suspensions were ordered for kindergarteners, a 70 percent increase from two years earlier. The writers find strong negative slope relationships between use of exclusionary discipline and subsequent academic outcomes, which are more likely to yield lower levels of achievement and spikes in dropout rates.

As shown in other studies, most of the harsh disciplinary actions are taken in response to low-level behaviors. Today Philadelphia criminalizes school behavior that was simply treated as a disciplinary issue a few years ago. In 2005–2006, 17 percent of incidents classified as "assault on students" resulted in police notification; in 2009–2010, this figure leaped to 42 percent. Students with disabilities are disproportionately subjected to out-of-school suspensions. In 2008–2009, there were 54 suspensions per 100 students with disabilities compared to 24 per 100 students without disabilities. "A very common disciplinary practice in Philadelphia is to refer students who break school rules to alternative schools" including schools operated by private companies. Some critics have raised concerns that Philadelphia schools rely upon disciplinary policies to rid their schools of low-achieving students.

In January 2004, the New York Department of Education entered into an agreement with the City Police Department and the Mayor's Office to launch the Impact Initiative to identify "high crime" schools and transfer control over school environments to the NYPD. By 2007, twenty-six schools were classified as Impact Schools. In addition, 21 percent of middle schools and high schools mandated total body scans of students by using metal detectors on a daily basis. Another set of schools monitored students with random, roving metal detectors. In the academic year 2006–2007, the school safety equipment budget for New York City jumped by 139 percent. It was within this context that in 2007 the New York Civil Liberties Union published "Criminalizing the Classroom: The Over-Policing of New York City Public Schools" to expose the costs—financial, educational, and human—of excessive policing in schools (Mukherjee 2007).

The Impact Initiative schools are high-poverty schools that are large and overcrowded, underfunded, focused on testing, and disproportionately serving students of color. These schools are characterized by higher-than-average numbers of suspensions and lower-than-average graduation rates. The New York Civil Liberties Union's extensive survey and interviews documented the effects of the Impact Initiative policing and found derogatory, discriminatory, and abusive comments and conduct; intrusive searches and confiscation of personal items; intrusion on instructional time; arrests of students for minor noncriminal violations; and retaliatory arrests of educators. Perhaps most critically, the NYCLU found that 77 percent of police interventions in the schools involved noncriminal incidents.

Throughout 2005 and 2006, City Council held hearings, students and community members protested, demanding transparency and accountability for the new "security" initiative. In November 2006, about 800 students from the Urban Youth Collaborative issued a students' Bill of Rights, demanding privacy and protection, the right to "attend school in a safe, secure, non-threatening and respectful learning environment ... free from verbal and physical harassment as well as intrusions into their bodily space and belongings by schools safety agents and police officers" (Mukherjee 2007, 9). Students in New York, like those in Philadelphia, complain about inappropriate touching and language. These policies of student humiliation echo across a number of cities: "They're treating us like criminals, like we're animals."

Zero-tolerance and surveillance policies in and around public schools are *not* reducing crime or violence in schools but rather interfering with both the academic culture and civil liberties of youth and educators, particularly those attending and working in schools for young people of color. In contexts of high-stakes testing, particularly precarious contexts, there is strong suspicion that administrators rely upon zero-tolerance policies to remove students whose scores will deflate school averages and that these administrators are reluctant to accept incoming students—transfers, those on parole or probation, teen mothers, or other youth perceived to be "at risk" of low test scores.

As a result of well-funded policy regimes of high-stakes testing and policing, we witness today expensive strategies that structurally exclude and remove youth rather than engage and embrace; that marginalize the professional insights of educators; that privilege the experience of outsiders—police and measurement "experts"—over educators, parents, and youth; that cultivate academic cultures of stratification, fear, humiliation, and deportation. Educators, parents, community members, and youth yearn for *public accountability* for educational justice, to be determined by those with the greatest stake in public education.

Testing regimes and policing are expensive policies that exacerbate achievement gaps, undermine the teaching environments in schools, and disproportionately hinder the educational and therefore economic outcomes for youth of color. Perhaps most critically, these policies lead increasingly to redefining young people of color and neighborhood schools as disposable. These policies consistently and systematically lead to growing dropout and pushout rates for poor students of color as well as school closings. Disposability and dispossession are not accidental outcomes but rather embedded in the policies of the day that privilege testing and policing "reform" over strategic learning investment in the poorest communities.

Importantly, testing and policing strategies are expensive, appear to serve low-income schools but actually accomplish the "taxing" of low-resource public schools to support private industry or private interests. That is, both policies require a shifting of public dollars out of classrooms largely serving low-income students, and a simultaneous, well-funded branding and containment of poor youth, particularly youth of color.

FOLLOW THE MONEY: CHEATING, PROFITS, AND STATE POLICY SCANDALS

There's gold in them there tests.

(Miner 2005)

The testing regime, including zero-tolerance policies, has radically constrained the educational trajectories of millions of youth, twisted the processes of both teaching and learning, constricted and endangered school culture, and structurally enabled the racial, ethnic, and class-based gerrymandering of public education sometimes in the name of "choice." It is easy to argue that audit culture has contributed systematically to the educational, economic, and civic dispossession of poor youth, youth of color, and immigrant youth in the United States. But that's not the full story. In addition to dispossession of the many, audit culture has contributed handsomely to the accumulation of wealth, real estate, political power, selective public schools, and enhanced cultural capital for a few. We turn now to the mechanisms of *accumulation* leading to dispossession that are activated within present-day "ed reform." The present discussion will try to track the money.

In 2002, the year of NCLB, PBS profiled "the four companies that dominate the business of making and scoring standardized achievement tests." Congress had set aside $400 million to support the development and administration of NCLB-required testing for grades 4–8. At the time, Harcourt Educational Measure, CTB McGraw Hill, and Riverside Publishing wrote 96 percent of the state-level exams, while NCS Pearson was the leading scorer. According to Bowker Annual, which reports on publishing and book revenues, in 1955 test sales were $7 million (adjusted to 1998 dollars). By 1997 that figure jumped to $263 million and by 2002 the estimates were between $400 and $700 million (PBS 2002).

In 2011, *New York Times* reporter Michael Winerip (2011b) exposed a new corporate/public education scandal:

> In recent years, the Pearson Foundation has paid to send state education commissioners to meet with their international counterparts in London, Helsinki, Singapore and … Rio de Janeiro. Staying in expensive hotels they meet with educators and top executives from Pearson, now one of the largest education companies in the world for standardized tests, packaged curricula and Prentice Hall texts. As publishers and testing companies enjoy a rising share of public subsidies for tests, scoring, teacher development packages, curricular packages, virtual and web based educational products, and now the "Common Core" adopted by more than 40 states, the question has been raised about the propriety of these trips as a signal of the deep and perhaps inappropriate intimacy of state education departments and the private sector. These trips, like the cheating scandals, may signal more than transgression and reveal, instead, a deep and growing collaboration—or purchasing of power—by the private sector, bleeding into the public education system. Pearson describes itself as "the leading provider of assessment and education data management services in North America…. Only Pearson offers complete and cohesive support to implement the new Common Core state standards.

Winerip explains that the Common Core standards—the new national standards to which states are rapidly signing on—have been developed by the Council of Chief State School Officers, the very public officials whom Pearson has funded to attend international conferences.

By December 2011, New York State's attorney general decided to investigate whether the Pearson Foundation "acted improperly to influence state education officials by paying for overseas trips and other perks" (Hu 2011).

Instigated by Winerip's investigative journalism,

> the office of the attorney general, Eric T. Schneiderman, issued subpoenas this week to the foundation and to Pearson Education seeking documents and information related to their activities with state education officials, including at least four education conferences—in London, Helsinki, Singapore and Rio de Janeiro—since 2008, according to people familiar with the investigation…. The attorney general's

investigation is specifically looking at whether foundation employees improperly sought to influence state officials or procurement processes to obtain lucrative state contracts, and whether the employees failed to disclose lobbying activities in annual filings with the attorney general's office. (Hu 2011)

Jack Jennings, well-respected president of the Center on Education Policy, compared the influence of publishing companies in education to the overinvolvement of pharmaceuticals companies on Congress: "We shouldn't let these companies—that make tests, textbooks and curriculum materials—buy the loyalty of educators the way the drug companies have bought the loyalty of doctors" (Winerip 2011b).

Profiting from Cheating

While the economic incentives to cheat have been well established for individual teachers and corporate fraud, we are now beginning to see how deeply implicated state and city policymakers are in securing no-bid contracts and in systematically misrepresenting—or failing to investigate—miraculous achievement gains that feed glowing headlines.

Brian Jacob of the Kennedy School at Harvard and Steven Levitt of the University of Chicago and American Bar Association published "Rotten Apples," an essay detailing their algorithm for predicting the level of test-cheating that *would* be committed by educators based on incentives for high achievement in a district. A decade ago they argued that "introducing high-stakes testing without appropriate safeguards will likely lead to widespread cheating; that local policies attributing more weight to standardized testing made it more likely that teachers would cheat" (Sorokin 2003). Corporate and individual cheating were predicted early in this generation of test-based "education reform."'

Soon after the passage of NCLB, stories of individuals accused of cheating populated the headlines. David Berliner (2009) detailed stories from Birmingham, Alabama, and Houston about emergent "cheating scandals." In Birmingham, more than 500 students from the high school who were not expected to do well on the standardized exam were dropped just before state testing. Wesley Elementary School, which won accolades for teaching low-income students how to read, was featured on an Oprah Winfrey show about schools that "defy the odds." In 2003 Wesley's fifth graders performed in the top 10 percent in the state on reading exams but as sixth graders the same cohort fell to the bottom 10 percent in the state. "Confronted with data, the Wesley teachers admitted cheating was standard operating procedure."

That same year:

The principal [Saraceno] of the Bronx's Herbert Lehman High School is charged with changing students' failing grades to passing. Teachers are accusing a Bronx high school principal hired with a $25,000 bonus to improve the school's academics of instead transforming the school into a "diploma mill." . . . As part of a Department of Education program to lure principals to the city's most challenging schools, she was given a bonus and the title "executive principal." At the time, this perplexed more than a few parents and teachers, who told the city's daily newspapers that they couldn't understand why a school with a "B" on its latest report card needed to offer its new principal an extra $25,000 a year. According to current and former teachers, Saraceno methodically set about increasing the schools 47 percent graduation rate by changing students' grades from failing to passing over the objections of their teachers and, in some instances, in violation of state regulations. (Phillis 2009)

In April 2011, Philadelphia journalist Dale Mezacappa, former president of the Education Writers Association, learned of Pennsylvania's erasure scan and requested statewide data on testing security and erasures to extract evidence about the extent to which Philadelphia colluded in overrepresenting spikes in achievement. On July 6, Mezzacappa and colleague Ben Herold posted their findings that a total of eighty-nine schools in the state, twenty-eight in Philadelphia, had been flagged for distinctly high rates of erasures and suspect gains in math and reading (Winerup 2011c).

In response to this exposé, on July 29, the *Philadelphia Public School Notebook* ran an article entitled, "Confessions of a Cheating Teacher" (Herold 2011). Herold explains, "The teacher who shared her story cautions that it can be difficult to understand the decisions made by people—teachers, administrators, students—in 'failing' inner city schools in the NCLB era without having first walked in their shoes. 'I thought I was really strong-willed and sure of what was right and wrong,' she said. 'My only defense would be that I lost track of what was right because it was so stressful to be there.'"

The circuits of erasure-scandals lit up the nation's newspapers in the early summer of 2011. On July 5 the news broke that 178 teachers and principals in the Atlanta public schools were accused of cheating to raise students' scores, according to the Georgia Bureau of Investigation. As the cheating progressed and student scores were on the run, the Atlanta system gained the attention, and resources, of the Gates and Broad foundations. Although forty-four schools were involved in the cheating scandal, many refused to cooperate with investigators. According to the *Christian Science Monitor*, an "administrator instructed employees to tell investigators to 'go to hell.' When teachers tried to alert authorities, they were labeled 'disgruntled.' One principal opened an ethics investigation against a whistle-blower" (Jonsson 2011).

From 2009 to 2011, twenty-two states and the District of Columbia have had confirmed instances of cheating. By highlighting individual teachers as culprits, the structural pressures on testing as a magical silver bullet for all that ails public education are rendered invisible; erased, so to speak. Readers will not be shocked to learn that there is a new blossoming private sector industry emergent at the intersection of testing and securitization, funded with public dollars, for testing security (Neill 2011).

The intensifying incentives for high test scores, which in turn germinates cheating scandals, have also been the triggering agent for an expansive for-profit industry of tutoring services. In a careful and rich multisite ethnography of for-profit tutoring organizations, Jill Koyama (2010) traces how a little noted feature of NCLB, the mandate for free tutoring for students in failing schools, has unleashed a wave of quiet transfers of money from public to private tutoring services, relatively unaccountable for quality or outcomes. Koyama studies the relation of a for-profit provider of after-school tutoring and forty-two of its New York City partner schools who were required to purchase the elite model of "school support organization models" for $66,675 per school, "thus seemingly penalizing the schools that apparently require the greatest assistance" (37). Koyama concludes that this policy mandate, by "attending to—defining, regulating, evaluating and remedying—school failure, according to NCLB, provokes a host of inadvertent, conspicuous and abstruse consequences or problems, not the least of which is more failure" (7). With the public, again, footing the bill while educators, parents, and the community have little say in how or why monies would be spent on these providers.

The points made by Koyama are confirmed by journalist Juan Gonzalez. He indicated that the New York City Department of Education paid a private company more than $21,000,000 in two years to tutor thousands of public school students at home. He documents that most of that money went for overhead at Champion Learning Center. Champion got $79 per hour to tutor each pupil for four hours a week, and yet Champion paid its part-time tutors an average of $17 per hour, many of whom were college students with no teaching experience. And then we learn, in October 2008, that the Department of Education spent $5 million a year for private couriers, largely to support the transport of "assessment and accountability" materials. According to Gonzalez (2008), "Couriers are being paid to pick up the tests from all schools, deliver them to the DOE computer center in Queens and then dispose of them. That's an average of $10,000 per day for every school day of the year." This reallocation of public dollars to private companies, authorized by NCLB, has been a serious under-the-radar, upward redistribution scheme tracked by few, but felt by many.

This rash of individual, corporate, and state-produced scandals was of course foreshadowed by Horace Mann Bond, Donald Campbell, Brian Jacob, Steven Levitt, David Berliner, and scores of educators in earlier eras. These educators, analysts, and methodologists did not consider cheating a transgression of the high-stakes testing industry but inherent to and constitutive of the industry, bolstered by national policy and fiscal incentives.

CORPORATE CHEATING AND THE FURTHER DELEGITIMATION OF THE "SCIENCE OF TESTING"

Moving out of schools and into corporate settings, there is ample evidence of routinized transgressions embedded in the practices of the high-stakes testing industry. Todd Farley, author of *Making the Grades: My Misadventures in the Standardized Testing Industry* (2009), writes,

> Testing companies fudge numbers all the time, whether reliability numbers (to show the industry is doing a more "standardized" job than it really is); validity

numbers (to show the industry is doing a more accurate job than it really is); or score distribution numbers (when test scoring companies work to ensure student results match the predictions of their own psychometricians).... In my career there seemed to be a major disconnect between the profit motive of the testing industry's major players (Pearson Education, McGraw Hill, Riverside Publishing, ETS K–12, DRC) and any altruistic goals for American education. For many years I scored students tests. I saw an industry primarily focused on meeting deadlines and completing contracts, with the importance of the correct scores being put on tests seeming to come in second to the rush to get any score put on them. My work in test development was no different, with the companies who employed me apparently willing to take huge short cuts in developing tests because meeting a contract's deadline was clearly more important than the quality of any assessment.

Farley (2011) continues with this belief as he ends an entry in the Huffington Post:

In any case, when next some standardized test scores are found to be incorrect or fraudulent (because they will) or some standardized testing company commits or tries to cover up another egregious error (because they will), perhaps then we can admit large scale assessment isn't the panacea it's often been touted to be. Perhaps then we can concede that an educational philosophy based on a system of national standardized tests isn't any Brave New World of American education, it's just a bad idea that even the Chinese are already turning away from as being too inefficient and antiquated. Caveat emptor. America. Buyer Beware.

COMMUNITY AND EDUCATOR DEMANDS FOR PUBLIC ACCOUNTABILITY

In discussions with educators who support high-stakes testing, the refrain is consistent, and we are sympathetic: in the poorest schools, somebody is finally paying attention to the educational needs of each child; at least with NCLB we can now disaggregate the data and understand the differential gains for different groups. Schools are finally being held accountable for their failure to educate. This may all seem true—but a wide-angle lens on the collateral damage of accountability regimes suggests that the very youth and schools intended to benefit are indeed often the most severely hurt. In the most extreme cases, those students end up losing their school; their educators may lose (or leave) a job; their communities lose a sacred public resource; and too many youth are permanently left behind—criminalized and without academic or vocational skills.

While test-based accountability regimes are reengineering the opportunity structures of America, we are beginning to hear push back from parents, educators, principals, and even a few brave politicians. Consider the testimony of Thomas Ratliff, member of the Texas State Board of Education, who testified in September 2011:

Educators and school board members across the state are becoming painfully aware of how much testing the Texas Legislature has inflicted on our local schools and our children.

Did you know, this year our public schools will spend almost 1 out of every 5 days conducting tests for the State of Texas? Yes, that's right, an average of almost one day a week, or nearly 20 percent of the school year. According to the Texas Education Agency, Texas public schools will spend 34 days out of the 185 day long school year conducting tests mandated by state government, an average of 4 days per student. Keep in mind; this figure doesn't include the number of days spent taking other tests (6-weeks tests, weekly quizzes, semester exams) or getting students ready to take the state's tests. Due to the high stakes nature of these tests, schools spend extra time getting their students ready to take the test by working on testing strategies, and other things that take away from learning the material. I think this is over the top....

To put a dollar figure on this problem, consider this. Texas spends $44 billion per year on public education. Of that, almost $1 billion is spent on testing days, just for the state. If you are looking for ways to make public education more efficient, this seems like a good place to start.

To be clear, I support accountability. Should there be some general measure of how our public schools compare to one another? Absolutely. But I also believe the State of Texas should be accountable to the parents of public school students and explain why we must endure so much *testing* at the expense of *learning*. (Ratliff 2011)

Communities want accountability. However, like Thomas Ratliff, a member of the Texas State Board of Education, parents, educators, and youth increasingly do not equate testing with accountability. They are asking for accountability that is public, democratic, reliant upon multiple outcomes, and responsive to the people closest to the ground. Few are fooled by testing regimes in drag as accountability, that encourage privatization, exile, and disenfranchisement of the poorest learners, while transferring public monies into private hands.

A report from the Public Agenda and the Kettering Foundation details public sentiment on the question of accountability: "Don't count us out: How an overreliance on accountability could undermine the public's confidence in schools, business, government and more" (Johnson, Rochkind, and DuPont 2011). The public wants accountability, desperately and deeply; they don't consider many institutions, public or private, to be responsive or effective. However, when accountability is externally defined, "it tends to disenfranchise those most directly affected by it" (4). Researchers found that the most problematic effect of the test-based accountability movement, from the perspective of parents and communities, has been the effect on "collective or civic learning." Thus it is ironic that "benchmarks and other performance measures used to demonstrate impact had a *deadening* effect on innovation" (5).

The writers of the Public Agenda report join thousands of researchers, community advocates, educators, parents, and students calling for accountability—a public model of accountability for deep-seated, historic, and structural problems that are *moral*, not *technical*, using a range of qualitative and quantitative measures of indicators that are locally meaningful, developed by those close to the ground—educators, parents, community, and youth—in which schools and accountability protocols are built on a sense of collective responsibility for knotty problems and innovative solutions.

Like Ratliff, educators too have been calling for public accountability, developing metrics by which teachers can collectively assess student work—papers, experiments, performances, public speaking—over time. To offer just one example: The New York Performance Standards Consortium involves a network of thirty public schools in New York State that engage in a rich and rigorous commitment to *performance assessments* for graduation (discipline based and interdisciplinary projects, exhibitions, essays, experiments in community, civic learning projects). These schools have been at the national forefront of changing the conversation about accountability, with student work, by educators, engaging both youth and their teachers in the complex tasks of teaching and learning. Committed to data-driven pedagogy, inquiry-based projects, and an ethic of collective reflection and revision by educators and youth, students are assessed through critical analysis of student work collected over time; examples of thoughtful revisions of research and writing; performance on teacher-constructed assignments and exams; performance as evaluated by teacher-developed and revised rubrics; completion of course requirements that involve complex texts and writing assignments; classroom discussions and participation; questions asked and comments offered during class; student participation in out-of-classroom interviews, field trips, and interactions with experts invited to make presentations; student self-assessments; and student sense of self as a learner, reader, writer, and a citizen of the community.

This organized set of indicators has been generated collectively by the educators in the consortium. These educators have developed a rubric for assessing student development across areas. While students in consortium schools must take two of the five mandated, content-based, state-designed exit examinations, called Regents examinations, in order to graduate, they are also required to satisfy a rich set of intellectual, ethical, and cultural projects in math, history, language arts, and science and to defend their work to committees of educators from the school, other high school educators, and a professor or other professional from the community. The students attending consortium schools represent the demographic montage of New York, but longitudinal evidence gathered by Martha Foote confirms that these students graduate and attend college, persist in college, and avoid remediation courses at rates far surpassing their traditional school peers (Foote 2005). The Performance Standards Consortium is but one example of a set of nonselective public schools with strong commitments to educational accountability and transparency, democratic pedagogy, public displays of student work, data-driven inclusion, and building an academic culture of inquiry and participation (Tashlik 2010).

Writing in *Educational Leadership* on measurement in public education, Mike Schmoker (2008/2009) profiled a number of innovations, including the work of the consortium schools: "Instead of test prep, students and teachers focus on work that culminates in four or more final projects in core academic areas: a literary analysis, a science experiment and related research project, an extended mathematics problem solving project and a research paper in social studies demonstrating use of argument and evidence" (73). "Rubrics listing criteria for satisfactorily accomplishing tasks like analyzing a literary work and performing scientific research were developed by consortium faculty, college professors and local professionals—who also identify exemplar anchor projects." In order to establish a process of validity across schools, every summer faculty from the consortium schools gather with college faculty and professionals to conduct moderation studies of 150 sample projects to fine-tune the rubric and generate shared criteria for assessing student work. Data reviews continue throughout the year, within disciplines and across.

As Schmoker argues, "Following the consortium model, we could easily create a system through which schools continue to administer standardized tests but subordinate the focus on test scores to assessments of . . . skills modeled on the Consortium's rubrics" (4).

Turning to the Chicago Consortium on Urban School Reform, we find another well-elaborated schema for public accountability in which individual schools in Chicago are assessed in terms of the five "essentials" of educational support: instructional leadership, professional capacity, family and community engagement, learning climate, and ambitious instruction, with clear indicators for each. Teachers, students, and sometimes parents and the community are surveyed to assess quality of student discussion, peer support for academic engagement, the extent to which a classroom has high academic expectations, and student-teacher trust. The consortium also conducts research on the critical elements of a school culture and a neighborhood that support educational innovation, quality, and sustainability, and they find, consistently, that levels of trust and respect in a building, between youth and teachers and, even more significantly, between educators, predict well the extent of school improvement that is likely to unfold over three years. Most powerfully, measures of school level "trust" and a sense of shared "collective responsibility" are among the best predictors of academic improvement over time.

As the Chicago Consortium and the Performance Assessment Consortium suggest, we are living in a time when policymakers join educators, parents, community members, and even students hungry for accountability—mutual, public, multiple-indicator accountability systems built on trust and collective responsibility. Indeed, one can imagine a host of alternative designs for public accountability that do or don't include standardized tests as one measure of assessment. The National Assessment of Educational Progress samples students on standardized tests, producing data on national and state trends but not imposing significant stakes on the life trajectories of individual students affected by present evaluation schema and their relationship to disinvestment and austerity policies. The Chicago Consortium encourages public performances of student work in schools and communities. A number of schools are advocating teacher-generated assessments in combination with low-stakes standardized tests. In a number of urban communities, progressive educators have begun to link arms with local advocates, students, and parents to generate assessment systems for rich, pedagogically engaging accountability; to mobilize for the transformation, not closing, of failing schools; to cultivate educational contexts of inquiry, democracy, and equity not testing, punishment, and exit; to resist the corporate evaluation and humiliation of educators with high-stakes test scores.

> *May 2011.* Embracing the latest new tool in the accountability universe, the governor, state chancellor and education commissioner ramrod a measure through the Board of Regents, mandating that up to 40 percent of teachers' and principals' evaluations be based on test scores.
>
> *November 2011.* New York is one of two states in the nation to post statistically significant declines on the National Assessment tests. John B. King, the education commissioner, says the state is certainly going in the wrong direction, but has a plan to spur students' achievement. "The new Common Core Learning Standards will help get them there," he says. (Winerip 2011a)

In this political context, even school principals are mobilizing to refuse to implement single testing measures of accountability or invalid indices of performance. When front-line bureaucrats speak loudly and collectively in opposition, it is indeed apparent that the past decade's flirtation with testing has been anything but educationally accountable. Consider the last installment in Michael Winerip's memoir of testing in New York State:

> *December 19, 2011.* Nearly a quarter of the state's principals—1,046—have signed an online letter protesting the plan to evaluate teachers and principals by test scores. Among the reasons cited is New York's long tradition of creating tests that have little to do with reality. (2011a)

Key questions of accountability do indeed need to be posed. The question, however, is not *if* schools should be held accountable but *for what, by whom,* and with *what consequence.* The more accountability processes involve multiple stakeholders; rely upon varied indicators of student engagement and performance and school culture and processes; encourage creativity and innovation rather than fear and punishment; and the more evidence is used to support rather than humiliate or stratify schools, the richer the accountability process and the more likely it is to cultivate democratic participation, educational transformation, and the sustainability of educational innovation.

REFLECTIONS ON HIGH-STAKES TESTING AND DISPOSSESSION

Perhaps we can all appreciate the initial impetus for a high-stakes testing movement, particularly in low-income communities where demands for educational accountability have been dismissed for generations. And yet now we bear witness as another simple demand for justice has been appropriated into a "scientific" and corporate movement for labeling and punishing youth, evaluating and dismissing educators, closing and privatizing public schools, legitimating inequality gaps. The fiscal, academic, and human costs associated with testing regimes are extraordinary and leaking profusely out of the classroom into publishing houses. We now have a generation of youth raised on tests, with scores burned into their souls, basting in a culture that has convinced a good portion of youth of color that they are less able to compete academically or economically. More than fifty years after *Brown v. Board of Education*, schools are more segregated and stratified than before; few think of their schools as intellectually nurturing—or accountable.

The heavy financial and labor commitments to *technologies of testing as educational practice* have facilitated discipline and punishment, particularly in low-income schools of color, and escorted a substantial cohort of youth out of high school prior to graduation, with few skills or labor market options. While testing does not singularly produce schools of failure (like guns don't kill), the intensive investment in and consequences of high-stakes testing dramatically widen inequality gaps, cultivating a generation of youth ill-equipped to compete in either the legitimate labor market or higher education.

Poignantly, there are two well-funded public sectors waiting to enlist these young people who are excessive to the economy and ineligible for the increasingly inaccessible world of higher education. The military, and prisons, await the new recruits, with ample public funding.

As we have argued in this chapter, the twinned dynamics of dispossession and accumulation of capital are at work in the redesign of public education. Testing is simply the technology by which the redistribution of capital—skills, bodies, opportunities, buildings, and democracy—has been legitimated. In a critical history of the present, we are witnessing the production of "disposables," the aggressive invasion of elite settlers demanding their exclusive rights to public schools, the accumulation of profit by corporations linked too intimately with state policymakers, and the proliferation of the testing-industrial complex in which publishers, test companies, scoring companies, test security organizations, private "turn around" experts, and increasingly online versions of test prep are extorting precious monies out of the classroom and into the accountability machine.

As poor and working-class youth, particularly youth of color, are dispossessed—that is denied engaging academic opportunities, deskilled, and hobbled educationally and economically—elite youth enjoy access to a wider and wider array of selective public schools. As low-income communities lose essential local resources (libraries, schools) and their democratic participation in educational governance is silenced, publishing house profits soar.

Public education has long had an ambivalent relationship to social inequality: largely reproductive but at moments deliciously transformative.

The scales have fully tipped: schools are becoming an explicit institutional engine for ramming inequality gaps into the bodies and souls, skills and opportunities, of low-income and elite youth.

Inequality will soon appear to be sadly inevitable, indeed natural and deserved. But fortunately resistance is on the rise.

FOR FURTHER READING

Dandrea, Ruth Ann. "About Those Tests I Gave You: An Open Letter to My Students." Spring 2012. http://www.rethinkingschools.org/archive/26_03/26_03_dandrea.shtml.
Fine, Michelle. *Framing Dropouts: Notes on the Politics of an Urban High School.* Albany: SUNY Press, 1991.

Chapter 6

Circuits of Dispossession and Accumulation in a Nation of Swelling Inequality Gaps

As prior chapters have documented, in the name of "ed reform," the historic braid of racial justice and educational choice has been unraveled. The language of choice has been co-opted to justify the reallocation of money and bodies pulled out of the public sphere via vouchers, charters, virtual schooling, or admission to an elite school well beyond the borders of the local neighborhood.

With sights on the capitalization of state-funded services, corporations, philanthropists, and neoliberal policymakers have unleashed a systematic devolution of public goods in the name of austerity, the transfer of public dollars into corporate hands, the strategic derogation and undermining of public sector workers and their unions, a transformation of the public labor force into short-term and part-time workers, the reclamation of community schools to be managed more efficiently by "outsiders" and to be accessible for more "deserving" students.

With the corporate purchase of mass media, audit culture's sound bites remind us routinely of the devastating failures of the public sphere and the magical promise of privatization. Ironically, while the scaffolding on the public sector is being torn down, in an ideological campaign to reduce government spending, the deficit grows. Public resources are being funneled into substantial investment in military, prisons, policing, and the hyper-securitization of public life.

Simultaneously, we are watching as the country eats our young, or some of our young. We bear witness, in particular, as new generations of low-income youth are increasingly socially metabolized by state institutions—education, social service, police, prisons, and the military—as excess, disposable and dispensable, not needed for a weak labor market, and not eligible for the pristine world of higher education.

We are acutely aware of corporations targeting public education as an economi-cally "white-hot sector," as the profit margins spike for evaluation firms, test security companies, after-school tutoring, virtual charters, for-profit charters, education management organizations, for-profit colleges, and a few large publishing houses associated with testing companies—all sustained handsomely with the redistribu-tion of public resources from neighborhood schools and classrooms to the expansive education marketplace.

DISPOSSESSION AND ACCUMULATION: TWINNED DYNAMICS OF POLITICAL ECONOMY

As the political economy of federal and state education policy shifts, it is important to reiterate the dual consequences: the *dispossession* of many and the *accumulation* of wealth by a few. Throughout this text we have argued that the *dispossession* of those living in poverty, communities of color, and immigrants is intimately linked to the *elite accumulation* of capital, real estate, opportunities, and bright futures for the young.

Dispossession—to be systematically denied resources, opportunities, trajec-tories once available—involves both fiscal *disinvestment* in education for children of poverty and *hyper-investment* of state resources in the criminalization of youth in these same communities. Thus, dispossession involves school closings, lack of access to gifted and talented programs and elite high schools, being tracked out of rigorous academic curriculum, diploma denial, and never or rarely enjoying a full complement of qualified experienced educators who remain in your school over time (see Chapter 3 for data on teacher turnover). At the same time, dispossession also involves the substantial fiscal investment of public resources into police, surveillance technologies, in-school and out-of-school "zero-tolerance" policies, Immigration and Customs Enforcement, and the "human security" apparatus of intensified policing and surveillance in low-income communities of color and immigrant communities. Dispossession practices are expensive in terms of the material costs of surveillance and containment, but also in the sacrifice of human capacity, desire, and engage-ment; talent lost; family dreams ripped apart; heightened fear of crime; managing community protest; the death of democracy, and its myth, in too many communities.

If dispossession is manifest in varied forms, so, too, is accumulation. As we have argued, wealth and power accumulate most obviously from corporate profits leeching off of the pain of poverty and the public purse. Concentration of wealth and power are increasingly accomplished in the more banal redesign of the public sphere to serve the children of elites, the reclamation of buildings, maximization of opportunities, and the ever-more inequitable redistribution of public resources across communities.

The combination of dispossession and accumulation reminds us of the gro-tesque inequalities through which we all try to craft lives of meaning: the para-sitic relations of wealth and poverty, but also, more optimistically, our profound interdependence and the fleeting opportunities for fights of solidarity across lines of race, ethnicity, class, and neighborhood.

The Bleeding of Dispossession across Sectors

We have also argued that dispossession cuts across the landscape of life sectors. A problem in one sector bears leaky consequence across varied spheres of life—especially if you are poor. The circuitry of dispossession in public education is triggered in large part through testing, policing, and underfunding, which, in turn, provokes *detachment* from public opportunities and institutions and *coerced engagement/containment* within institutions such as juvenile/criminal justice and/or the military.

In their original article on circuits of dispossession, Michelle Fine and Jessica Ruglis (2008) documented how the singular policy mandate of high-stakes exit examinations required for graduation can unleash a wave of negative outcomes for low-income high school pushouts, exiting prematurely from high school with neither the skills to negotiate a living-wage job nor eligibility for higher education. Fine and Ruglis further detailed the evidence on the empirical relationships between "diploma denial" and a number of physical health conditions (coronary heart disease, high blood pressure, diabetes), mental health conditions (depression and anxiety), pregnancy outcomes (young people without diplomas are more likely to be teen parents, and have a second child during adolescence than those who graduate), unemployment and underemployment, lack of health insurance, homelessness, involvement with violence, criminal justice involvement, and death (Fine and Ruglis 2008). That simple condition of being a high school dropout or a student who was pushed out—which we know is heightened in contexts of finance inequity, high-stakes testing, over-policing, high turnover of teachers, and school closings—cascades for many into a flood of troubling education and economic outcomes, health conditions, parenting practices, low voting and community participation, and high criminal justice involvement. To further complicate matters, dropout status interacts with race/ethnicity such that all of these outcomes are dramatically worse for black and Latino dropouts and pushouts than those who are white or Asian.

The leakage of troubles across sectors is common knowledge in low-income communities, and something of a surprise to people who live with resources. Middle-, upper-middle-class, and wealthy people use both collective public and private resources to erase, remedy, buy out, or insulate themselves from education problems, difficulties with the police, or health care issues. By so doing, the relatively affluent are able to contain the collateral damage. But for people living in communities low on resources and high on marginalization, troubles bleed. More to the point, the disruptive, dispossessing consequences hemorrhage in the following ways:

- When public policies diminish the likelihood of high school graduation, one can document educational consequences but also economic, civic, health, criminal justice, and even evidence that parenting styles and voting patterns are affected (Fine and Ruglis 2008);

- When technologies of the prison-industrial complex flood communities via racial profiling, stop and frisk, police surveillance in and out of school, and the everyday criminalization of youth, there are cumulative negative consequences for young people's demonstrated trust in government and the public sector, beliefs in education, internalization of the social contract, their attitudes toward work, relations with neighbors, willingness to grant police legitimacy and therefore their willingness to participate in helping to solve crimes or seek assistance when they need protection; and

- When children lose parents to the mass incarceration or to deportation, when they are removed from homes and placed in shelters or foster care, the tremors of family disruption destabilize school and family, affecting physical health, psychological well-being, anxiety, sense of belonging, and exacerbating a profound sense of human insecurity.

A circuits of dispossession and privilege framework allows us to understand that when poor communities are targeted with policies that undermine well-being—policies that reduce the likelihood of accessing or graduating from a quality high school; policies that criminalize and overincarcerate youth and parents; policies that scrutinize and detain undocumented immigrant parents; policies that curtail health care for families—the weight of dispossession can be felt politically, economically, socially, educationally, and personally. And, as noted below, the shadow of dispossession is cast broadly, threatening our collective human security.

THE COLLECTIVE IMPACT OF SWELLING INEQUALITY GAPS

Neoliberal policy has a clear and disparate impact on poor and working-class communities, communities of color, and immigrant groups. And yet there is a growing body of literature suggesting that by systematically dismantling safety nets for the most vulnerable among us, we all grow vulnerable to the consequences of inequality gaps. That is, with all the gated communities, security systems, selective educational options, policing, freedom from the state, and protection that money can buy, the 1 percent live in a constant state of insecurity; they are not safe if the 99 percent are systematically denied rights, entitlements, state resources, and benefits.

As noted earlier, British epidemiologists Richard Wilkinson and Kate Pickett (2009) argue that severely unequal societies, like the United States, (re)produce high rates of "social pain" distributed collectively and unevenly. In 2011 there was a spreading global recognition of, and outrage against, extreme inequality gaps. Throughout 2011, this critical analysis could be heard in movements of "indignidos" in Spain, protests for liberation and democracy in Cairo, for labor justice in Wisconsin, against austerity in Greece, against economic injustice in the United Kingdom, against police brutality in the Bronx, and for the 99 percent in Zuccotti Park, New York City.

The epidemiological evidence presented in *The Spirit Level* (Wilkinson and Pickett 2009) demonstrates that the *size* of the inequality gap is directly proportional to the material, geographic, social, and psychological distance between the wealthiest and the most impoverished. Large inequality gaps enable various forms of social suffering to saturate communities at great distance from those who could be held accountable for remedy. Policies that widen inequality gaps jeopardize us all. And in that space of detachment and dissociation, threats to our collective well-being metastasize.

NEOLIBERAL EDUCATION POLICY AND THE WIDENING OF INEQUALITY GAPS

In this volume we have tried to make visible *how* seemingly neutral state policies, and then institutional practices, can reproduce and exacerbate inequality gaps if they are neutered of equity commitments. Whether we consider high-stakes testing, over-policing in schools, the undermining of teachers' professional rights and stability, school closings, handing public school buildings over to corporate management, funding virtual charters, gutting Affirmative Action policies, denying undocumented children education or health care, dismantling collective bargaining agreements, reversing desegregation orders, implementing a stratified system of "choice," or refusing to legislate finance equity, much less if we add in all the ways in which state policy is now being driven by corporate and philanthropic interests, we begin to see how both the public and private sectors are collaborators, so to speak, widening inequality gaps and securing adverse consequences folded into the political DNA of future generations.

At this point—or perhaps before—we may be critiqued for sounding conspiratorial, for suggesting that politicians, philanthropists, and corporations meet with the express aim of disadvantaging the most vulnerable children. Well, to be clear, we do not believe that politicians, philanthropists, and corporations *intend* to undermine the well-being of our collective democracy and devastate low-income communities of color. But intent matters little when the outcome is driven in large part by their shared class interests and consequent policy direction. We are disturbed, shocked in fact, that in the face of relentless evidence that these neoliberal policies are fundamentally corrosive to our most vulnerable students, democratic institutions, and our collective well-being—that public and private "ed reformers" refuse to change course. Consequently, the state and allied corporate interests must be held accountable for their relentless commitment to a policy agenda that undermines low-income communities, hobbles democratic participation, and threatens our collective well-being in the face of mountains of evidence of adverse impact and alternative strategies.

THE INTIMATE WOUNDS AND REVERBERATIONS OF DISPOSSESSION FROM PUBLIC SCHOOLS

We know that present policies restructuring public education often cut deep, leaving behind scars and keloids on the souls of young people, generations, and communities;

banishing and curdling dreams; metabolizing desire into despair and alienation. We also know, from working in communities, that many young people of poverty, their families, and community advocates are generous, fueled with radical desires and redemptive commitments, often more gracious than might be expected. They are still willing, after generations of policy betrayal, to dream, trust, and struggle for educational justice. Despite generations of growing inequality, evidence of betrayal, dispossession, and a city, state, and nation that have all but painted "Disposable" on their backs, they cling to the belief that tomorrow might be better and are willing to fight in many ways to reclaim their human rights to educational justice.

THROUGH THE EYES OF A YOUNG ADULT, GRADUATING FROM A FAILING SCHOOL

We open this section on the intimacies of dispossession—the scars and the resistance—reprinting the words of Melissa Kissoon (2011), an advocate for educational justice, the keynote speaker at an Alternatives to School Closings rally in New York City:

> My name is Melissa Kissoon and I am a 19 year old graduate of Franklin K. Lane High School in Brooklyn. I am also a youth leader with Future of Tomorrow and the Urban Youth Collaborative. As youth organizers, we won the fight for student Metro cards in 2010, and we also created 4 high school student success centers, which is a place where students can go for help with going to college.
>
> I am here today to talk to you about the effect phasing out a school has on students with first-hand experience, and to urge all of us to consider alternatives to phasing out, or closing, a school. I have gone through a high school phase out. In my first two years of high school, there were clubs and extra credit activities to help students get ahead or to help struggling students. Despite Lane's reputation, in my opinion Lane was improving and, for me, it was a good school. Then one day the principal and deans got us together to tell us our school is phasing out, which meant that they would be putting another school into our building and we would no longer accept any new students or freshman. Then later on that year we found out the building would be incorporating not one school but *four* other schools. They informed us about all these changes *after* the decisions were made, leaving students and parents with no input. Once the four new schools came, it was hard to be proud of a school that was no longer ours. The four schools came and they were given the fourth floor in our building and, to prove that this school was really no longer ours anymore, we weren't allowed to go to the 4th floor at all, and if you were caught on the other schools' floor it would be considered trespassing. Then when the next year came, and there were more students in the new schools and fewer in our school, the DoE decided to split the rest of the floors in half. So for example, if your classroom was around the corner, you could no longer just walk over to your room because that hall technically belonged to another school,

so you'd have to go upstairs and around the back and then go back down stairs to make it to your class. As a result of this, many students became late for their classes, got in trouble with their teachers and sometimes missed certain pop quizzes teachers give the first five minutes of class. Another result of the school phase out led to Lane's programs to be taken away. There were small learning communities focused in my school like a law program, a vision technology program, and a cooking program. As the phase out continued these programs did not. And most of the schools' teachers either left or retired. As a senior during this time this made acquiring personal recommendations extremely hard, because in my past years I had teachers who consecutively taught me for two semesters, which would mean that they not only knew me the best but they have witnessed my growth. Instead I had to settle for recommendations from teachers who taught me within the same semester, so they really didn't have too much to say about me or my growth as an individual. This was an unfair process that was brought on to us without any notice or say in the matter. Nobody told us—the students—our school was failing until suddenly they told us they were closing us down, and I would hope that in the future no other school would have to go through what my school went through.

As we may know, most students who have gone through a similar situation to this, are low-income students of color, primarily Black and Latino, as well as West Indian and other targeted groups. The zone schools we go to are usually the low-performing ones. The higher performing schools are the specialized high schools or high schools with high-income students that are mostly for more privileged kids compared to those in neighborhood public schools. This creates an ongoing cycle, because it is hard to become privileged when you come from a poor education system. And this is the mentality of most students, which is honestly why most students give up on school so quickly. When school districts close schools, they are sending a message to low-income students of color that is: "We're going to give up on you, rather than supporting you." And it is understandable that the DoE may assume phasing out a school is actually improving the schools in the long term, but what about the current students? In a recent report made by the Urban Youth Collaborative, UYC, of the 21 phased-out high schools in New York City, the 33,000 students who were in their final years, only 9,592 actually graduated. In schools the dropout rates were high, including my own and at another school, the dropout rate reached 70 percent in the year the school closed.

Although I graduated and I'm in college now this is not a typical situation of a student who has come from a high school phase out. I can honestly say, I look back at the last four years of my life and I feel robbed of my high school experience. My school was no longer MY school; I was basically being kicked out of a school that made a promise to support me and give me all I need to graduate. Students must be consulted about the use and future use of their school. We must be included in decisions about OUR education.

We are glad for today's conference to talk about other solutions for low-performing schools. We know that there are many alternatives to closing schools. Equitable funding is essential—giving attention and resources to low-performing schools so we can transform them. This will truly support students, and give them and their schools a real chance to succeed! Thank you for your time.

NEOLIBERALISM AND CIRCUITS
OF INTIMATE DISPOSSESSION

If only Melissa were atypical. As has been described in the two prior chapters, in schools throughout urban communities, particularly in low-income communities of color, in the most marginalized schools, we hear official plans to close and then reopen the building for other children. We rarely hear about the scars, betrayals, shock, humiliation, resilience, and resistance that so many young people—and educators—carry as they limp out of the building.

So Melissa speaks for many when she eloquently points out that the neoliberal message to poor youth of color is unambiguous—we are not here to support you; don't trespass; your teachers are gone; relationships shattered; you are the product of failure; we are starting again; you will be erased (Ayala and Galletta 2012).When public schools are closed with neither community nor educator (nor student) input, when public schools are repossessed for a charter network or selective admissions or put to another use entirely, the message is transparent.

As we have reviewed in this volume, school closing is but one policy that provokes the singeing of aspirations and opportunities for low-income youth of color, facilitating a sense of alienation for many and exile for some. But quite a few, like Melissa, rally. This is particularly evident in those young people who are actively engaged with community and activist youth organizations, who enjoy a close relationship with a teacher, or live with parents who insist on basic academic achievement and human rights for their children. But many young people don't rally. They have read the political tea leaves too well. They have internalized the message that this is no longer their school, their community, their government. Democracy is not made for them.

In a project called Polling for Justice (PFJ), a participatory action research project designed with youth and adult allies, we set out to examine *how* these neoliberal policy initiatives—high-stakes testing, over-policing in schools, denial of health care, housing insecurity, mass incarceration, and racial profiling that includes stop-and-frisk policies—affect the educational, political, and psychological lives of youth in New York City (Fox et al. 2010). We draw theoretically on notions of *structural dispossession* developed by David Harvey (2004) and elaborated by Fine and Ruglis (2008), and we then track across 1,200 New York City surveyed youth, how privatization, discipline and punishment policies, and structural realignment of public education move under the skin of poor and working-class youth. We ask: Who profits, who pays, and who is resisting the systematic hijacking of the public sector. In our analysis we attend closely to the ways that gender, sexuality, class, race/ethnicity, immigration status, and neighborhood facilitate or mitigate the collateral damage of dispossession.

POLLING FOR JUSTICE: PARTICIPATORY INQUIRY ON DISPOSSESSION, RESILIENCE, AND RESISTANCE

As noted earlier, Polling for Justice (PFJ) offers a powerful window into the capillaries that connect social policy and lives, mediated through community, power relations, and institutional life. In the PFJ research, presented briefly below, a group of activist researchers, youth, and community organizers set out to document how young people across a landscape of wild diversities experience, embody, internalize, and resist neoliberal reforms of the early twenty-first century in New York City. Interested in the uneven distribution of resources, opportunities, and consequences, we wanted to understand how the retreat of the state from social welfare, mobilized since the Reagan years, has swollen the stress load on poor and working-class youth while disabling the very relationships and institutions that might provide support for youth in crisis. And we wanted to understand how so many survive, triumphant, in the ashes (Fox et al. 2010; Fox and Fine 2012; Stoudt, Fox, and Fine 2012).

Polling for Justice (PFJ) was designed to investigate how urban youth experience, respond to, and organize against the profoundly uneven opportunities for development across the five boroughs of New York City. Our inquiry focused on four policy sectors: education, health care, housing/family stability, and criminal justice, and it was explicitly constructed to gather and funnel social science evidence into organizing campaigns for youth justice—violence against girls and women, police harassment, college access, high-stakes testing, and access to comprehensive sexuality education, to name just a few (see Table 6.1).

With quantitative and qualitative measures, PFJ surveyed more than 1,200 New York City youth in order to:

1. document the *geography and demography of dispossession and privilege* by detailing empirically where and for whom social policies, institutions, and practices enable and constrict opportunities for youth development across the boroughs of New York City;
2. track the *cross-sector consequences of dispossession* by investigating how dispossession in one sector (e.g., not earning a high school diploma) adversely affects outcomes in other sectors (e.g., economic, health, and criminal justice outcomes);
3. chronicle the ways in which youth and adult allies *mobilize to resist,* negotiate, and challenge collectively these policies and practices; and
4. design activist *scholarship to "be of use"* in varied organizing campaigns for youth justice and human rights policy struggles.

And then, in response to a number of campaigns against school closings and charter openings, we added a fifth goal:

5. to examine the extent to which *school closings and charter opening map onto zones of dispossession*; that is, to assess the extent to which high dropout/discharge

Table 6.1 Responses of New York City Youth to the Uneven Distribution of Resources, Opportunities, and Consequences

Sector	Policy Triggers to Dispossession (Examples)	Outcomes	Differential Impact	Buffers
Education, e.g., dropouts/ pushouts, suspended students, or those with GEDs	Finance inequity High-stakes testing High teacher turnover Sense of belonging/ alienation Access to engaging, inquiry-based curriculum and pedagogy	Graduation Educational aspirations Grades Relationships with educators Plans for college Suspension/expulsion/ GED	We analyzed data by race/ ethnicity, class/mother's education, neighborhood, school size, performance assessment vs. high-stakes Regents examinations	Positive relationship with a teacher and/or involvement with a community-based organization made a huge difference in educational outcomes for even the most dispossessed youth
Criminal justice, e.g., those who have had negative interactions with police in last six months	In-school policing Zero tolerance Racial profiling Stop and frisk	Negative interactions with police: legal, verbal, sexual and/or physical Positive interactions with police Trust in government	There were vast differences in negative interactions with police by gender, race/ethnicity, class, neighborhood, and sexual orientation	Involvement with an activist youth organization reduced and mediated some of the negative impact of negative interactions with police

Health care, e.g., those with no access to insurance	Lack of access to insurance Distrust of medical systems Exposure to health and sexual health education	Caring for self: Seeking medical assistance as needed Engaging in safe sex Rates of alcohol/drug use Involvement in violent interactions Levels of depression, anxiety, and "worries"	Levels of dispossession, in interaction with race/ethnicity, sexuality, and neighborhood, were highly associated with negative "risk" behaviors	Youth who were involved in a community-based or activist organization were far less likely to place themselves in harm's way even if highly dispossessed
Family stability, e.g., those who are homeless, are in foster care, or have a parent in prison or a parent who has been deported	Parent incarcerated or deported Have to move out of home Lived in foster care/homeless shelter	Trust in family Human (in)security	Youth whose mothers had been pushed out of school/cropped out had much more disrupted home environments, more exposure to violence, police harassment, involvement in foster care/homelessness	But not all—many young people whose mothers left high school prior to graduation have persisted through to graduation and college

145

rates are associated with heavy police presence, surveillance, and criminalization of youth and then to consider the extent to which these are communities declared educational disasters by the DOE, where schools are being closed and selective admissions or charter schools opened.

We organized the data to examine what we call *cumulative dispossession*, trying to capture empirically the demographic and geographic landscape of dispossession, and then the extent to which youth who have been pushed out or dropped out of schools, for instance, and also have no health insurance, have had negative encounters with police, and disrupted home lives were in fact more likely to report depression, risky sexual engagements, involvement with violence, and lower levels of psychological well-being.

We created a scale ranging from 0 to 4, a simple additive metric of cumulative dispossession across the four sectors. Overlaying levels of dispossession with demography and geography, we analyzed the uneven distribution of dispossession (Fox et al. 2010). To determine the collateral consequences of dispossession, we calculated negative outcomes (violence, depression, use of alcohol and drugs, unsafe sex) and differential impact by level of dispossession and demographics (race/ethnicity, class/mother's level of education, sexuality, gender, immigration status, neighborhood). Finally we sought statistical and ethnographic evidence of interventions that buffer dispossession in the lives of vulnerable youth.

While we have written about the data in a number of articles and chapters, for the purposes of this argument, it is important to confirm that the collateral consequences of dispossession are grossly uneven by class, race/ethnicity, neighborhood, gender, and sexuality.

The Geography and Demography of Dispossession

With community members helping to analyze the data, PFJ presented in local neighborhoods citywide maps to display the dramatically uneven distribution of adverse impact (see Figure 6.1). With an analytic eye on class, gender, race/ethnicity, sexuality, immigration status, disability status, and neighborhood, we reviewed the geography of police harassment. We mapped, for instance, evidence on the frequency of negative encounters with police by neighborhood and sexuality and learned of the chronic, devastating negative experiences that lesbian, gay, bisexual, and transgender (LGBT) youth have with police (especially in the Bronx).

From the quantitative mapping, we launched a set of data-driven focus groups in specific neighborhoods where we found "hot spots" of dispossession (e.g., high rates of school pushouts; high rates of criminalization of youth of color; extremely high rates of surveillance on LGBT youth, particularly LGBT youth of color). In these focus groups, young people were asked to interpret, for and with us, the distributions and circuits of injustice we had documented. We learned how young people make sense, resist, and resign themselves to practices we considered outrageous.

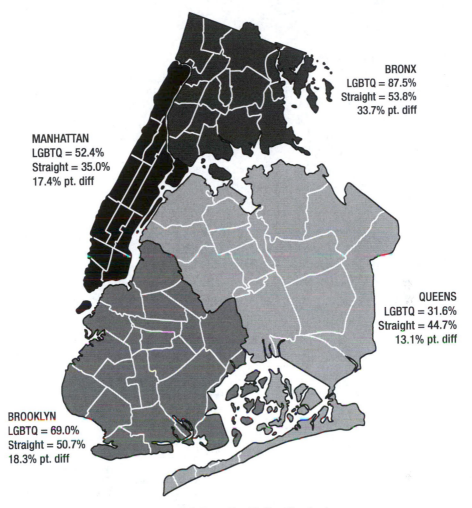

Figure 6.1 Negative Police Contact

INTERVIEWER: So how do you explain the high rates of negative interactions between police and LGBT youth in Brooklyn?

YOUNG MAN: I'm black and I'm gay. I'm easy prey.

At the same time we heard amazing stories of solidarity, connection, and clever reversals of surveillance (photo videos of police brutality) that help young people remain buoyant, actively imagining a different tomorrow.

The Collateral Damage of Dispossession

Even as these policies are unevenly distributed, across groups we found that the more policy-driven forms of dispossession accumulate within young bodies and communities, the more youth are likely to report participating in "risky" behaviors, including unsafe sexual practices, violence, drug and alcohol use, and the apparently benign but in fact dangerous behavior of not getting themselves out of harm's way.

Figure 6.2 displays the linear relationships between circuits of dispossession and risk-taking behaviors. Youth who were most highly dispossessed (group 4) were nearly six times more likely to engage with violence, more than four times as likely to engage in unsafe sex, and almost three times as likely to use illegal drugs than youth who did not report experiences of dispossession (group 0).

Turning to psychological indicators, youth in the most dispossessed group (group 4) were twice as likely to report symptoms of clinical depression, using standardized depression scales, and higher levels of human insecurities, using a home-grown assessment of anxiety scale, when compared with youth in the least dispossessed group (group 0).

These data were gathered using a cross-sectional design; we therefore can make no claims to causality. The patterns, however, are highly suggestive. For every indicator we studied, those youth who scored as "highly dispossessed" by education

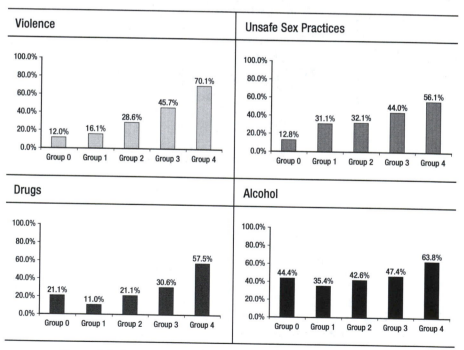

Figure 6.2 Circuits of Dispossession by Risk-Taking Behaviors

(pushed out, suspended, or expelled), housing/family stability (homeless, in foster care, or parent in prison or deported), criminal justice (negative interactions with police), and health care (no access to health insurance) reported much higher rates of negative outcomes (for detailed findings see Fine et al. 2010)

Is Demography Destiny?

Finally, while we gathered substantial information that suggests race/ethnicity, class, sexuality, and neighborhood are highly associated with the differential impact of social policy and that dispossession is not color blind, we also learned much about resilience and mediators.

While the adverse consequences of dispossession are impossible to deny, the relationship between dispossession and risk taking is not perfect. Indeed 70 percent of the youth with the most cumulative dispossession (group 4) engaged in or were victimized by violence, but 30 percent were not; 44 percent did not engage in unsafe sex practices, 42 percent did not use drugs, and 36 percent did not drink alcohol (Fine et al. 2010). If there is substantial evidence of "damage," there is more substantial evidence of resilience, resistance, desire—and interventions that mediate dispossession and collateral consequences.

We felt it was important to probe our data for mediators; to determine if there are any social interventions that help cushion the negative blows of dispossession. And indeed we learned that involvement in youth organizations and strong connections with educators function as buffers for youth. That is, even though they were extremely vulnerable to policies that threatened their housing, education, family, health care, and involvement with police, those youth who had relational opportunities with adults and peers, and took advantage of them in schools or community contexts, were less likely to report high levels of clinical depression and "risky" behaviors.

Policies that trigger dispossession put us collectively at risk—and some much more than others. These "risky" behaviors are typically viewed as "bad choices" initiated by "at risk" youth. Polling for Justice, however, has contested this interpretation by linking the origins of social problems to structural inequalities and social policies that systematically disrupt the lives of large numbers of poor youth and youth of color and in turn place them at risk. Even after mountains of evidence on adverse impact have been gathered, policymakers have refused to reset their course and simultaneously embarked on an intensified austerity regimen to cut more deeply into the very programs that provide continuity of relationships with educators and social supports to buffer young people from the harsh winds of structural dispossession.

INTIMATE DISPOSSESSION AND THE SHRINKAGE OF EDUCATIONAL POSSIBILITIES

Schools are today sites for classed and racialized dispossession, for many youth; where they learn, as Melissa did, that they are not considered relevant to the renaissance of the city—doesn't quite matter which city. For poor and working-class youth, encounters with public institutions—schools and police—are increasingly civics lessons where young people learn that the blades of race, class, and ethnicity cut the cloth of public resources, determining who receives, and who is denied, a rich public education, freedom to walk the streets without being stopped or frisked, to stand in groups on street corners without being thrown to the ground, to dream about college or a meaningful work life.

Like children who learn to love in homes scarred by violence, youth in schools that are underresourced, test-driven, heavily policed dropout factories are being asked to learn in contexts of humiliation, betrayal, and disrespect. Neither fully internalizing the evidence of their dispossession nor fully resisting it, these children are learning their perceived worth in the larger social hierarchy. They are learning, further, that public services are inherently inferior to private ones; that cumulative disadvantage and disinvestment are systematic moves of the state.

Our analytic purpose, however, demands that we not remain singularly fixated on the experience of public institutions and those the institutions serve. This relatively constricted focus would by definition ignore the relationship between larger social and economic forces and institutional experiences of dispossession and disposability. For this reason we must presently jump scale from institutions to the policies embedded in the dynamics of a larger political economy. As inequality gaps grow, housing and economic security in turn becomes ever-more precarious, and poor and working-class children are more likely to see their neighborhood schools shuttered. In this context, state policy moves are stunningly reproductive. In the name of accountability, expensive testing and public "safety" regimes have been put in place that fundamentally undermine the likelihood of graduation and college access in poor, black, and Latino communities. Then, in the name of public responsibility, departments of education, encouraged by NCLB and state policy, have declared these sites to be educational hazard zones. Youth are pushed out and drop out at disproportionately high rates, and increasingly schools in these communities are closed as policing intensifies and testing scores designate new sites of failure.

Simultaneously, educational opportunities are increasingly migrating to white and wealthier neighborhoods where the fertile soil of social, political, and economic advantage grows over time and, in turn, an ever greater abundance of advantage is harvested. Cynically or foolishly, mayors, bolstered by philanthropic and corporate support, declare progress. Meanwhile, in communities of concentrated poverty, schools are closing, youth are losing their neighborhood place of learning, parents live further and further from their child's school, and security guards determine who enters, who leaves, and who stays. The intellectual, economic, and civic consequences of such a radical redistribution of resources are substantial; the psychological and existential weight is severe.

And yet, in these "revolting" times, as you heard from Melissa and will hear about in our final chapter, resistance is high; surprising solidarities are being forged between educators and parents, and poor and working-class communities are demanding public space, reclaiming public institutions, and insisting on educational justice.

FOR FURTHER READING

Fox, M., & M. Fine. "Circulating Critical Research: Reflections on Performance and Moving Inquiry into Action." In *Critical Qualitative Research Reader,* edited by G. Cannella & S. Steinberg, 453-465. New York: Peter Lang Publishing, 2012.

Fuentes, Annette. "Arresting Development: Zero Tolerance and the Criminalization of Children." Winter 2011/2012. http://www.rethinkingschools.org/archive/26_02/26_02_fuentes .shtml.

Ravitch, Diane. "School 'Reform': A Failing Grade." *New York Review of Books,* September 29, 2011. http://www.nybooks.com/articles/archives/2011/sep/29/school-reform-failing -grade/.

Stoudt, B., M. Fine, and M. Fox. "Growing Up Policed in the Age of Aggressive Policing Policies." *New York Law School Law Review* 56 (12) (2011): 1331–1370.

Chapter 7

Contesting Public Education

AUSTERITY AND THE INTENSIFYING FIGHT FOR A COLLECTIVE FUTURE

We are at a moment in which there is a growing recognition of our profound inter-dependence, the damage that has already befallen the fragility of public education as a system, and the need for radical actions for solidarity and sustainability. Science writer Janine M. Benyus (1997) lectures on social problems as she asks, "How would nature solve this?" (197). For instance she has written on how the mighty oaks survived Katrina. Standing tall, almost unbowed, she tells us, oak trees grow in communities, expansive, bold, and comfortably taking up lots of space. While they appear autonomous and freestanding, the truth is that they are held up by a thick, entwined maze of roots, deep and wide. These intimate underground networks lean on each other for strength, even and especially in times of natural disaster. We find ourselves at a time of deeply unnatural political disaster; someone is shearing the nourishing tangle of roots that sustains us all.

As this book has made clear from the beginning, the problems of systems including education will require a far-reaching and ambitious agenda of strategic investment. The difficulty of neighborhood schools in poor communities of color is not a new phenomenon. If we are to understand this deepening crisis we cannot separate it from the political-economic context. Clearly, serious effort to solve the problem will not come from policy or presidential fiat from afar. Rather the spark and power for such change must come from the overlapping of communities embroiled in the consequences of neglect and ever-harsher Social Darwinist policies working in collaboration with allies who recognize shared fates—educator networks; unions across sectors; youth movements across neighborhoods.

To mount such a far-reaching campaign, however, demands that the strictures of present policy assumption be broken. More to the point, the *naturalized policy landscape*—which assumes that nothing but market options and austerity, nothing but ever-more starved public options, and nothing more than what is available now can ever be available again—must be re-gardened. The roots are being pruned by interventions sold as fertilizer. The image, however, of austerity as fertilizer is increasingly giving way to an alternate image—of austerity as toxin.

Attempts to depict austerity measures, in education as elsewhere, as natural and as inevitable are beginning to fail. The geography of the commons grows as groups such as the Occupy Wall Street (OWS) movement reclaim public spaces in the city. Home foreclosures turn middle-class members into squatters and political activists. And usurpation of public school space by corporatized charters provokes resistance that unites parents, neighbors, and community organizers. On November 17, 2011, thousands of people across race, class, and gender divides, of various levels of educational obtainment and political affiliations, joined together to protest the regimen of austerity at the site of the most powerful symbol of free market economics in the United States and perhaps the world today: Wall Street. The signs of the Occupy Wall Street participants bobbed in a sea of people, naming issues and demands that cohered into a larger collective cry at being locked out from a stable future. The placards demanded more jobs, not corporate bailouts; investment in schools, not war; ending student debt and the mortgaging of our children's future; health care as a right, not a privilege; and food stamps as an entitlement that assures reprieve from hunger. Participants united around calls for the highest income earners to pay their fair share of taxes. Dotting every part of the landscape was a demand to redistribute dollars from the wealthy to the middle class and poor to finance job creation and services. Through private conversations and public chants, members of the rally pointed to the commons as the site for correcting economic and political imbalances produced by the market. And so they marched from the portals to Wall Street into the heart of the bestial finance industry and occupied the streets. Their messages were clear, and their willingness to be arrested to dramatize the urgency of the situation inspiring. Arrests that day numbered in the hundreds.

The political winds have begun to shift. The Occupy movement provided a space and place for otherwise disparate groups to find the common ground to resist the losses of jobs, services, and, more largely, hope. Their political work is structured around a people's mic, decisionmaking by committee, and collective leadership as a corrective to the corruption associated with concentrations of power. OWS emphasizes militant tactics or acts of civil disobedience and disruption to draw attention to its message of inequality and the urgent need for income redistribution. Finally, the Occupy movement has, on the basis of both its tactics and message, given renewed prominence to mainstream political discussion about taxation and social services.

The choices of tactics, movement structure, alliance formation, celebration of the commons, and elevation of inequality as the issue of the day are bold, underscoring urgency to radically disrupt circuits of privilege for a minority of citizens in a moment of deepening crisis for the vast majority. In a short period of time the growing public influence of OWS has reignited the political imagination of many citizens redrawing their sense of social change boundary. OWS is not without profound contradiction. For example, how can it extend its reach and power without a centralized decisionmaking structure? How can it influence policymaking if it firmly insists on remaining an outsider group? What are the roles of leadership in presenting and influencing the shape of a message? How can it promote a change agenda without a series of specific demands that accompany its call for redistribution? Clearly, these questions will have to be addressed, but it is important to remember that OWS is in its infancy. The questions presently being raised are part of the fundamental DNA of most movements in their earliest stage of development. What remains remarkable is the rapidity of the movement's circulation through the larger culture, influencing movement organizing, electoral political discourse, and legislative agenda. Although OWS has helped to channel discontent into a political movement, it is important to remember that the politics of austerity and the economics of privilege continue. OWS, while presently critical to the reversal of present trend, remains largely untested in relationship to this persistent and growing threat.

LANDSCAPES OF AUSTERITY

In the midst of new resistance, austerity policies continue to rule the day not only in America but as well in Western Europe in the global economic crisis. Advocates of austerity presume no other source of revenue is available to sustain or expand public services or hiring. Quite simply, present revenue streams are considered to be the only source of present or potential revenue. Therefore, to balance budgets caught in the high-velocity windstorm of economic turbulence, we must cut programming. Is it as fixed a universe as advocates of austerity would have us believe? What if the immutable, naturalized imagery of the budget landscape is as much a fabrication of the present as a Renoir painting is a fiction of the past?

The political decision to forego tax revenue from the wealthy continues to have powerful reverberations in the United States. It triggers deficit financing, budget cutting, contraction of the public sector workforce, and a restructuring or rationing of public services. Tax codes, which at one time were a tool for redistributing resources from the wealthy to the middle class and poor, have been retooled to produce relief and favored status for the most affluent. The gutting of this once powerful mechanism for redistribution has come at great cost. Most concretely, taxes on the wealthiest sectors of the society have been traded off in favor of slashing public budgets and refiguring public services. Such policymaking has largely been at the expense of the poor and middle class.

Throughout the United States the budgets of universities are being slashed while tuition rises and the census of students is either capped or grows to arrest the bleeding of austerity. At the City University of New York (CUNY), for example, the number of students has increased from 230,000 to 270,000 over approximately seven years. At the same time "rational" tuition increases will be instituted between 2011 and 2016 to raise tuition by 25 percent. These increases will have a disproportionate effect on poor students of color. Importantly, a majority of students at CUNY are black or Latino and over 40 percent have family incomes under $30,000. These policies have been accompanied by capping practices at community colleges contending with student bodies that are less and less able to be contained by available classroom space. It is not unusual for students to be sitting on radiators or in the hallway because the seating inside the classroom cannot accommodate them; in effect they have been locked out of a learning relationship through an austerity-driven spatial rearrangement of the course.

The austerity policies being enacted in higher education are also affecting its workforce. The proportion of university faculty who are cheaper and part-time has swelled during the last twenty years. This point is perhaps most vividly illustrated by the fact that less costly, part-time faculty teach over 50 percent of the courses in most public universities across the country. While part-time positions increase in number, full-time positions are cut. At CUNY, between 1975 and 2012 the number of full-time faculty declined from 12,500 to 7,000. In 2000, the number of full-time faculty totaled about 5,700. Although many part-time faculty are prized by academic departments for their expertise and commitment, they are often unable to carry a full load of faculty responsibility outside of the classroom. Departmental committee membership, reference letters for graduating students, office hours, and advising are but a few of the tasks shouldered by an ever-smaller full-time faculty cohort.

Clearly, these dynamics affect the quality of education offered to students. As well, they represent a speedup or increase in workload, further compounded by increased class size and a ratcheting up of publication and fund-raising standards for tenure. The latter point is especially salient as the number of full-time tenure-bearing positions decline and graduates of doctoral programs nationwide increase. As the competition for scarce positions intensifies, so, too, does the standard for granting a faculty member job stability, or tenure. The proportion of faculty positions in higher education that offer tenure has declined from a high in the 1950s of approximately 100 percent to the present rate, which has dipped below 30 percent. The new image of public higher education, then, is of a part-time faculty member, teaching ever-larger classes in buildings less able to accommodate those who are registered, running from class to class to make ends meet, and frequently unable to meet with students or colleagues outside the classroom. Or of an instructor teaching in pajamas, online, to faceless students accruing credit, and debt, without ever meeting a faculty member. This imagery is tightly aligned with new realities of austerity policy, the disproportionate cheapening of classroom experience for poor students of color, increasing the workload of full-time faculty, expanding the proportion of less expensive part-time faculty, admitting more and more students at the same time the number of full-time faculty disappear, and shoehorning students into facilities that can no longer adequately cope. The degradation of the quality of public higher education parallels the experiences of K–12 and health care. Austerity policy is a virus that, when unleashed, produces similar symptoms and outcomes of service decline across the various sectors of the welfare state. What we are witnessing is a hollowing out and radical restructuring of public services.

As the commons, or public sphere, disappears, an increasing number of working and poor people are dislocated from some public institutions and redirected to others. It is not an accident, for example, that the trend lines of increased incarceration and school dropouts have occurred simultaneously or during the approximate thirty-year period in which the welfare state, and, more specifically, public education has been remade as result of policies of austerity. This context in part explains how more and more students of color are pushed off the commons or out of public education and into situations that increase the likelihood of crime and imprisonment. In an earlier era rural peasants in England were displaced by the wealthy from the communal lands that sustained them. They migrated to urban areas, surrendering traditional ways of life and working as cheap labor, ever-more vulnerable to the volatility of emergent industries and factories. Many disappeared into almshouses or prisons. Similarly, as young people of color today are pushed out of a public school commons given over to corporate interest and ideology, they are trapped between diminished market opportunity and incarceration. Poor people of color are marked as increasingly disposable.

The abandonment of the commons is a phenomenon intimately linked with the government role in insulating working people from the exploitation of the marketplace. As Cindi Katz (2008) argues, "Neoliberal capitalism and what George Lipsitz (2006) with typically perfect pitch, calls the 'social warrant of hostile privatism,'... lubricates, naturalizes and sustains [a landscape of racialized, gendered, and classed inequality that is] in every way reductive. They close off and narrow possibilities in the spaces of everyday life" (18, 16). The social reproduction protections of the state include "labor laws, social programs of the welfare state and subsistence resources" that make workers less dependent on their wages (Collins 2012, 2). This "protective covering of the state" was won through social movement campaigns of the 1930s and 1960s. These class tensions ultimately yielded a state apparatus that shielded workers from some of the most primitive forms of capital accumulation. As Jane Collins (2012) notes, "Primitive accumulation is not just about the amassing of capital for productive investment—it is the attempt of capitalists to reinstate the radical separation of workers from the means of production, to remove their covering. Although in theory capital accumulation does not need primitive accumulation, in practice, it is required whenever the working classes create obstacles to the accumulation process" (7).

Katz elaborates further on the human landscapes in which capital accumulation and dispossession erode community, capacity, and the health of our social formation. Katz writes on essential nurturing elements of social reproduction, which are

> the broad material social practices and forces associated with sustaining production and social life in all its variations. It is the stuff of everyday life as well as the structuring forces that constitute any social formation.... How social reproduction is accomplished and by whom, as much as what it properly includes, are social questions that have been the focus of labor, community and household struggles.... Neoliberal imperatives ... have been associated with concerted attempts by the state

and capitalists to offload responsibility for social reproduction onto individuals and households as well as civil society organizations such as community groups, religious institutions and non-governmental organizations. (Katz 2008)

In discussing the "crisis of social reproduction," with her analysis situated in the recovery theater of post-Katrina New Orleans, she argues that five elements of social reproduction are under siege: environment and infrastructure, health care, education, housing, and the organization of social and criminal justice. These are, of course, the roots that Beynus described earlier.

A strong relationship exists between the dismantling of social reproduction protections and the new disequilibrium and restructuring of global capital. As the US economy sinks and becomes ever-less competitive internationally, it has predictably focused on labor-saving devices or technology to increase productivity as well as reduced wages to restore historic rates of profit making. It is within a context of economic crisis and empire decline that the wages and benefits of private sector workers have been slashed, ostensibly to restore competiveness internationally. It is well known, however, that wage reductions at the base of the income pyramid have been accompanied by a growth in wealth and salary at the very top, exacerbating wealth inequality. But the working class is not powerless. It is still a challenge for members of the economic and political elite to slash private sector worker wages— government programming protects public workers from market exploitation and enables all workers to prolong their resistance to this regime of income decline through various forms of state resource support, union protection, legislation, and social reproduction. If the private sector wants to break worker resistance to wage reduction, it must dismantle the state apparatus providing protections from the exploitation of the marketplace. New programming and investment levels have been devised to accommodate an epoch of austerity policy. Of particular concern to this discussion is how market dynamics and austerity are reinventing state social reproduction functions regarding public education.

REFORMING THE STATE IN AN ERA OF AUSTERITY

James O' Connor (1973) and Ian Gough (1979) have noted that the state or government in an advanced capitalist economy has a number of primary functions. Certainly its primary responsibility is to support the process of capital accumulation. That is accomplished through arms of government that set economic policy including, but not limited to, establishing interest rates, providing loans to failing companies, and promulgating income tax codes. Another responsibility of government, particularly in advanced economies, is to reproduce the larger society's workforce presently and into the future. More concretely, there is a need to evolve a healthy, educated workforce socialized into the norms and values of the social order. Clearly, there is much variation across societies regarding the project of social reproduction. For example, the education, health care, and social welfare systems in Western Europe are very different than the structures and policies developed in the United States. What remains consistent, however, is the existence of a state apparatus throughout Western Europe and in the United States to address this social need. The state also performs the function of social control. It is entrusted with the responsibility of maintaining social peace. The maintenance of social control is daily enacted, for example, through policing on the streets of urban areas, surveillance of public schools declared unsafe, prosecution of crimes through the judiciary, and incarceration of rule violators. It is important to remember that intensifying control measures, in contradiction to intent, often produce the tinder that explodes in dissent and conflict. In the past three decades this part of the state budget has swelled. That is particularly the case in public schools. This growth has been driven by the expansion of the prison system, an explosion in the incarceration rates of young men of color, and the massive presence of policing and surveillance technologies in sites of education. A final function of the state is that it must legitimate its policies to the social order. It is within this legitimating frame that policies of strategic investment are displaced by market and technological solutions, such as charter schooling and testing accountability.

We are in a moment when historic understandings between the social order and its citizenry regarding the meaning of basic state functions are being radically rewritten. The penetration of the state and its policy decisionmaking by concentrated wealth was discussed in earlier chapters. It is sufficient to note at this point that on the basis of new election laws, strategic philanthropic giving, and the migration of foundation officials to high-level government positions that the state has lost a significant amount of its autonomy. In a sense the state has been encircled by a web of money and influence, a suffocating and impermeable framework, that is enclosing the policy options once available to decisionmakers. The choice for policymaking that serves short-term corporate interests and erodes redistribution to the working and middle class is perhaps the most essential outcome in this shifting locus of state decisionmaking. This enclosure of policy options and, ultimately, the commons has had a particularly powerful impact on the social reproduction functions of the state.

The programs that have offered at least a modicum of resource protection to working people are being dramatically diminished on the basis of disinvestment, rationing, restructuring, and deprofessionalization. This is occurring across many sectors of the welfare state. For example, resources available for food stamps and unemployment insurance have been constrained at the same time that need has exploded. Certainly these trends have also been evident in health care as diagnosis must match insurance reimbursement formula. It is on this basis that doctors and nurses have less and less discretion in their decisionmaking, the time in hospitals is shortened, reliance on technology increases, and signs of success are increasingly measured by levels of expenditure. These trends occur within a context where more and more of the health care dollar is spent on insurance company middlemen, private providers, and technology. Clearly, the quality of the health care being provided to citizens is being radically reformed or deformed. Specific understandings regarding medical care are rewritten in the name of productivity, efficiency, and austerity. In turn, the meaning of the social reproduction function of the state in relationship to health care is dramatically changed as patients' time with practitioners and in hospitals is reduced, pills become a cheaper alternative to access, and many professionals are deskilled in an environment of cheapened, ever-more mechanized forms of care.

The story unfolding in K–12 public education, although different in detail, is very similar in broad outline to that which has more or less already been told in health care. Austerity in public education has elevated the fantasy—and legitimated the enactment of—no-cost or budget-neutral reform. The technologies of testing, virtual learning, and accountability have become the mantra of the new reformers despite evidence they are expensive, no evidence that they are effective or accountable even on their own terms, and highly disruptive to the goal of providing deeply rooted, sustained educational practice and inquiry for all children. In a long and ugly history of national experiments with children and adults of color, these initiatives are accompanied by a commitment to launching privatizing experiments in public education. As noted earlier, these experiments include both charters and the recently reinvigorated voucher reform. Finally, this sea change occurs within an environment that attacks teachers, slashes their salaries and benefits, and witnesses a 50 percent turnover of their number in large urban areas approximately every six years. The decline in the circumstance of teachers is not only measured by the numbers; it is also inflected in their day-to-day, qualitative experience. The emphasis on test taking has produced classroom environments ever-more uniform in curricula and mechanized in pedagogy because of the singular attention paid to raising scores. A number of reports have suggested that teacher skill, discretion, and aspiration recede in such circumstance. This arid classroom environment may in part explain both the churning of teachers and the ever-greater reliance on "professional tourists" such as Teach for America "interns" who make a two-year commitment to the work.

The implicit assumption is that little relationship exists between teacher skill development occurring in the classroom over time and the academic progress of students. Such assumption in turn clears the path for an ever-changing, increasingly short-term, and cheaper workforce. Critically, the volatility and inexperience of the workforce heighten the prospect for its docility, which in turn increases the likelihood that uniform, ever-more rote forms of curricula that deprofessionalize will not be resisted.

Importantly, policies of austerity also produce a cheapened, fluid workforce with little long-term commitment to the classroom. The essential relationships of students and teachers, sustained over time, and the always fragile partnerships of schools and parents developed in community, are uprooted by reforms dedicated to short-term educators, school closings and reopenings, unregulated systems of choice (for schools, not students). We are witnessing the dramatic shearing of complex relations between schools and the communities—the relations we used to call democracy. With short-term educators and "teacher proof curriculum," instruction is routinized and cheapened and the teaching workforce deskilled and destabilized; the aspirations of public education regarding the social reproduction of students are also radically transformed. As the test score becomes both the ends and the means of the learning culture, every other part of the public education experience that does not serve such ends is excised. And so art, music, foreign language, and physical education are rendered vulnerable—especially in the poorest communities where test drill is normative. As well, complex, less easily measured learning associated with writing and critical thinking is increasingly underemphasized. It is ironic indeed that the social reproduction of critical thinkers, literate writers, and engaged citizens who are fluent in many languages is disappearing from our public school system in a moment when the global economy demands that its highest-paid workers increasingly have such capacity. This logic suggests that the overwhelming majority of the students embedded in the public school system's new culture of austerity and corporatist practice are not being educated for the limited high-paying jobs in the "new global economy" but rather for the expansive low-wage jobs in the service sectors. The ever-more delimited opportunities for high-wage jobs in the marketplace are mirrored in the cheapened value of the new teaching workforce and socialization experience of curricula in public schools.

Although this market dynamic has a powerful explanatory logic, it is but part of the larger story. The present restructuring of public education is also a consequence of the drive to capitalize large parts of the commons during a period of economic crisis. As noted in earlier chapters, in a period of diminished competiveness and profit making, which threatens the very foundation of the American economy, the liquidation of public assets is increasingly seen as the short-term answer to long-term crisis. The crisis of the economy is perhaps most powerfully illustrated by the fact that an increasing share of the profit generated by the economy, 41 percent, is harvested from a sector of the economy yielding no social value, the finance industry. By electing the public education reform engine of charter schools, vouchers, testing, and measureable forms of accountability, we have surrendered any prospect for significantly enlarging the academic capacity of the vast majority of public school students. There is another way, one that values the role of public goods while simultaneously understanding that public education must be profoundly altered on the basis of evidence, involvement of parents and students in the life of the school, introduction of complex forms of curricula, teacher capacity development, transformative strategic investment, and a commitment to education as a public not a private good. Some part of the political contestation being waged by OWS, parent and community groups, teachers for social justice, and youth organizing throughout the country is about the meaning of a public good in general and public education more specifically. What is being challenged is the presumption that public goods are an artifact of an earlier era, an anachronism in the language of Rick Santorum, rather than precious resources enhancing citizen capacity that cannot be reproduced by either market principle or transaction.

THE VALUE OF A PUBLIC GOOD

The present discourse regarding the state and the public goods it delivers has asserted that both are unproductive, inefficient, and essentially a drag on an economy already distressed. This logic legitimated the hollowing out of a range of public goods. This restructuring of public goods was intended on the one hand to diminish the protections afforded to workers and on the other to shift from a paradigm of redistribution to corporatist consolidation of control over public assets and policymaking. Importantly, historic policies of redistribution were not simply about tax dollars flowing from the wealthy to the middle class and poor. Redistribution also insinuated itself into a medical care system that created greater equity between social classes. It also was evident in enriched classes in math, writing, and critical thinking in public schools. This redistribution of knowledge and skill across classes marked at least a part of the public education experience. We of course do not want to romanticize the history of public goods. The redistribution of access to quality health care and transfer of skills and knowledge through public education was deformed by racism, sexism, and political battles, which consistently traded off universal rights for more circumscribed and selective service provision. That said, redistributive policies, although highly flawed, were an outcome of pitched battles between unions and business interests in the 1930s and movement politics of the 1960s. As noted earlier, redistributive public goods are now being replaced by corporatist services.

Questions of equity are less and less evident in policymaking regarding public goods. To the contrary, it is simply part of the new reform gospel that public goods are by definition inferior to services acquired privately. Private hospitals, charters, and vouchers share the common conceit that the private sector can provide better services with less money, thus their greater compatibility with a politics of austerity. How those services are constituted, what kinds of change they are likely to produce, the differential dispersion of corporatist service by race and class and the kinds of vulnerability it promotes remain unexplored. This much is clear: the "new" corporatist public good is structured to minimize worker protection from the exploitation of the marketplace, be it a slotting into low-wage service sector jobs or the rationing of resources.

Public goods are also distinguished from the market by their greater reliance on collaborative rather than competitive forms of transaction to produce outcomes. For example, for teachers and students, classroom pedagogy demands various forms of collaboration to produce new skill sets and knowledge. Equally important, scholars have documented collaboration between parents and neighborhood schools as a particularly effective way to improve the academic performance of students. Finally, we cannot expect to promote a new learning culture within schools without collaboration between students. Principals can attempt to unilaterally impose new initiatives, but more often than not, tacit and overt resistance by teachers and students will doom the venture. Shared ownership and collaboration are essential to the reconstitution of a learning environment.

The outcomes associated with a public good are complex and not as easily reduced to a singular, uniform marker of success as in the marketplace: profit. More to the point, in every school the needs of learners are different and complex.

To the extent that schools support students' deep learning, a set of conditions have to be in place, as documented by the Consortium on Chicago School Research (Lupesco et al. 2007), including a sense of community, shared pedagogical commitments among educators, strong leadership, complex assignments, and intensive work with families as well as community. There is no evidence that school closings enhance students' achievement. The hard truth is that educators need to be well supported in an environment where they can provide and ask for help. They need to create a similar context in their classrooms where students are known, needs are recognized, and gifts are appreciated; where standards are high, support is deep, and assessments are varied. These requirements are not especially compatible with the presently simple, and too often cheap, drive-by interventions of the testing regime, single-variable teacher evaluations, school closings and reopenings, and heavy policing.

Critically, the ability of the teacher to work across this range of learning needs and dimensions is tightly aligned with professional skill level. Equally important, the effectiveness of the instructor is dependent upon supervisory support, capacity development, and the number of students in the classroom at any given moment. The latter point is especially salient. As the size of a class grows, instructor capacity to adequately address the full range of student learning needs and to maximally exploit complex learning assignments is minimized. There is an association between strategic investment in class size, particularly in the poorest communities, and teacher capacity to use their skills and discretion to deliver a public good tailored to meet the complex learning needs of students. Clearly, such conditions are not met through budget austerity policy in public schools.

As policymakers demand that public goods mimic the marketplace, we are losing the very essence of a public good and simultaneously the social or collective good it can produce. As public equity recedes and is replaced by a glorification of private goods, we witness the simultaneous and related growth of inequality. As complex public goods are reduced to cheapened, ever-more mechanical and uniform services, the prospect of expansive capacity development and new opportunity incubated by a commons dims. Finally, as the space for collaborative efforts to produce a collective good is supplanted by competition for test scores, rationed charter school seats, public assets, and scarce jobs, the possibility of public goods providing a space for building new forms of collectivity and solidarity fades. The transformation of the commons—from a space of generative production of redistributive public goods to corporatist services that are handmaidens to the intensified exploitation of the marketplace—is well under way. As in the past, the only hope of slowing this juggernaut and resetting policy direction is to build social movements that offer a vision, politics, and program agenda aligned with the interests of working and poor people. Only by developing a power commensurate to that which has been accumulated by concentrated wealth and governing elites can grassroots groups hope to alter the present arc of reform and the diminished life chances of the largest number of Americans.

CONTESTED TERRAIN: WHICH SIDE ARE YOU ON?

The commons is the most hotly contested battleground today between social classes in advanced capitalist economies. The stakes in America are especially high because its welfare state historically offered far fewer protections to working people than those policies developed in, for example, Western Europe. American austerity policy, which has catapulted a free fall of slashed budgets and degraded service, threatens the very existence of the tissue of protective resources and legislation that has insulated working people from the intensified exploitation of the market. As was noted in the last section, this is occurring at precisely the moment in which market forces are most turbulent, demanding a transfer of public assets, reduced wages, and working conditions to restore profit margins. The American struggle over welfare state functions and protections is especially important because it offers a signal to the rest of the world just how far political and economic elites are prepared to go in restricting access to, restructuring, and liquidating the commons.

The future of the commons will not simply be determined by governing elites. To the contrary, welfare state functions and protections emerged out of struggles between class interests regarding the distribution of resources. These social movements demanded that resources be redistributed to enlarge and enforce economic and social rights. Struggles with dominant economic interests yielded both victory and defeat. Most critical to this discussion, however, is that an expansion of the commons and the protections it offers did not come without struggle or the counterposing of working-class power with concentrated wealth's growing influence over state policymaking.

At the present moment, however, there is a substantial imbalance between the power of governing elites and working groups. For years, the power of unions as measured by their dues-paying membership has declined. Simultaneously, the activist base of unions has diminished. The weakened power of worker organizations is also evident in the diminished presence of student organizations in an era of increased debt and tuition throughout higher education. Equally important, grassroots groups from churches to community-based organizations are finding it increasingly difficult to retain, much less expand, their base because of the increased pulls on the lives of poor and working people. Perhaps the most compelling counterpull for many regarding participation is the need to work multiple jobs to survive. This desire to turn inward, although understandable in an era of mounting political and economic pressure, is also counterproductive given the array of forces arrayed against all things public and progressive. Broad-based coalition fights on the shared ground of tax policy and welfare state revenue are essential if we are to reverse policies of disinvestment and service degradation. Alternatively, small armies fighting alone on single issues are doomed to fail both in the short and long term.

Ultimately, the fight for the commons will determine the extent to which working people are protected by a state apparatus or abandoned in favor of an ever-greater redistribution of public assets upward and more primitive forms of capital accumulation resulting in intensified exploitation. That is an especially taut battle line and ultimately each of us will have to choose not only where we stand but also what we are prepared to invest in this expansive and historic struggle.

For public education, the choices are stark and clear. To what extent are educators prepared to stand with the poorest communities of color particularly, and all schools generally, to change the learning conditions of public schools through substantial strategic investment? How can we make certain that such investment promotes deep participation in, and ownership of, schooling by parents, the nurturing of restless inquiry or question posing as an essential trait of an educated citizen, critical thinking as fundamental to sustaining a democracy, and curricula that addresses the diverse racial and class histories of its students? How are we prepared to resist definitions of crisis that lead to policies of exit from public schools (and lead toward charter schools and vouchers), punitive forms of teacher evaluation, student assessment that significantly reduces the complexity of what needs to be learned and taught, an exiling of multicultural curricula as in the case of Tucson, and threats on the heads of children of undocumented adults as in Alabama? How do we contest the continuing degradation of public education and increased concentration of the most needy learners in parched sites of intensifying disinvestment and reimagine, rebuild, and reenergize the commons? In what ways are we prepared to challenge the rote, cheapened forms of accountability, curricula, and instruction engineered by the present culture of testing? How are we prepared to fight school closing policies, which on the one hand neglect contextual factors producing low test scores while on the other disproportionately and negatively affect poor children of color? How do we confront the call for a college education for all at precisely the moment when access is being reduced and the quality of classroom instruction cheapened? Equally important, if K–12 is a gateway to college and economic stability, how can we not challenge the soaring student debt that increasingly accompanies college attendance? How do we enlarge both the dollars available for financial aid and access to those resources for the neediest students? To what extent are we willing to resist expansive transfers of public assets to private entrepreneurs in the new education marketplace? What quality and kind of education are we demanding from public managers? How committed are we to struggle with and invest in a public good as complex as public education over the long haul? What kinds of data are we prepared to collect and disseminate to scale up best practices? Clearly, these questions highlight the multiple challenges to activist engagement and the difficulty of promoting meaningful durable educational change. That said, these are but some of the questions that demand not simple answers but a political willingness to fight privately and publicly for forms of change that address the real needs and condition of public education in the poorest communities of color. Such a stand must be contrasted to policymaking based largely on the blinder of ideological predisposition, allure of technological magic bullets, and the craven self-interest of profit making.

Part of this decisionmaking will depend on our politics. It is foolish to presume that we will simply weigh and assess the choices in a hothouse of cumulative micro impressions or data where all choices are equal. To the contrary, all choices are not equal. If we choose redistribution of resources to and public education strategic investment in very poor communities of color, we are making a political decision. That decision privileges the most disadvantaged communities, assumes that the government is a better site than the marketplace for developing public goods such as education, promotes redistributive tax policy, and is betting on public investment in schooling as a way to both increase academic capacity and job opportunity.

That said, it is also clear that schools cannot unilaterally solve the persistent, complex problems of an economy and empire in crisis. Public education alone cannot solve the migration of jobs to other parts of the world in a global economy. It cannot magically fix the conditions in surrounding communities and larger society that spawn estrangement, destructive behavior, and various forms of dispossession. Finally, schools cannot independently promote a pathway to a more robust democracy. No single institution can address the multiple and complex issues afflicting the larger social order. Altering present conditions will take substantial time, the building of a broad powerful movement and the germination of political leaders prepared to take the risks necessary for change. What we do know, however, is that public education is a primary front line in the battle to remake the larger economy and the commons. Once we make the political and personal choice to resist, we must also select a place to stand and fight. This book has made the case that public education may be an especially critical space of contestation because of its resources, central role in reproducing a labor force, and vital place in the iconography of American democracy. Our struggle is to evolve the vibrant, participatory, democratic energies that build communities, sustain families, enrich individual lives, and enlarge institutional practice—a struggle that is recharged daily through acts of solidarity, redistributive justice, and political struggle. The logic of choosing sides and a specific place for struggle is richly described by the activist, scholar Arundhati Roy. "What is happening to our world is almost too colossal for human comprehension to contain. But it is a terrible, terrible thing. To contemplate its girth and circumference, to attempt to define it, to try and fight it all at once, is impossible. The only way to fight it is by fighting specific wars in specific ways" (as quoted in Harvey 2004, 167).

Roy discusses the dimensions and historic significance of the present struggle:

> Privatization is essentially the transfer of productive public assets from the state to private companies. Productive assets include natural resources [*and the commons*], Earth, forest, water and air. These are the assets that the state holds in trust for the people it represents.... To snatch these away and sell them as stock to private companies is a process of barbaric dispossession on a scale that has no parallel in history. (167)

For the purposes of this discussion we can simply substitute commons and education for natural resources and apply the frame and logic offered by Roy. As we think about the change platform that should frame the campaign for public education, we should begin with the four proposals recently sketched by Linda Darling-Hammond (2012):

First, we need to recognize that the growing income gap, unemployment and poverty must be addressed if we are to close the education gap and maintain a stable democratic society....

Second, we must finally address the outrageous disparities in school funding that set us apart from other industrialized nations.... This should include benchmarks for early childhood education, well-qualified teachers, high-quality curriculums and equitable instructional resources....

Third, we should equalize learning opportunities outside school including high-quality preschool education and enriched summer learning opportunities for all students. A major study at Johns Hopkins University found that one-third of the achievement gap between affluent and poor high school students is present at the start of the first grade and two-thirds occurs because of summer learning loss for low income students....

Fourth, we must invest in the quality of our educators. Since federal supports for teacher training were dramatically reduced in the '80s, teacher shortages in schools serving low-income students have increased to the point where there is a revolving door for teachers in these schools. (14–15)

Other items might be added to this list including increasing teacher salaries, as has occurred in countries with especially effective public education systems, creating less dependence on local taxes and more on federal taxes to finance public education in the poorest communities of color, and creating financial incentives to draw the most experienced and effective teachers to the neediest communities. The exact nature of the change platform or list, however, is less important than the actual work of building the power to challenge present policy. In the absence of movement organizations dedicated to altering present policy direction and promoting investment in public schools, we can fashion the most compelling set of policy proposals but they remain inert. What animates policy proposal is the power of campaigns advancing a political, education agenda.

THE STRUGGLE FOR A REDISTRIBUTIVE STATE

The present struggle for redistribution of economic resources and political power from concentrated wealth to a broad citizenry is a struggle for racial, class, and gender justice; this will not be won quickly or easily. The necessary social movements to win such transformative change are in their very infancy of power accumulation and structural development. In this moment what has been refreshing and invigorating for many progressives, however, is the emergence of the Occupy movement. OWS has applied the lens of justice, a feature that has all but disappeared in our larger culture, to the spreading cancer of economic inequality and political oligarchy. It has been a powerful corrective to a naturalized policy landscape where participants are unwilling to discuss either the implications of growing inequality or its relationship to austerity policy. Those issues have been forced by OWS into every level of policy discussion regarding student debt, inequality, sustainability, and shared fates. From New York State where Governor Cuomo was forced to salvage at least part of a "Millionaires" tax he was prepared to abandon to President Obama's recent U-turn on progressive taxation, the revenue discussion is beginning to shift, if ever so slightly. Equally important, the joining of fairness with attention paid to need and equity on the uneven playing field of policymaking is no longer seen as naïve but increasingly necessary. Clearly, this shift is presently modest and met with an intensifying resistance by the Right.

In a spate of recent articles in the *New York Times,* for example, the movement platform or policy discussion of redistribution through state mechanisms was sharply contested. In an article entitled "Education Gap Grows between Rich and Poor, Studies Say," Charles Murray noted, "Inequality is more of a symptom than a cause.... When the economy recovers you see all of these problems persisting for reasons having nothing to do with money and everything to do with culture" (Tavernise 2012). Framing the problems of education, unemployment, student debt, health care, and other social problems as cultural, not economic, phenomena became prominent—if highly controversial—after 1965 when Senator Daniel Patrick Moynihan (1964) argued that "family life in the black community constituted a 'tangle of pathology.'" "Culture of poverty" arguments have persisted for so many decades, despite their insidiously racist and classist assumptions, because they imply that breakdowns in values as well as norms, rather than economic inequalities and political-economic injustices, explain present social conditions. This old story line resurrected by Murray is accompanied by yet another resurfaced by Douglas Besharov, who argues that the problems are too complex to be solved by the state: "The problem is a puzzle, no one has the slightest idea what will work" (Tavernese 2012). Yet we can, in fact, solve persistent problems of public higher education access through elimination of student debt, degradation of service through subsidies of health care, learning delays through the creation of early childhood education programming, capitalization of public assets through the regulation of private sector avarice, and deep distrust of the state through programs that promote equity of investment and participation.

The right-wing has emphasized a cultural frame that shrouds race and class injustice and then promotes the notion that the complexity of today's social problems is beyond the capacity of the state to solve. The right-wing highlights past failures of public programs as a way of discounting the demands of progressive social movements. Equally important, it implicitly presents the market as the only alternative to state failure and the rewarding of "job creators" with an ever-greater proportion of wealth as the answer to the ills of the economy. In effect, it is a policy prescription for maintaining the status quo of steady decline for working people across the country in income, education, and debt level. Paul Krugman responds to Murray's arguments in the same issue of the *New York Times* by noting, "So we reject the attempt to divert the national conversation away from soaring inequality toward the alleged moral failings of those Americans being left behind. Traditional values aren't as crucial as social conservatives would have you believe—and in any case, the social changes taking place in America's working class are overwhelmingly the consequence of sharply rising inequality not its cause" (2012).

Only powerful social movements tethered to a progressive platform for change can produce the redistributive policies necessary to promote the economic and social U-turn urgently needed to revitalize our schools, communities, and democracy. Policies of economic redistribution through more progressive tax structures, which place more dollars in the pockets of poor and middle-class citizens, although necessary, are insufficient. The present crisis will not be solved in its entirety by moving capital from one group of individuals in society to another.

Part of the present struggle has to do with the function of the state in a capitalist society in a moment of crisis. Conversations are emerging inside and outside of electoral politics. For example, Elizabeth Warren in her run for senator of Massachusetts is advancing a political agenda of corporate regulation, while unions across the country are working to build alliances with community groups to advance a common agenda for rebuilding and reinvesting in public schools and public services in the poorest communities. Simultaneously, local campaigns are emerging in neighborhoods across the nation calling for an alternative to the spreading virus of foreclosure and eviction.

Will these emergent battle lines help the state perform strategic functions that promote the interests of working people? More specifically, will the state invest in the future of working-class people through stronger regulative policies and quality public institutions including public schools, higher education, health care as well as a range of social services? How can the state be restructured to pollinate innovation by amplifying the voices of grassroots groups at various stages of program development and implementation? In what ways can the state act to redistribute dollars away from surveillance and control activities of prisons or policing inside schools and to the education of the poorest? Regarding the larger environment, will the state be accorded the discretion and resources to address the mounting threat and damage of the ecological crisis? The public sphere and natural environment are the bases of our common fate; as they are imperiled so, too, is any prospect for a hopeful future.

A basic assumption of this book is that corporations and concentrated wealth cannot address these crises. They are too decentralized, self-interested, and short term in their thinking to effectively answer the questions that need asking. Only the centralized apparatus of the state can begin to seriously address these pressing questions. Yet it is important not to romanticize the recent history of the state. Too often the state has overemphasized policing functions over other forms of investment. Additionally centralized decisionmaking has trumped the need for democratic participation and its potential to create a better fit between community need and state programming. Naomi Klein (2011) recently indicated that one of the great failures of the Left is not understanding that state power can be just as corrupt as corporate power. She adds that we have to have learned those lessons of the past. A state amputated from progressive social movements cannot be expected to independently wrestle free from the intensifying demand of corporate interests in a moment of crisis. Clearly the state must be held accountable to meet the needs of middle-class and poor communities. However, that can only be accomplished by strong social movements committed to principles of democratic participation, satisfactory forms of strategic investment, and transformative levels of wealth redistribution. Such an agenda will meet stiff resistance and have contradictions that will never be fully resolved. However, the question before us is whether we surrender to present trend or struggle through movement politics to reclaim a democracy and public space that redistribute power and resources and thus enact some part of the promise of America regarding justice and enfranchisement. This vision can only be accomplished through the accumulation of power on the political battlefield. It is to that part of the story we now turn our attention.

The Emergent Political Battle Lines

Even as we move past the 2012 presidential election, the political battle to transform public education and more generally the role of the state is being won by the Right. Up to now mass political discourse has been successful in concealing the issue of inequality and deifying a market-based solution to private and public problems. This, in turn, has led to the vilification of the state, regressive taxes, disinvestment in public services, and policies of austerity. Slowly, such belief is being challenged by a cross section of social movements. Wisconsin workers—during legislative decisionmaking to restrict union membership and slash public employee benefits—staged a defiant takeover of the state capitol in February 2011. This act of civil disobedience was organized and directed by graduate students at the University of Wisconsin in Madison. In turn it led to electoral tactics to delay the passage of legislation and the recall of key legislators. Although at best these actions produced mixed results, they represent a departure, a new beginning of meeting the ever-more harsh policy proposals of the Right with sharply militant and inspired tactics. Subsequently, the tactics of Wisconsin pollinated other sites. For example, in New York, students, unions, and community groups joined in a brief takeover of the state capitol in Albany. Prior to that, thirty-one faculty and students of the City University of New York (CUNY) were arrested protesting budget cuts. The protest was organized by CUNY's faculty and staff union, the Professional Staff Congress. In spring 2011 the state capitol in California was also deluged by students protesting dramatic increases in the tuition of the state's university system. These uprisings reminded many of the critical role students can and must play in the development of a broad social movement politics.

The organizing during the spring of 2011, however, was only a prelude to the national emergence of the Occupy Wall Street movement. From Oakland, California, to New York City to Miami, Florida, and hundreds of cities and towns in between, Occupy sites surfaced and in many instances flourished. They shared a commitment to taking over public space—enlisting the support of labor, students, and community groups—as well as highlighting growing inequality. The movement's focus on the single message of the top 1 percent of wage earners snaring an ever-larger share of income and wealth resonated with the larger public. Quickly major media outlets dedicated more and more of their airtime to this movement story. *Time* magazine named *Protester* as the collective person of the year. Critically, the Occupy movement refused to develop a leadership hierarchy and instead relied on an expansive democratic committee decisionmaking structure. Its firm commitment to horizontal decisionmaking and encampments in public spaces constituted a large part of its movement identity. As well, it engaged in acts of defiant civil disobedience, for example, in resisting police efforts to dismantle public encampments and in attacking centers of concentrated wealth such as Wall Street. The Occupy movement's willingness to confront both the issue of inequality and sites of concentrated wealth has attracted a large following especially among college students. As Graeber, a leader of the Occupy movement, wrote, "We are watching the beginnings of the defiant self-assertion of a generation of Americans, a generation who are looking forward to finishing their education with no jobs, no future, but still saddled with enormous and unforgivable debt.... Is it really surprising they would like to have a word with the financial magnates who stole their future?" (Graeber 2011).

In considering movement politics, it is important to reconsider the wisdom of Roy when she remarks that the scope of what we are resisting is so great, so rapidly changing, that it is hard to comprehend, no less struggle against in its entirety. She suggests we wage our fights around specific issues, be it the frontal attack on public workers and their unions, the degradation of K–12 public education, the foreclosure of housing for the poor and middle class, an ever-more restrictive health care system less and less able to meet the needs of ill people, the sustained funding of mass incarceration and criminalization, or soaring tuition. Simultaneously, we must build into our work an integration of otherwise disparate struggles to achieve coherent analysis and, over time, a larger umbrella to reclaim public space, multiracial democracy, human rights, and the commons. Otherwise we are doomed to forever work in fragmented sites of resistance, never recognizing the larger possibility of a broader collective struggle, which joins issues into a common platform and political work. That broader movement may, however, have to await the development of strong local and regional campaigns on specific issues. This is especially frustrating when we are faced with the present broad assault of capital, which is rapidly dissolving both the commons and large sectors of the private sector. How can we be patient in our organizing when the present moment is so imperiled and our living conditions so radically altered? Yet we must engage in this local, painstaking organizing work if we are to accumulate necessary power over the long term.

At the same time, we must acknowledge that the present moment may be rewriting old rules regarding movement formation. More specifically, the subtle composition of creating a movement may be breaking with historic pattern. For example, a broad, strong movement may emerge at a single point in time with little warning or apparent local foundation. It may simply pollinate rapidly in relationship to a set of intensifying oppressive conditions that demand immediate attention. And so present movements may be in a catch-up relationship to the building need for corrective action shared by a multitude of otherwise disparate citizens. It is the urgency of oppression and intense desire for action that may create rapidly expanding circles of solidarity both embodied and virtual. That is one scenario. Many would argue that is precisely what the Occupy movement represents.

We would agree that the sense of oppression, lost hope, and need for action has joined many otherwise estranged and isolated citizens to this growing social movement. That said, OWS is in the very earliest stage of its development. Equally important, if history is any indicator and it usually is, OWS politics will need to have a deeper root system locally than has been the case and evolve a more effective structure to guide trans-local work—that is, horizontal, national work—before it can effectively challenge any part of the Right's agenda. Presently, OWS is in an early, albeit promising, stage of tactical, strategic, and structural experimentation. It has offered critical support to labor and community groups. Yet its future remains uncertain. In the euphoria of finally watching a movement lift off into public consciousness, the Left must not mistake promise with reality. OWS's small base, limited structural reach, singular emphasis on the issue of inequality as compelling as it may be, and absence of a change platform limits its capacity. We are not dismissing OWS; to the contrary we think its emergence is critically important to the ongoing evolution of a broad, effective social movement. At the same time we are not confusing OWS with the existence of such a broad movement in its present form; at the moment it simply cannot effectively challenge any part of the Right's agenda. Some part of the root system that will help to grow OWS—or more likely the next stage movement it will morph into—is in our estimation occurring around issues of public education.

Public education campaigns offer an especially rich example of contemporary organizing that can inform the next stage development of OWS. These campaigns have a singular urgency built around issues that matter to poor people. Additionally, unlike OWS, the organizing is structured vertically and horizontally to direct campaigns, has created clear platforms for change, and evolved from local to regional struggles. Importantly, this movement can also learn from OWS as it has been unable to penetrate the public's consciousness or build national reach into its work. Critically, however, public education organizing has involved a growing number of very poor citizens in campaigns to resist and reverse the ongoing collapse of neighborhood schooling. Finally, these campaigns are being waged at the most intense point of frontal assault on the role and function of the state, public education.

Public Education, the Front-Line Struggle to Re-Create the Commons

It is important to reiterate that the degraded conditions of public schools in the poorest communities produce teacher turnover leading to underprepared classroom instructors, the continuing decay of physical plants, ever-greater student-teacher ratios in the classroom, and ever-more rote forms of learning. And so the inequality gap reported in the larger culture is mirrored by differences in investment, academic experience, and outcomes between poor communities and their more affluent counterparts. The robust and statistically significant relationship between academic outcomes and social class was most recently documented by a group of Stanford researchers led by Sean

Ahearn. Clearly, poor communities, especially those of color, are not lacking in an explosive abundance of public education issues around which they might organize. Their task, however, is to craft a framework for transformation and build an effective organizing campaign around it. Underpinning the genesis of such campaigns are communities summoning the political will and hope that in a moment of deepening cynicism about the prospects of public education, especially for poor children, that such a fight is not only worth waging but essential. Despite the concentrated right-wing effort to atomize collective aspirations for public education into choice and exit, the will to stand and fight for better public schools has in recent years grown.

The authors of *Community Organizing for Stronger Schools* (Mediratta, Shah, and McAlister 2009) have developed perhaps the most comprehensive and rigorous research on the structure and impact of recent campaigns. In a cross section of sites including Oakland, Miami, Austin, eastern Pennsylvania, Chicago, the Bronx, and Los Angeles, over 1,000 qualitative interviews and quantitative surveys were conducted. As well, seventy-five observations of leadership development sessions, public actions, and negotiations were incorporated into the study design. Archival documents also offered a window into organizational practices. Secondary district-level data such as dropout rates, graduation rates, and demographic data were systematically dissected. Finally, over 1,700 articles of local media on education issues were analyzed to establish context for a number of the campaigns.

Most critical to this discussion is determining the kinds of impact(s) this cross section of organizing work had on local as well as regional policymaking. Kavitha Mediratta, Seema Shah, and Sara McAlister (2009) note that organizing increased the responsiveness of district officials to the needs of low-income parents of color and that district resource allocations reflected demands to preserve or expand equity (24). These redistributive policies both reallocated existent resources and in a number of places, such as Los Angeles, increased the size of the investment in public education. New policy initiatives at each of these sites, or districts, were consistent with the platforms or reform proposals of community groups. These platforms for change included, but were not limited to, the following: (1) teacher and principal development to increase parent engagement, (2) teacher recruitment and retention programming, (3) amendments to testing and promotion policies, and (4) small school creation through new fiscal mechanisms. Although differences in approach and outcome exist across sites, the authors indicate that the findings consistently point to the impact of the organizing campaigns on underserved African American, Latino, and other low-income immigrant communities. These outcomes are echoed by Mark Warren and Karen Mapp in their book *A Match on Dry Grass: Community Organizing as a Catalyst for School Reform* (2011).

It is important to note that in three of the cities intensively studied as part of a case study project, dynamic interplay between organizing campaigns and the development of invigorated public school learning was documented. More specifically, in Austin, Miami, and Oakland, change campaigns emphasized building teacher-parent partnerships, opportunities for greater community participation, and increased instructor capacity. It has been very difficult to join teachers and community groups in a common struggle for improving public education. These groups have often warred with each other over the obligations of unions beyond member wage increases or to the communities they serve and the boundary between community participation and professional expertise. These tensions were addressed in the motion of a campaign and deepening sense of shared fate. For example, in New York City as parents and teachers built relationships of solidarity in a struggle for public investment in a South Bronx neighborhood's schools, the boundaries of relationship shifted. Increasingly, teachers began to trust parents to participate in the hiring of professionals and drafting of contract language while parents advanced an agenda to create a new tier of teaching career with a higher salary for teachers with greater expertise. New understandings germinating from allied campaigns and deepened understanding of common fate have also occurred in fights over charters, vouchers, and virtual learning. Critically, not all parents have seen their fate bundled with public teachers or parents. Parents in charter schools or seeking vouchers to parochial schools have often engaged in forms of public battle with stakeholders in the public sector. Important to this discussion, however, the changed relational cultures produced within targeted public schools as a result of organizing campaigns, in turn, produced dramatic increases in student achievement scores. The relationship between organizing for more equitable financing of public schools, the development of a robust learning culture, and academic outcomes is clear on the basis of this most recent evidence. And yet, few of these lessons are being incorporated into a systematic practice that either informs or shapes public school reform.

Some part of the question regarding the multiple benefits of organizing is linked with participatory policy development, rooted with and in communities, and how such outcome is achieved. Much of the discussion regarding organizing and education reform has focused on the metanarrative of organizing and its impact. Most frequently, the discussion pays almost exclusive attention to the external campaign, its powerful players, critical events, and specific outcomes. Conversely, little attention is systematically paid to the conscious use of specific internal and external organizing practices and their contributions to building effective campaigns and school systems. That is, organizing and policy work are typically separated but it may be important to gather an archive of examples in which organizing and local campaigns have been mobilized not only in resistance—against budget cuts and school closings, against gross measures of teacher evaluation and charter takeover of public school buildings—but also for policy formulation, finance equity, performance assessment in schools, multicultural curricula, school discipline policies that don't require police, and to recruit and sustain strong teacher experience and expertise in the poorest communities, as was the case with the lead teacher experiment in the Bronx.

A campaign implemented in the South Bronx of its ninth school district was particularly compelling because of its layered, nuanced approach to organizing. The campaign developed by the Community Collaborative to Improve School District 9 (CC9) built a coalition of community-based agencies, parents, university partners, and the United Federation of Teachers (UFT). It emphasized multiple levels of internal organizing necessary to build the power to launch an effective external campaign for educational justice. These threads of this internal organizing work included (1) building a collaborative of community-based agencies (CC9) as a vehicle for enlarging parent power; (2) promoting university-community collaboration to aid fund-raising and technical capacity development; (3) establishing community ownership of the change campaign through an invigorated democratic decisionmaking culture, lowering of access costs to participation through available day care, meals, language translation, and rigorous leadership development; and (4) forging alliance with teachers and their unions around issues of common concern.

The power of CC9 was also built and threaded through a series of tactical and strategic decisions. For example, its campaign focused on increased investment within the classroom. Its lead teacher campaign demanded an infusion of lead, or expert, teachers into the poorest communities of color to mentor less-experienced instructors through the incentive of increased pay. This initiative was seen as a primary corrective to the rapid turnover of teachers in the district, the relationship between churning and low levels of student achievement, the need to build an alliance with teacher unions, and the articulated objectives of the Department of Education of the City of New York to heighten investment in teacher capacity. Parents expected and data suggested that such an intervention would upgrade teacher expertise, increase professional life expectancy, reward lead teachers with higher salaries, and result in higher test scores. The demand promised both broad benefits and accountability accruing from a specific strategic investment. This promise was realized as various indices both quantitative and qualitative in each of the ten targeted schools jumped dramatically two years after the introduction of the lead teachers. Importantly, the campaign that was waged to advance investment or equity in very poor schools was also strategically choreographed. On one hand, it featured a series of public events that announced the grassroots muscle and powerful alliances supporting CC9's agenda. These packed rallies were a mélange of speeches by elected officials expressing commitment, exhortations by parent leaders to ignite passions, chanting at ever greater decibel levels by parents, and performances by students to exemplify what the fight was about. Each of these events increased the pressure on DOE to reach a settlement with the community. These public events occurred simultaneous to private negotiations between DOE and parent leaders. The use of private negotiation and public event by CC9 was yet another dimension of its conscious strategic thinking (Fabricant 2010).

It is essential to excavate the deep practice and experience of education justice organizing if we are to transport the lessons of specific campaigns. We know that for a campaign to influence academic outcomes, it must effectively promote strategic investment in the poorest schools, create new forms of relationship between parents, teachers, and students thus transforming the learning culture, and build organizations that increase autonomous parent power. Clearly, promoting equitable investment is paramount. Presently, the education organizing literature etches broad contours of a number of campaigns but reveals little about aspects of these struggles most salient to building parent power, producing alliances, influencing issue selection, sustaining community involvement, structuring campaign tactics, and finally maximizing new forms of investment in public education. These choices and practices need to be systematically enunciated if we are to evolve sturdier foundations for erecting ever-more powerful campaigns that challenge the presently inequitable distribution of resources to public schools.

Relying on organizing as the primary strategy for forcing increased investment and redistributive policies is fraught with dilemma. To begin with, parents, particularly those from the poorest communities, daily contend with multiple, compelling demands on their scarce time. Helping parents to focus their scarce time on school reform represents a significant challenge for organizers. Equally important, many parents' experience with teachers and local schools has engendered both distrust and cynicism. Finding ways to re-grid these relationships from tacit hostility to a growing regard capable of blossoming into collaboration represents yet another locus of organizing challenge. For example, the American Federation of Teachers (AFT) is attempting to build alliances in five cities between local unions, neighborhood organizations, and parent leaders on issues most affecting the quality of public education, including, but not limited to, investment in classroom ratios, teacher capacity development, assessment, and curricula. Local community-organizing initiatives are not yet of sufficient scale to gather the power necessary to alter city or regional policy. These issues of scale will need to be carefully considered in relationship to complex differences in school culture, regional norms, and the strength of union presence that may influence the development and implementation of a program. A growing issue is that parents are increasingly divided in their fealty to charters as contrasted to traditional public schools or the fate of their individual child as compared to the larger neighborhood's future. Critically, effective organizing demands that divisions be addressed in the motion of a campaign and focus not be squandered on what divides but rather what joins otherwise fragmented individuals and groups. Much of the local organizing presently under way in K–12 and the national work being undertaken by the AFT shares this trait.

Other issues in no particular order of importance that represent an undertow to mounting powerful organizing campaigns include, but are not limited to, the following items. Sustaining parent participation after their initial engagement in a campaign is difficult. Parents often migrate back to earlier points of equilibrium after a campaign concludes, thus undermining the long-term fate of the larger organizing work, and educators often forget to sustain the collaboration with parents after the victory has been won. Finding the funding necessary to support and sustain an organizing campaign in an increasingly hostile and conservative political environment is an especially daunting challenge. Equally important, such support is difficult to locate when present policy hegemony has caused a cross section of foundations to disregard investment and organizing as a serious approach to resurrecting public education. The job of organizers is not simply to build bodies of power attached to a particular school building but as well to transform public education. By building a relationship to schooling as well as specific schools, the organizers emphasize the importance of an enlarged sustained participation of parents in learning, the nurturing of inquiry, and complex curricula. Critical to such a project, however, is the fact that developing a cohort of organizers who remain with the work for an extended period of time is imperiled by more intense job demands and an unstable work environment. Like teachers, organizers turn over too rapidly because of low salaries, difficult working conditions, and frustration. Also, like teachers, their departure creates a tear in the fabric of expertise and continuity so critical to weaving effective campaigns over time. Finding ways to sustain organizers' relationship to both the work and the specific organization, although critical, remains elusive given both the nature of the work and the instability of the funding. The present instability of the economy and diminishment of other job options may paradoxically offer some hope of extending an organizer's tenure in one place. That said, necessity must also be joined to the satisfactions associated with such choice if it is to have any longer-term benefit to an organizing campaign (Fabricant 2011a).

This summary of dilemmas associated with organizing as a primary strategy for advancing a reform agenda, although realistic, is chilling. Given the challenge that has been enumerated, can we realistically expect community organizing to offer a way out of the present morass of misguided public education policymaking? The gritty reality of both the present challenge facing public education in very poor communities of color and the present limitations of community organizing as a strategy to halt and reverse decline are best articulated by parents caught in the crosshairs of this struggle. A parent leader of CC9 articulated this tension when she noted,

> Look, we are trying to fix problems that have hurt the schools here for longer than I can remember. I went to the schools in this neighborhood and now I am a parent sending my kids to the same schools. For years, I have watched and fumed as my kids haven't been given what they need to make it as students. I've tried to talk to the administrators to do it their way. It hasn't worked, can't get it done by myself with no power. I've got to join up with other parents in the same situation to change things. It's the only way. I know it's going to be a long fight, but what other choice do I have, how can I look my kids in the face if I don't give it my best shot. Organizing parents and building power is our best shot. (Fabricant 2011a)

EMERGENT LANDSCAPES OF ORGANIZING: RETHINKING THE POLITICS AND PRAXIS OF PUBLIC EDUCATION

There is an urgency associated with building the power necessary to challenge the agenda of the Right to radically restructure the basic functions of public education and more largely the welfare state. To address this agenda demands that a social movement of breathtaking scope and power be built. This work will be both arduous and uncertain. In our estimation, however, any movement building intention during this epoch of an increasingly barbaric capitalism must combine an ambitious platform for change with an equally compelling strategic vision of movement building. What follows is a preliminary sketch of some of the issues that must be considered as we enlarge and deepen our work. Critically, a large part of this work must be spearheaded by public unions because of their relatively substantial war chest, membership base, and the common ground they share with emergent movements regarding the enlargement and enhancement of public services.

1. *A progressive income tax structure:* The demand for progressive income tax structures needs to be announced in every corner of the country. The relationship between growing inequality, the radical restructuring of the tax codes since Reagan, and the consequent crisis of the public sector needs to be driven home in every campaign. In the absence of this discourse we are playing on the Right's side of the field. No new revenue by definition means budget cutting. Critically, new revenue can produce multipliers of benefit beyond jobs and benefits for present public employees. It can also mean jobs for the construction trade on infrastructure projects and enhanced quality of services for a cross section of communities if the revenue is invested strategically and effectively. A progressive taxation program has the single greatest potential for creating alliances across class, race, and union divides. That collectivity is urgently needed.

    The class war that is being waged on workers needs to be refocused on the wealthy paying their fair share. That is the kind of moral high ground that we can and must seize. The counter arguments from the Right that the wealthy will relocate if taxes are raised have been empirically disproven. However, we must be prepared to rebut the counter arguments that will be raised. Otherwise the class issue will be framed in precisely the way Chris Christie has named it: "We have public workers with high salaries and rich benefits and then we have all of the other workers" (Fabricant 2011b). That framing and the locus of the battle must be changed if we are to move from defense to offense.

2. *An increased willingness to engage in direct action to extend rights and wages:* If we have learned anything from Wisconsin and OWS it is that direct action is highly compatible with stalling the right-wing blitzkrieg and rallying public support. We cannot expect the Democratic Party to save us from this onslaught. They will only ally with labor to the extent that they understand labor as powerful. Backroom negotiations with Democrats and corporate leaders in the hope of producing negotiated settlements are necessary during this period but increasingly unavailable and insufficient. Quite frankly, such negotiation must be joined to labor developing and flexing an ever-more militant muscle. That is a large part of the lesson of Wisconsin. We cannot engage in such actions indiscriminately. They must be strategically and tactically selected at the opportune moment. That said, labor leaders must be willing to risk organizing, mobilizing, and deploying

members in ways that disrupt business as usual. As educators, our work lives are being radically restructured and disrupted. If our unions and leaders are to have any legitimacy over the short and long term, they must respond in kind.

3. *Creating alliances between public workers and the communities they serve:* Labor, service workers, and community-based agencies cannot win this war alone. At the moment, these groups simply do not have the soldiers or war chest to engage in anything but guerrilla warfare. To move from tactics of disruption to a power that has the potential to transform political discourse and policy, we must create common cause with a cross section of communities—adults and youth—touched by, for example, the public education services we deliver. Too often, however, community members are on the other side of a fault line separating them from public workers whom they blame for the ever-more degraded education, health care, and social services they receive. Consequently, labor must begin to develop town hall meetings that, on the one hand, describe the factors that are corrupting services and, on the other, discuss the common fate of workers and community members locked in a downward spiral of public services and standard of living. That discussion must be part of an ongoing union-sponsored campaign. We also need to be alert to the ever-greater investment that corporate reform foundations and patrons will make in moving increasingly starved CBOs to their side of the debate. That likely battleground must be incorporated into our early thinking when working to build such alliance.

4. *Rethinking partnership through the prism of union contracts:* Clearly, if labor is to grow its power, community members are an indispensable part of the army that must be built. However, too often community members, served by public employees such as teachers or health care workers, have seen public agencies and public workers as adversaries. Too often unions are perceived as unresponsive, untrustworthy, and unwilling to listen to the experience, expertise, and recommendations of those they serve. Autonomy and distance has been a working assumption of professional life. The contradiction, however, is that the trust necessary to build relationship and alliance is not primarily created from expertise or objective distance. Rather it is created through new forms of attentiveness to those we serve. Only such attentiveness and solidarity over time can provide a basis for community members and CBOs taking the risks necessary to form an alliance with labor. A new course can be set if we listen less to those in power, who invariably structure negotiations to produce a next round of concessions, and more to community members and their grounded understanding of what it will take to improve public institutions.

This attentiveness must also inform the development of contract demands, which join community desire with union negotiations. Moments will exist where the union and communities disagree on elements of a contract. It is within this context that sometimes off-the-record, difficult discussions will need to take place between unions and service users about equally cherished but not compatible values (e.g., equity and seniority). Consequently, in the near term, we must begin to create a dialogue that allows differences to be aired and modifications to be made that considers both the needs of union members and the quality of services delivered to communities. Only in this way can more enduring alliances be built.

5. *Risk taking and the reinvention of the work of unions:* Over the past four decades of ever-more dramatic decline in the membership and power of unions, we have witnessed the simultaneous atrophying of labor imagination and risk taking. Increasingly unions collect dues, negotiate contracts, provide services, and enforce their contracts in a hostile political environment. As the prospects for enhanced contracts diminishes, too often the corrective for leadership is to become ever-more insular—more defensive, self-interested, and myopic about what needs to be done. This is evidenced by the relatively low levels of investment in organizing, demobilization of members, extravagant and often empty national and regional conferences as well as an almost exclusive focus on traditional corridors of power to solve problems. Exceptions to such trends do exist. Service Employees International Union (SEIU), for example, has invested in organizing new forms of alliance between community groups and labor. The AFT is just beginning to make a similar commitment to enlarging its community work. The Professional Staff Congress, the union of faculty and professional staff at CUNY, has engaged in the difficult work of internal organizing, or animating its base, in anti-austerity campaigns while building alliances with emergent student groups on tuition, debt, and the enhancement of learning conditions. The California Federation of Teachers launched an effective member and community campaign to mobilize resistance to recent austerity initiatives.

This crisis is teaching us all over again that we cannot trust formal power as we have in the past to solve present problems. By and large our wages and rights are seen as the enemy of entrenched political and economic power. We must outline a different kind of progress and innovation in education, health care, and other services. Some part of our task also requires that we learn from the practices of the Right. For example, the Broad and Gates foundations have consciously created pipelines that connect their agenda to leadership development programs channeling graduates to critical positions throughout the nation. Unions must be "equally strategic and develop progressive leadership pipelines for students interested in public education careers" (Fabricant 2011b).

If parents, unions, and community-based groups promoting investment in public education are not seen as the engines of innovation and progress, they will fail. That means we must not simply defend the public sphere, but attack our adversaries to extend what is available. We can do this by creating far-reaching and innovative programs that address the present crisis on the basis of innovative, empirically validated practice, and strategic investment. We must be the champions of both our members, the communities we serve, and emergent social movements with which we can ally. As well we must be willing to cross swords with those who can afford to pay but refuse.

Risk taking also means that increasingly we will have to act rapidly in situations that may not be entirely clear. Crisis demands action. We would add it demands action that is increasingly able to inspire members to commit themselves to ever-greater levels of struggle, because that is what it will take to win. We would be remiss if we did not at least mention how difficult it has been over the past thirty years to engage community and union members in a collective work. Other pulls on people's lives in an increasingly unpredictable social world have resulted in their creating a protective armor that shields them from new commitments. That, too, however, is changing as lives are being disrupted by radical forms of austerity. We are in a moment of opportunity that may allow us to use this disruption to promote new forms of resistance.

This is by no means a recipe or prescription. There is no simple way out of this class war unless we exit public services. Exit is not a viable option, however, if we care about the larger collective, including family, friends, colleagues, and strangers in need and the stitching that holds together our collective not-quite democracy. We need to rebuild the collective power of labor, community groups, and emergent social movements by restructuring our line of attack, platform for change, organizations, alliances, contracts, and willingness to engage in new risk-taking behaviors. That experimentation is critical in a moment such as this one of retreat and peril. What we are asking represents a very tall order. We are suggesting that in a moment of crisis that threatens our survival we reinvent ourselves. We have no choice but to engage in the survival work of the moment. But only by reinventing our work as we struggle to stay alive can we build the kind of transformative change that on the one hand engages those delivering and receiving public services and on the other builds partnership with, for example, young people increasingly drawn to social movements because of the load of student debt and unemployment they are increasingly made to bear. Only a broad base of deep participation will yield a power commensurate with the attack on every vestige of the public sector and, most specific to this book, public education. That is the organizing work we must build and the fight we must wage if we are to reverse the momentum of the Right and win a future of collective purpose.

FOR FURTHER READING

Fabricant, Michael. *Organizing for Educational Justice: The Campaign for Public School Reform in the South Bronx.* Minneapolis: University of Minnesota Press, 2010.

Fruchter, Norm. *Urban Schools, Public Will: Making Education Work for All Our Children.* New York: Teachers College Press, 2007.

Karp, Stan. "Challenging Corporate Ed Reform: And 10 Hopeful Signs of Resistance." October 18, 2011. http://www.rethinkingschools.org/archive/26_03/26_03_karp.shtml.

Karp, Stan. "School Reform We Can't Believe In." April 14, 2010. http://www.rethinkingschools.org/archive/24_03/24_03_NCLBstan.shtml.

Mediratta, Kavitha, Seema Shah, and Sara McAlister. *Community Organizing for Stronger Schools: Strategies and Successes.* Cambridge: Harvard Education Press, 2009.

References

The Advancement Project. (2010). "Test, Punish and Push Out: How Zero Tolerance and High-Stakes Testing Funnel Youth into the School-to-Prison Pipeline." Accessed March 3, 2011. http://www.thestrategycenter.org/blog/2010/02/03/advancement-project -releases-new-report-test-punish-push-out.

American Educational Research Association, American Psychological Association, and National Council on Measurement in Education. (1999). *Standards for Educational and Psychological Testing.* Washington, DC: American Educational Research Association.

American Psychological Association. (2010). "Appropriate Use of High-Stakes Testing in Our Nation's Schools." *American Psychological Association.* Accessed June 11, 2011. http:// www.apa.org/pubs/info/brochures/testing.aspx.

Anand, B., et al. (2002). *Keeping the Struggle Alive: Studying Desegregation in Our Town, A Guide to Doing Oral History.* New York: Teachers College Press.

Anyon, J. (1997). *Ghetto Schooling.* New York: Teachers College Press.

Appleman Williams, W. (1980). *Empire as a Way of Life: An Essay on the Causes and Character of America's Present Predicament, along with a Few Thoughts about an Alternative.* New York: Oxford University Press.

Associated Press. (2012). "Panel Says Schools' Failings Could Threaten Economy and National Security." *New York Times,* March 20: A14.

Avitia, D., et al. (2009). *NYC Schools under Bloomberg and Klein: What Parents, Teachers, and Policymakers Need to Know.* New York: Lulu.

Ayala, J., & A. Galletta. (2012). "Documenting Disappearing Spaces: Erasure and Remembrance in Two High School Closures." *Peace and Conflict: Journal of Peace Psychology* 18(2): 149–155.

Ayers, W., B. Dohrn, & R. Ayers, eds. (2001). *Zero Tolerance: Resisting the Drive for Punishment in Our Schools. A Handbook for Parents, Students, Educators, and Citizens.* New York: New Press.

Baines, L., & G. Kent Stanley. (2006). "The Iatrogenic Consequences of Standards-based Education." *The Clearing House* 79(3): 119–123.

Baker, B. (2011). "Take Your SGP and VAMit, Damn it!" *School Finance 101,* September 2. http://schoolfinance101.wordpress.com/2011/09/02/take-your-sgp-and-vamit -damn-it/.

Barkan, J. (2011). "Got Dough? How Billionaires Rule Our Schools." *Dissent,* Winter. Accessed April 7, 2011. http://dissentmagazine.org/article/?article=3781.

Bell, D. (1992). *Faces at the Bottom of the Well: The Permanence of Racism*. New York: Basic Books.

Benyus, J. M. (1997). "Recognizing What Works: A Conscious Emulation of Life's Genius." In *What We See: Advancing the Observations of Jane Jacobs*, edited by S. Goldsmith & L. Elizabeth, 195–204. Oakland, CA: New Village Press.

Berliner, D. (2009). "Why Rising Test Scores May Not Mean Increased Learning." *Washington Post*, October 1. Accessed October 1, 2009. http://voices.washingtonpost.com.

Bond, H. M. (1959). *The Search for Talent*. Cambridge: Cambridge Graduate School of Education, Harvard University Press.

Bowles, S., & H. Gintis. (1976). *Schooling in Capitalist America: Educational Reform and the Contradictions of Economic Life*. New York: Basic Books.

Bracey, G. W. (2005). *Charter Schools' Performance and Accountability: A Disconnect*. Tempe: Education Policy Studies Laboratory. http://nepc.colorado.edu/files/EPSL-0505-113 -EPRU.pdf.

Bracey, G. W. (2004). *City Wide Systems of Charter Schools: Proceed with Caution*. Tempe: Education Policy Studies Laboratory.

Campbell, D. T. (1976). *Assessing the Impact of Planned Social Change*. Hanover, NH: Public Affairs Center, Dartmouth College.

Collins, G. (2011). "Reading, 'Riting and Revenues." *New York Times*, May 12: A29.

Collins, J. (2012). "Theorizing Wisconsin's 2011 Protests: Community-Based Unionism Confronts Accumulation by Dispossession." *American Ethnologist* 39(1): 6–20.

Cooper, M., & M. Thee-Brenan. (2011). "Majority in Poll Back Employees in Public Sector Unions." *New York Times*, March 1: A1.

Costigan, A. (2005). "Choosing to Stay, Choosing to Leave: New York City Teaching Fellows After Two Years." *Teacher Education Quarterly*, Spring: 125–142.

CREDO. (2009). Multiple Choice: Charter School Performance in 16 States. Stanford: CREDO. http://credo.stanford.edu/reports/MULTIPLE_CHOICE_CREDO.pdf.

Crocco, M., & A. Costigan. (2007). "The Narrowing of Curriculum and Pedagogy in the Age of Accountability: Urban Educators Speak Out." *Urban Education* 42(6).

Dagenhart, D., et al. (2005). "Giving Teachers a Voice." *Kappa Delta Pi Record* 41(3): 108–111.

Darling-Hammond, L. (2012). "Redlining Our Schools: Why Is Congress Writing Off Poor Children?" *The Nation*, January 30: 11–15.

Delpit, L. (2006). *Other People's Children*. New York: New Press.

Dillard, J. F., & L. Richula (2005). "The Rules Are No Game: From Instrumental Rationality to Administrative Evil." *Accounting, Auditing & Accountability Journal* 18(5): 608–630.

Dillon, S. (2011). "Tight Budgets Mean Squeeze in Classrooms." *New York Times*, March 7: A1.

Dillon, S. (2009). "Education Chief to Warn Advocates That Inferior Charter Schools Harm the Effort." *New York Times*, June 22: A10.

Du Bois, W. E. B. (1899). *The Philadelphia Negro*. New York: Lippincott.

Du Bois, W. E. B. (1910). *The Crisis: A Record of the Darker Races*. Accessed January 10, 2010. http://www.thecrisismagazine.com/.

Economic Policy Institute. (2011). "Disturbing Racial Wealth Gap." Accessed September 23, 2011. http://www.epi.org/news/disturbing-racial-wealth-gap/.

Education Notes Online. (2011). "Brandeis High School: Diary of a School Designed for Closure." Accessed January 8, 2011. http://ednotesonline.blogspot.com/2011/01/ brandeis-high-school-diary-of-school.html.

Eggers, D., & N. Clements Calegari. (2011). "The High Cost of Low Teacher Salaries." *New York Times,* May 1: WK12.

El-Amine, Z., & L. Glazer. (2008). "'Evolution' or Destruction? A Look at Washington, D.C." In *Keeping the Promise? The Debate over Charter Schools,* edited by L. Dingerson, B. Miner, B. Peterson, & S. Walters, 53–66. Milwaukee: Rethinking Schools.

Fabricant, M. (2011a). "Organizing for Equity." *American Educator* 35(1): 36–40.

Fabricant, M. (2011b). "Reimagining Labor: The Lessons of Wisconsin." *Working USA: The Journal of Labor and Society* 15(1): 235–241.

Fabricant, M. (2010). *Organizing for Educational Justice: The Campaign for Public School Reform in the South Bronx.* Minneapolis: University of Minnesota Press.

Fang, L. (2011). "Selling Schools Out: The Scam of Virtual Education Reform." *The Nation,* December 5: 11–18.

Farley, T. (2011). "Standardized Testing: A Decade in Review." *Huffington Post,* April 4. Accessed April 4, 2011. http://www.huffingtonpost.com/todd-farley/standardized -testing-ade_b_846044.html.

Farley, T. (2009). *Making the Grades: My Misadventures in the Standardized Testing Industry.* San Francisco: Berrett-Koehler Publishers.

Ferge, Z. (2000). "What Are the State Functions Neoliberalism Wants to Get Rid Of?" In *Not for Sale: In Defense of Public Goods,* edited by A. Anton, M. Fisk and N. Holmstrom, 181–204. Boulder, CO: Westview Press.

Ferguson, N. (2009). "How Great Powers Fall." *Newsweek,* December 7: 1.

Fine, M. (1991). *Framing Dropouts: Notes on the Politics of an Urban High School.* Albany: SUNY Press.

Fine, M., R. Roberts, M. Torre, & D. Upegui. (2001). "Participatory Action Research Behind Bars." *Critical Psychology: The International Journal of Critical Psychology* 2: 145–157.

Fine, M., & J. Ruglis. (2008). "Circuits of Dispossession: The Racialized and Classed Realignment of the Public Sphere for Youth in the U.S." *Transforming Anthropology* 17(1): 20–33.

Fine, M., B. Stoudt, M. Fox, & M. Santos. (2010). "The Uneven Distribution of Social Suffering: Documenting the Social Health Consequences of Neo-liberal Social Policy on Marginalized Youth." *European Health Psychology* 12 (September): 30–36.

Finnegan, M. (2011). "With Construction Stopped, Charter Fight Continues." *The West Side Spirit,* June 1.

Foote, M. (2005). "College Performance Study." *The New York Performance Standard Consortium.* Accessed April 7, 2011. http://performanceassessment.org/consequences/ collegeperformancestudy.pdf.

Fox, M., & M. Fine. (2012). "Circulating Critical Research: Reflections on Performance and Moving Inquiry into Action." In *Critical Qualitative Research Reader,* edited by G. Cannella & S. Steinberg. New York: Peter Lang Publishing.

Fox, M., K. Mediratta, B. Stoudt, J. Ruglis, M. Fine, & S. Salah. (2010). "Critical Youth Engagement: Participatory Action Research and Organizing." In *Handbook of Research on Civic Engagement in Youth,* edited by L. Sherrod, J. Torney-Purta, & C. Flanagan, 621–650. Hoboken, NJ: John Wiley & Sons Publishers.

Frankenberg, E., & G. Siegel-Hawley. (2009). "Equity Overlooked: Charter Schools and Civil Rights Policy." *The Civil Rights Project.* http://civilrightsproject.ucla.edu/research/ k-12-education/integration-and-diversity/equity-overlooked-charter-schools-and-civil -rights-policy/frankenberg-equity-overlooked-report-2009.pdf.

Fruchter, N. (2007). *Urban Schools, Public Will: Making Education Work for All Our Children.* New York: Teachers College Press.

Gabriel, T. (2011a). "More Pupils Are Learning Online, Fueling Debate on Quality." *New York Times,* April 6: A1.

Gabriel, T. (2011b). "Teachers Wonder, Why the Scorn?" *New York Times,* March 3: A1.

Galletta, A., & W. E. Cross. (2007). "Past as Present, Present as Past: Historicizing Black Education and Interrogating 'Integration.'" In *Contesting Stereotypes and Creating Identities: Social Categories, Social Identities, and Educational Participation,* edited by A. J. Fuligni, 15–41. New York: Russell Sage Foundation.

Galletta, A., & V. Jones. (2010). "Why Are You Doing This? Questions on Purpose, Structure, and Outcomes in Participatory Action Research Engaging Youth and Teacher Candidates." *Educational Studies* 46: 337–357.

Gangi, R., V. Schiraldi, & J. Ziedenberg. (1999). *New York State of Mind? Higher Education vs. Prison Funding in the Empire State, 1988–1998.* Washington, DC: Justice Policy Institute, The Correctional Institute of New York.

GAO. (2009). *Schools Use Multiple Strategies to Help Students Meet Academic Standards, Especially Schools with Higher Proportions of Low-Income and Minority Students,* November 16. http://www.gao.gov/assets/300/298455.pdf.

Giroux, H. (2006). *Stormy Weather: Katrina and the Politics of Disposability.* Boulder, CO: Paradigm Publishers.

Glass, G. V. (2008). *Fertilizers, Pills & Magnetic Strips: The Fate of Public Education in America.* Charlotte: Information Age Publishing.

Goldstein, D. (2011a). "Brill's Discontent." *The Nation,* August 29/September 5: 14–18.

Goldstein, D. (2011b). "The Test Generation." *The American Prospect,* April 4. Accessed May 5, 2011. http://prospect.org/article/test-generation.

Gonzalez, J. (2010). "Public sentiment has turned against Mayor Bloomberg's dictatorial school reforms." *New York Daily News,* January 27. Accessed January 28, 2010. http://articles.nydailynews.com/2010-01-27/local/29437061_1_low-performing-schools-special-education-james-eterno.

Gonzalez, J. (2008). "Department of Education Spends $5M a Year on Couriers." *New York Daily News,* October 29. Accessed October 29, 2008. http://www.nydailynews.com.

Gootman, E. & R. Gebeloff. (2008). "A Plan to Test the City's Youngest Pupils." *New York Times,* August 26: B1.

Gough, I. (1979). *The Political Economy of the Welfare State.* New York: Macmillan.

Graeber, D. (2011). "Occupy Wall Street Rediscovers the Radical Imagination." *Guardian,* September 25. Accessed September 26, 2011. http://www.guardian.co.uk/commentisfree/cifamerica/2011/sep/25/occupy-wall-street-protest.

Gramsci, A. (1971). *Selections from the Prison Notebooks.* London: Lawrence and Wishart.

Granek Guttell, S. (2001). "Why Teachers Stay, and Leave." *New York Times,* June 20. Accessed October 3, 2011. http://www.nytimes.com/2001/06/25/opinion/l-why-teachers-stay-and-leave-960578.html.

Green, E. (2010). "Building a Better Teacher." *New York Times,* March 7: MM30.

Gwynne, J., & M. de la Torre. (2009). *When Schools Close: Effects on Displaced Students in Chicago Public Schools.* Chicago: Consortium on Chicago School Research at the University of Chicago (October): 1–3.

Hacker, J., & P. Pierson. (2011). *Winner-Take-All Politics: How Washington Made the Rich Richer—and Turned Its Back on the Middle Class.* New York: Simon & Schuster.

Halbfinger, D. (2011). "Christie Declares 'New Normal' in Budget Proposal." *New York Times,* February 23: A16.

Hamilton, L. S., B. M. Stecher, & K. Yuan. (2008). *Standards-Based Reform in the United States: History, Research, and Future Directions.* New York: Rand Corporation.

Hancock, L. (2011). "Tested: Covering Schools in the Age of Micro-Measurement." *Columbia Journalism Review* (March/April). Accessed August 15, 2011. http://www.cjr.org/cover_story/tested.php?page%3D1&page=6.

Harvey, D. (2005). *The New Imperialism.* Oxford: Oxford University Press.

Harvey, D. (2004). *A Geographer's Perspective on the New American Imperialism: Conversations with History.* Berkeley, CA: UC Institute of International Studies.

Hass, N. (2009). "Scholarly Investments." *New York Times,* December 6: ST1.

Hayek, F. (1944). *The Road to Serfdom.* Chicago: University of Chicago.

Herold, Benjamin. (2011). "Confessions of a Cheating Teacher." *Philadelphia Public School Notebook.* Accessed March 1, 2011. http://thenotebook.org.

Herrada, E. (2012). Peace and Conflict: "Email diary from Detroit." *Journal of Peace Psychology* 18(2): 173–176.

Herrera, L. (2011). "In Florida, Virtual Classrooms with No Teachers." *New York Times,* January 18: A15.

Hobsbawm, E. (1994). *The Age of Extremes: The Short Twentieth Century, 1914–1991.* New York: Vintage Books.

Horgan, J. (2011). "Why We Lie." *New York Times,* December 25: BR12.

Hout, M., & S. W. Elliott, eds. (2011). Incentives and Test-Based Accountability in Education. National Research Council. Washington, DC: The National Academies Press.

Hu, W. (2011). "Testing Firm Faces Inquiry on Free Trips for Officials." *New York Times,* December 21: A29.

Jacob, B. A., & S. D. Levitt. (2003). "Rotten Apples: An Investigation of the Prevalence and Predictors of Teachers' Cheating." *The Quarterly Journal of Economics*: 843–877.

Johnson, J., J. Rochkind, & S. DuPont. (2011). "Don't Count Us Out." *Kettering Foundation and Public Agenda.* Accessed January 15, 2012. http://cbe.bentley.edu/sites/cbe/files/don't-count-us-out.pdf.

Jonsson, P. (2011). "America's Biggest Teacher and Principal Cheating Scandal Unfolds in Atlanta." *Christian Science Monitor.* Accessed December 11, 2011. http://www.csmonitor.com/USA/Education/2011/0705/America-s-biggest-teacher-and-principal-cheating-scandal-unfolds-in-Atlanta.

Katz, C. (2008). "Bad Elements: Katrina and the Scoured Landscape of Social Reproduction." *Gender, Place and Culture* (15)1: 15–29.

Katz, C. (2001). "Vagabond Capitalism and the Need for Social Reproduction." *Antipode* 33(4): 709–728.

Kauffman, D., S. M. Johnson, S. M. Kardos, E. Liu, and H. G. Peske. (2002). "Lost at Sea": New teachers' Experiences with Curriculum and assessment. *Teachers College Record* 104(2): 273–300.

Kissoon, M. (2011). "Partnership for Student Advocacy Blog," September 29. Accessed September 30, 2011. http://www.pfsany.org/news/meet-melissa-kissoon/.

Klein, J. (2011). "The Failure of American Schools." *The Atlantic,* June: 77.

Klein, N. (2011). "Occupy Everywhere: Michael Moore, Naomi Klein on Next Steps for the Movement against Corporate Power." November 25. Broadcast on *Democracy Now!*

http://www.democracynow.org/2011/11/25/occupy_everywhere_michael_moore_naomi_klein.

Klein, N. (2007). *The Shock Doctrine: The Rise of Disaster Capitalism.* New York: Picador.

Koyama, J. P. (2010). *Making Failure Pay: For-Profit Tutoring, High-Stakes Testing, and Public Schools.* Chicago: University of Chicago Press.

Kozol, J. (1972). *Free Schools.* New York: Houghton-Mifflin.

Kristof, N. (2011). "Pay Teachers More." *New York Times,* March 13: WK10.

Krugman, P. (2012). "Money and Morals." *New York Times,* February 10: A27.

Labaree, D. (2011). "Targeting Teachers." *Dissent* 58(3): 9–14.

Libby, K. (2009). "From the Vault." *Schools Matter,* November 6. Accessed November 6, 2009. http://www.schoolsmatter.info/2009/11/from-vault_06.html.

Lieberman, R. (2011). "Why the Rich Are Getting Richer: American Politics and the Second Gilded Age." *Foreign Affairs* (January/February): 154–158.

Lipman, P. (2009). *Making Sense of Renaissance 2010 School Policy in Chicago: Race, Class and the Cultural Politics of Neoliberal Urban Restructuring.* Chicago: Great Cities Institute.

Lipman, P. (2004a). "Education Accountability and Repression of Democracy Post-9/11." *Journal for Critical Education Policy Studies* 2(1). Accessed May 5, 2011. http://www.jceps.com/?pageID=article&articleID=23.

Lipman, P. (2004b). *High Stakes Education: Inequality, Globalization, and Urban School Reform.* New York: RoutledgeFalmer.

Lipman, P., & D. Hursh. (2007). "Renaissance 2010: The Reassertion of Ruling-Class Power through Neoliberal Policies in Chicago." *Policy Futures in Education* 5(2): 160–178.

Losen, D. J. (2011). "Discipline Policies, Successful Schools, and Racial Justice." *National Education Policy Center.* Accessed December 11, 2011. http://nepc.colorado.edu/publication/discipline-policies.

Lupescu, S., H. Hart, T. Rosenkranz, N. Montgomery, & S. Sporte. (2007). "2007 Individual School Survey Report." *Consortium on Chicago Schools.* Accessed May 9, 2010. http://ccsr.uchicago.edu/ISR/7777/details7777.pdf.

Marcuse, H. (1964). *One Dimensional Man:* Studies in the Ideology of Advanced Industrial Society. Boston: Beacon Press.

Martinez, B. (2011). "State Court Ruling Paves Way for School Closings." *Wall Street Journal,* July 22.

McCoy, A. (2010). "Tomgram: Alfred McCoy, Taking Down America." *TomDispatch,* December 5. http://www.tomdispatch.com/archive/175327/%20http://www.huffingtonpost.com/alfred-w-mccoy/the-decline-and-fall-of-t_1_b_792570.html.

McKinley, J. (2011). "Aid Cuts Have Texas Schools Scrambling." *New York Times,* February 15: A16.

Medina, J. (2010). "At Top City Schools, Lack of Diversity Persists." *New York Times,* February 5. Accessed February 5, 2010. http://cityroom.blogs.nytimes.com/2010/02/05/at-top-city-schools-lack-of-diversity-persist/.

Medina, J. (2009). "City's Schools Share Their Space, and Bitterness." *New York Times,* November 30: A1.

Mediratta, K., S. Shah, & S. McAlister. (2009). *Community Organizing for Stronger Schools: Strategies and Successes.* Cambridge: Harvard Education Press.

Meier, D. (2005). "Creating Democratic Schools." *Rethinking Schools.* Accessed July 9, 2011. http://www.rethinkingschools.org/special_reports/quality_teachers/demo194.shtml.

Mickelson, R. A., & S. S. Smith. (1998). "Can Education Eliminate Race, Class, and Gender Inequality?" In *Race, Class and Gender,* 3rd ed., edited by M. L. Andersen & P. H. Collins, 328–340. New York: Wadsworth.

Miner, B. (2011). "Just Say No to Voucher Expansion." *Journal Sentinal,* March 12. Accessed March 12. http://www.jsonline.com/news/opinion/117830148.html.

Miner, B. (2005). "Keeping Public Schools Public: Testing Companies Mine for Gold." *Rethinking Schools.* Accessed January 15, 2011. http://www.rethinkingschools.org/special_reports/bushplan/test192.shtml.

Miron, G., & L. Dingerson. (2009). "The Charter School Express: Is Proliferation Interfering with Quality?" *Education Week* 29(6): 29–30, 36.

Molnar, A. (1996). "Charter Schools: The Smiling Face of Disinvestment." *Educational Leadership* 54(2): 9–15.

Molnar, A., & D. Garcia. (2007). "The Expanding Role of Privatization in Education: Implications for Teacher Education and Development." *Teacher Education Quarterly* 34: 11–24.

Moynihan, D. P. (1964). "The Negro Family: The Case for National Action." *United States Department of Labor.* http://www.dol.gov/oasam/programs/history/webid-meynihan.htm.

Mukherjee, E. (2007). *Criminalizing the Classroom: The Over-Policing of New York City Public Schools.* New York: NYCLU & ACLU.

Neill, M. (2011). "Testing, Cheating and Educational Corruption." *Fair Test.* Accessed December 11, 2011. http://fairtest.org/sites/default/files/Cheating_Fact_Sheet_8-17-11.pdf.

Neville, H. A., J. G. Yeung, N. R. Todd, L. B. Spanierman, & T. D. Reed. (2010). "Colorblind Racial Ideology and Beliefs about Racialized/University Mascot." *Journal of Diversity in Higher Education* 4(4): 236–249.

New York Civil Liberties Union. (2011). *Education Interrupted: The Growing Use of Suspensions in New York City Public Schools.* New York: NYCLU.

NYC Department of Education. (2009). *More Than 80 Percent of Students Admitted to a Top Choice High School for Fourth Consecutive Year,* March 29. Accessed December 11, 2011. http://schools.nyc.gov/Offices/mediarelations/NewsandSpeeches/2008-2009/20090325_hs_admissions.htm.

NY1 News. (2009). "Struggling Manhattan High School to Close." February 4. *New York 1.* Accessed February 4, 2009. http://www.ny1.com/content/top_stories/93362/struggling-manhattan-high-school-to-close/.

O'Connor, J. (1973). *The Fiscal Crisis of the State.* New York: St. Martin's Press.

O'Donnell, D. (2009). *Letter to Joel Klein.* February 26. Available at http://www.tilsonfunds.com/Personal/KeepingthePromiseWhitePapers.pdf. http://graphics8.nytimes.com/packages/pdf/nyregion/2009/20090305_KLEIN.pdf.

OECD. (2010). *PISA 2009 Results: Overcoming Social Background—Equity in Learning Opportunities and Outcomes (Volume II).* http://dx.doi.org/10.1787/9789264091504-en.

Orfield, G. (2010). *Choice without Equity: Charter School Segregation and the Need for Civil Rights Standards.* Los Angeles: Civil Rights Project at the University of California, Los Angeles.

Orfield, G. (2008). "Race and Schools: The Need for Action." *Civil Rights Project/Proyecto Derechos Civiles. University of California, NEA Research Visiting Scholars Series.* Spring, vol. 1b. Accessed February 3, 2011. http://www.nea.org/home/13054.htm.

Otterman, S. (2011). "Tests for Pupils, but the Grades to Teachers." *New York Times,* May 24: A1.

Otterman, S. (2010). "Schools' Supporters Fear They Weren't Heard." *New York Times*, January 28: A28.

Payne, C., & T. Knowles. (2009). "Promise and Peril: Charter Schools, Urban School Reform, and the Obama Administration." *Harvard Educational Review* 79(2): 227–239.

PBS. (2002). "The Testing Industry's Big Four." Accessed January 11, 2011. http://www .pbs.org/wgbh/pages/frontline/shows/schools/testing/companies.html.

Pérez, M. (2011). "Two Tales of One City: A Political Economy of the New York City Public High School Admissions Process." Doctoral dissertation. City University of New York.

Pérez, M. (2009). "Latina Parents, School Choice, and Pierre Bourdieu." In *Theoretical Encounters in Educational Research*, edited by J. Anyon, 135–148. New York: Routledge Press.

Peterson, B. (2011). "Testimony by Bob Peterson to the Wisconsin Assembly Committee on Education." *Rethinking Schools*. April 19, 2011. Accessed 20 April 2011. http://www .rethinkingschools.org//cmshandler.asp?special_reports/voucher_report/v_testimony .shtml.

Phillis, A. (2009). "Bronx High School Changed Grades to Graduate More Students." *Gotham Schools*. Accessed October 28, 2009. http://gothamschools.org/2009/10/28/bronx-high -school-changed-grades-to-graduate-more-students/.

Ratliff, T. (2011). "Texas State Board of Education." Accessed September 12, 2011. http:// www.texasisd.com/article_117027.shtml.

Ravitch, D. (2011a). "A Moment of National Insanity." *Education Week*, March 1. Accessed May 1, 2011. http://blogs.edweek.org/edweek/Bridging-Differences/2011/03/dear_ deborah_lucky_for_you.html.

Ravitch, D. (2011b). "School 'Reform': A Failing Grade." *New York Review of Books*, September 29. Accessed October 2, 2011. http://www.nybooks.com/articles/archives/2011/ sep/29/school-reform-failing-grade/.

Real Direct (2011). "New York City Neighborhoods: Upper West Side." Accessed February 3, 2012. resources.realdirect.com/neighborhoods/new-york-city-neighborhoods-upper -west-side.

Resmovits, J. (2011). "Murdoch Education Affiliate's $2.7 Million Consulting Contract Approved by New York City." *Huffington Post*, July 15. Accessed July 15, 2011. http://www.huffingtonpost.com/2011/07/15/murdoch-education-affiliate-contract -approved_n_900379.html.

Rettig, J. (2009). "How to Choose a Charter School." *US News and World Report*, December 9. Accessed June 2, 2011. http://www.usnews.com/education/high-schools/ articles/2009/12/09/how-to-choose-a-charter-school?page=2.

Richtel, M. (2012). "Teachers Resist High-Tech Push in Idaho Schools." *New York Times*, January 4: A1.

Robbins, L. (2011). "Lost in the School Choice Maze." *New York Times*, May 6: MB1.

Rothstein, R. (2011). "A Bet on No Child Left Behind." *Washington Post*, September 27.

Saltman, K. (2007). "Schooling in Disaster Capitalism: How the Political Right Is Using Disaster to Privatize Public Schooling." *Teacher Education Quarterly*. Spring 2007: 131–156.

Saul, S. (2011). "Profits and Questions at Online Charter Schools." *New York Times*, December 13: A1.

Schaniberg, L. (1997). "Firms Hoping to Turn Profit from Charters." *Education Week* 17(16): 1.

Schemo, D. J. (2004). "Nation's Charter Schools Lagging Behind, U.S. Test Scores Reveal." *New York Times*, August 17. Accessed October 12, 2011. http://www.nytimes.com/ 2004/08/17/education/17charter.html?pagewanted=all.

Schmoker, M. (2008/2009). "Measuring What Matters." *Educational Leadership* 66(4): 70–74.

Schrag, P. (2011). "Vouchers: They're Baaaaaack!" *The Nation,* June 20: 25–26.

Shrock, R. (2004). "The Perils They Face: Using Key Texts to Prepare Passionate Teachers for an Unfriendly World." *Teacher Education Quarterly* 31: 65–71.

Simon, M., & L. Dingerson. (2011). "Dismantling Schools—Disrespecting Communities." *The Ford Secondary Education and Racial Justice Collaborative.* Accessed December 11, 2011. http://www.fserjc.org/dismantling-schools/.

Sirin, S. R., & M. Fine. (2008). *Muslim American Youth: Understanding Hyphenated Identities through Multiple Methods.* New York: NYU Press.

Sizer, T., & G. Wood. (2008). "Charter Schools and the Values of Public Education." In *Keeping the Promise? The Debate over Charter Schools,* edited by L. Dingerson, B. Miner, B. Peterson, & S. Walters, 3–16. Milwaukee: Rethinking Schools.

Smith, N. (2009). "The Revolutionary Imperative." In *The Point Is to Change It: Geographies of Hope and Survival in an Age of Crisis,* edited by N. Castree, P. Chatterton, N. Heynen, W. Larner, & M. W. Wright, 52–65. West Sussex, UK: Wiley-Blackwell.

Sorokin, E. (2003). "Study: High Stakes Test Lead to Cheating." *Harvard Crimson,* November 21. Accessed June 1, 2011. http://www.thecrimson.com/article/2003/11/21/study-high-stakes-test-lead-to/.

Stoudt, B., M. Fox, & M. Fine. (2012). "Contesting Privilege with Critical Participatory Action Research." *Journal of Social Issues* 68(1): 178–193.

Strauss, V. (2011). "Conversations with Obama, Duncan on Assessment." *Washington Post,* October 3. Accessed October 3, 2011. http://www.washingtonpost.com/blogs/answer-sheet/post/conversations-with-obama-duncan-on-assessment/2011/10/02/gIQATtyYGL_blog.html.

Tashlik, P. (2010). "Changing the National Conversation on Assessment." *Phi Delta Kappan* 91(6): 55–60.

Tavernise, S. (2012). "Education Gap Grows between Rich and Poor, Studies Say." *New York Times,* February 10: A1.

Toch, T. (2009). *Sweating the Big Stuff: A Progress Report on the Movement to Scale up the Nation's Best Charter Schools.* http://scholasticadministrator.typepad.com/files/sweating060309.doc.pdf.

Trivers, R. (2011). *The Folly of Fools: The Logic of Deceit and Self-Deception in Human Life.* New York: Basic Books.

Urban Youth Collaborative. (2006). *Bill of Rights.* www.urbanyouthcollaborative.org/rights.html.

Viadero, D. (2009). "Study Casts Doubt on Strength of Charter Managers." *Education Week* 29(14). Accessed November 11, 2011. http://www.edweek.org/ew/articles/2009/12/03/14charter.h29.html.

Warren, J. R., & E. Grodsky. (2009). "Exit Exams Harm Students Who Fail Them—and Don't Benefit Students Who Pass Them." *Phi Delta Kappan* 90 (9): 645–649.

Warren, M., & K. Mapp. (2011). *A Match on Dry Grass: Community Organizing as a Catalyst for School Reform.* Oxford: Oxford University Press.

Waters, J. K. (2011). "Competing for the Virtual Student." *THE Journal,* July 7. Accessed July 8, 2011. http://thejournal.com/articles/2011/07/26/competing-for-the-virtual-student.aspx.

West, C. (1993). *Race Matters.* Boston: Beacon Press.

Western, B., & B. Pettit. (2010). *Collateral Costs: Incarceration's Effect on Economic Mobility.* Washington, DC: Pew Charitable Trusts.

Wilkinson, R., & K. Pickett. (2009). *The Spirit Level: Why Greater Equality Makes Societies Stronger.* New York: Bloomsbury Press.

Winerip, M. (2011a). "10 Years of Assessing Students with Scientific Exactitude." *New York Times,* December 19: A24.

Winerip, M. (2011b). "When Free Trips Overlap with Commercial Purposes." *New York Times,* September 18: A15.

Winerip, M. (2011c). "Pa. Joins States Facing a School Cheating Scandal." *New York Times,* July 31: A11.

Wolff, D. (2009). "Speculating on Education." *Counter Punch,* September 25. Accessed November 10, 2011. http://www.counterpunch.org/2009/09/25/speculating-on -education/.

Woodson, C. (2010). *The Miseducation of the Negro.* New York: Tribeca Books.

Youth United for Change and Advancement Project. (2011). "Zero Tolerance in Philadelphia." Accessed November 8, 2011. http://www.atlanticphilanthropies.org/sites/default/files/ uploads/Zero%20Tolerance%20in%20Philadelphia%20(2).pdf.

Zhao, Y. (2006). "Are We Fixing the Wrong Things?" *Educational Leadership* 63(8): 28–31.

Index

About the Authors

Michael Fabricant is Professor in the Silberman School of Social Work, Hunter College, and **Michelle Fine** is Distinguished Professor of Psychology, CUNY Graduate Center in New York. Both are the authors of important books on education and social policy.